VILLAGE SCHOOLS
A History of Rural Elementary
Education from the Eighteenth to the
Twenty-first Century in Prose and Verse

An object lesson in a rural school in England, c1890

VILLAGE SCHOOLS
A History of Rural Elementary Education from the Eighteenth to the Twenty-first Century in Prose and Verse

Edited and Introduced by
John Proctor

OXFORD
UNIVERSITY PRESS

OXFORD

UNIVERSITY PRESS

Great Clarendon Street, Oxford OX2 6DP

Oxford University Press is a department of the University of Oxford.
It furthers the University's objective of excellence in research, scholarship,
and education by publishing worldwide in

Oxford New York

Auckland Cape Town Dar es Salaam Hong Kong Karachi
Kuala Lumpur Madrid Melbourne Mexico City Nairobi
New Delhi Shanghai Taipei Toronto

with offices in

Argentina Austria Brazil Chile Czech Republic France Greece
Guatemala Hungary Italy Japan South Korea Poland Portugal
Singapore Switzerland Thailand Turkey Ukraine Vietnam

ISBN-13: 978-0-19-597996-1
ISBN-10: 0-19-597996-6

Typeset in Times
Printed in Pakistan by
Ibn-e-Hassan Off Set Printing Press, Karachi.
Published by
Ameena Saiyid, Oxford University Press
Plot No. 38, Sector 15, Korangi Industrial Area, PO Box 8214
Karachi-74900, Pakistan.

And soon they all say,
"Such, such were the joys
When we all—girls and boys—
In our youth-time were seen
On the echoing green".
William Blake, *Songs of Innocence*, 1789

Who would suppose that Education were a thing which had to be advocated on the ground of local expediency, or indeed on any ground? As if it stood not on the basis of everlasting duty, as a prime necessity of man.
Thomas Carlyle, *Chartism*, 1842

It is the duty of every civilized government to educate the masses, and if you have to face a certain amount of danger, face it boldly in the name of duty and... you will have the whole educated public with you in the struggle... therefore fear not, do not listen to the alarmist that you will make yourselves unpopular if you advocate and fight the cause of elementary education...
M.A. Jinnah, in support of the Elementary Education Bill, Bombay, 1912

Nothing is more encouraging than the way the villagers appreciate, and describe to me as I tour, a really good teacher. The boys come crowding to the school, and so do the girls; he is spoken of with reverence by the villagers; and his little charges are happy and good mannered and do him credit in after-life. What more could a teacher desire than a life of such usefulness? True it does not tend to great distinction, but to be loved and honoured by one village is more than many a great man can boast.
F.L. Brayne, *The Remaking of Village India*, 1929

By education I mean an all-round drawing out of the best in child and man —body, mind and spirit. Literacy is not the end of education nor even the beginning. It is only one of the means whereby man and woman can be educated. Literacy in itself is no education.
M.K. Gandhi, on the Wardha basic education scheme, India, 1936

CONTENTS

PREFACE

The contemporary voice that captures the essence of experience—
whether one can 'hear the people talking'—in verse or in prose—was
the criterion for the selection of each item in this village schools'
'history-anthology'. Observers reminisce about dame schools, common
day schools, one-teacher schools, inspectors and inspections; the
National, British and Board schools; the Muslim maktab and the Hindu
pathsala. They recall some of the humour and pathos; sometimes the
daily chatter or jubilation; sometimes the disgruntlements of pupils
and teachers or the embarrassment of not being able to pay the weekly
school fee; the 'presumptuous hen'; the damp coats and shawls that,
without a school cloakroom, all day 'send out a gentle steam as if it
were washing-day next door'; the stack of new slates 'grey with ashen
dust'—and the old—'...smooth and shiny on the front and greasy on
the back', and squeaky slate pencils; the Bengali inkpots swinging from
strings tied to boys' fingers as they walked to school in the mornings;
some disastrous lessons; the winter mud and the summer dust on
wooden shoes; the more recent cod liver oil and malt—delivered by the
dessertspoonful—and, too, the day-to-day patient teaching and learning
that made it all worthwhile. They recall, too, the poverty that pupils
and teachers endured as a national system of education slowly and
grudgingly followed behind the rural and urban transformations that
took place during the centuries with which this book is concerned.

That which cannot easily be contained within official documents or
formal histories may be found in personal memoirs. Here they provide
a conspectus of experiences illustrating the transitions in elementary
education in the countryside of the United Kingdom and abroad—and in
the latter we include, in particular, British India and the modern Islamic
Republic of Pakistan. The collection has not necessarily been assembled
in a scholarly manner—rather, its assembly may be compared with the
piecing together of an ever-expanding jig-saw puzzle for which, one
may be sure, many equally vivid—and representative—pieces lie in
libraries and old books' bookshops. From the latter have come Syed
Wajid Ali's rare pupil's perspective of a nineteenth century maktab and
pathsala—happy experiences—and other pieces, perhaps not seen for
periods of time measured in half-centuries. The memoirs are generally,

although by no means all, remarkably affectionate considering the limitations, inherent until modern times, of formal rural education.

It is intended that, in a comparative and historical context, the reader will find a coherent contribution to the understanding of the history of rural elementary education. The gradual eradication of child labour in the UK—and its parallels in modern developing countries—is seen as a significant result of the rigorous imposition of a compulsory (and an increasingly beneficial) national education system. By modern definitions, forms of child slavery and exploitation were a not uncommon feature of rural life in England even into the late nineteenth century.

A further purpose of this book is to give support to modern village schools. The contrast between the colourful, well-lit and activity-oriented village primary schools of the modern western world and the damp and gloomy hovels of past years is marked. Although often under threat of closure for economic reasons, small schools have many virtues. The reader is best left to judge, however, whether peering, so to speak, over the shoulders of people who experienced them, in one capacity or another, at some period in the last three centuries, is the best way to encourage such support. I hope, however, that it will.

I gratefully acknowledge the assistance of a number of people in compiling this history-anthology, including, in England, William Ingles, John Gray, Sue Thomas and my brother, David Proctor; Gavin Kerr and Richard and Doris Silver in New Zealand and Ruth Bavington and Apphia Paul in Pakistan. *Village Schools—A history of rural elementary education from the eighteenth to the twenty-first century in prose and verse*, is dedicated to my wife Susan and our children, Benjamin, Thomas and Annie, now embarking upon their school careers in Pakistan, and to the teachers and pupils, past and present, of the ninety-five pupil Christian Foundation School in the village of Raja Jang—to which all royalties are directed. This school, for the children of rural labourers, including brick-kiln workers, carters and agriculturists, first opened in January 1995. Raja Jang, described by the government Gazetteer of 1883–84 as 'a place of no importance', is ten kilometres east of Raiwind in the wheat and sugarcane district of the glorious Punjab of Pakistan.

John Proctor
Lahore
June 2005

1

INTRODUCTION

It is not unreasonable to suppose that most of the ancestors of the modern English were unable to read with any degree of fluency if they were born in the nineteenth century or earlier.[1] While the later Victorian period, from 1871, provided schools where the voluntary societies did not have them[2], and compulsory attendance from 1880, no more than a minority of the population could both read and write for the purpose of effective communication.[3] In the earlier Victorian period, less than 25 per cent of children had any school experience, and whatever they had was usually of limited duration, perhaps one to four years with irregular attendance. This pattern continued until 1871,[4] when between that year and 1900, school attendance in England and Wales rose from 1.2 million to 4.7 million, although perhaps a million more children should have been in school during this period.[5]

Similarly, beyond the United Kingdom, the great mass of people in the mid-nineteenth century were illiterate: '...with the exception of the Germans, the Dutch, Scandinavians, Swiss and the citizens of the USA, no people can in 1840 be described as literate. Several can be described as totally illiterate, like the Spaniards, the Portuguese... and except for the Lombards and Pietmontese, the Italians.'[6]

Where school attendance is voluntary, similarities abound between nineteenth century Europe and modern developing countries. These include rural-urban and regional imbalances in school provision (there may not be enough schools or schoolteachers and schools in rural areas may be too far from home—especially for girls); differences in attendance between boys and girls and high dropout rates in rural and urban areas with early leaving due, in the main, to children beginning full-time work. Early leaving is also attributed to the poor quality of teaching and learning.

Burgeoning populations and movement to the cities create educational needs that may only be redressed by state intervention; private or voluntary provision, as seen before 1871 in England, and as sometimes proposed as a solution in developing countries today, is unable to keep pace with needs.

Where the common rights of children are neither assumed or upheld by the law, children will be economically exploited: the nineteenth century factory and farming systems in England introduced child slavery on a scale previously unknown. It was not until the imposition of a national system of education that exploitation, including some of its more shocking forms, for example the employment of boys and girls, sometimes as young as five years, as members of the bought-and-sold agricultural gangs' system of eastern England, was brought under control. Education was intended only for a privileged class: popular education, its opponents said, would lead to discontent and dissidence; it was not required and should not be encouraged. Parents and employers, as in the poorer countries today, saw themselves as economic beneficiaries of child employment. One old man in 1842, for example, said of his youth—about 1770—'These had really been the days of infant slavery. The creatures were set to work as soon as they could crawl—and the parents were the hardest of taskmasters.' Nevertheless, he was against reform, comparing the cruelties he had endured with the 'light toil and positive comfort of the [1842] factory child.'[7]

A commonly held view was expressed by William Cobbett (1763–1835), author of *Rural Rides*, publisher of the *Political Register*, and a man-of-the-people, held in fond regard by succeeding generations:

All this increase of education [mainly through the agency of the monitorial schools] has not been productive of any good, and I venture to say that there is not a single country gentleman who will not say that the fathers of the last generation made better labourers, better servants and better men than their sons of the present generation. This proves that the labouring classes are much better without that intellectual enjoyment which [educators] are anxious to provide for them than they are with it... By useful employment the youth gains habits of obedience and industry, but send him to school, to a drunken master or to a sober conceited coxcomb of a schoolmaster and he will only learn habits of idleness and become too great in his own conceit to labour.

– William Cobbett, 1834[8]

In a period of change, Cobbett failed to see that the industrial revolution would affect all individuals. Many other people, too, considered child labour in the countryside essential. A Mr Ball, for example, stated in the

House of Commons in 1856: 'Those who are conversant with agriculture know that if we deprive the farmer of the labour of children, agriculture can not be carried on. There is no machinery by which we can get the weeds in growing crops out of the land. It can only be done by the employment of children, and if that employment is stopped the land will be choked with weeds, the crops will much decrease and a national calamity will be the result.'[9] Life, for labourers and their children, was as hard in the countryside as it was in the new factories:

> Or will you deem them amply paid in health,
> Labour's fair child, that languishes with wealth?
> Go then! and see them rising with the sun,
> Through a long course of daily toil to run;
> See them beneath the dog-star's raging heat,
> When the knees tremble and the temples beat;
> Behold them, leaning on their scythes, look o'er
> The labour past, and toils to come explore;
> See them alternate suns and showers engage,
> And hoard up aches and anguish for their age;
> Through fens and marshy moors their steps pursue,
> When their warm pores imbibe the evening dew;
> Then own that labour may as fatal be
> To these thy slaves, as thine excess to thee.
>
> – George Crabbe, *The Village*, Book I, 1783

The dog-star is Sirius, which, when seen at its brightest in August, portended fevers.

By the Education Acts of 1870 and 1880, children were at last in school, more or less, by the end of the nineteenth century.[10] Until twelve years of age, from 1898, when the minimum school-leaving age was raised, and from fourteen years in 1918 (fifteen in 1944 and sixteen years in 1973), urban children were not in full-time employment. In the rural areas, however, children of all ages continued in seasonal employment until, to a far less degree, the second half of the twentieth century. An Act of 1873 even permitted this form of rural employment, although, as permission to work was contingent upon school attendance, little notice was taken of it. E.M. Sneyd-Kynnersley, for example, inspecting schools in Norfolk in the 1870s, reported that to find only 36 children out of 121 in school who have made the required 125 or more attendances (out of a possible 210—and later, 250), was not unusual. George Ewart Evans, an oral historian in East Anglia, in describing the tasks of the child descendants of George Crabbe's villagers in a typical late nineteenth century year, noted:

> The farmers wanted cheap labour and the parents wanted money; and those two facts conspired to keep many children out of school when they should have been at their desks. In fact many of them must have spent as much time working on the land as they did at school. The third entry in the school log-book [of a village school in Suffolk] reads: 'Numbers low. Boys wanted for field work'. A few weeks later a number of children were absent harvesting beet—cattle beet or mangle-wurzels. In November the head teacher wrote: 'Forty-five boys given permission to go out *brushing*'. The boys were away acting as brushers at a partridge shoot, beating the undergrowth with sticks to rouse the birds and drive them on to the grounds. And so it went on all through the year. In January the teacher was worried because boys and girls were absent picking up stones and flint chips from the fields. They were paid for doing this by the farmers who carted away the stones to use as metal lining for the roads. In February and March they were often out of school employed in crow-keeping, bird keeping or tending, as the entries put it. That meant they were out scaring birds—rooks, crows, magpies and pigeons—keeping them away from the fields that had just been sown with spring corn. In many years they were out doing this again in the month of June, when the corn was just beginning to ripen.[11]

Children would also be employed on agricultural tasks early in the morning before attending school and, after school, continue this work until late at night. The increasing use of machinery on the land, from the 1930s, was a major factor in the decline of the use of child labour in the fields of England.

~~*~*~*~*

As a background to the memoirs within this anthology, it will be helpful to look at the various kinds of schools attended, or observed, by the authors. Despite the dreadfulness of private and voluntary school provision (even the seven per cent early Victorian economic elite suffered—unless tutored at home—see, for example, 'Temple Grove', 1834, in this volume), the alternative for the poor majority—early, constant and repetitive labour—was far worse.

The dame schools (widows, who often held these schools, were known as 'dames') were the most common—in 1837, in Manchester for example, according to the local Statistical Society, there were 230 of them, where reading, writing and sewing were taught. They are often derided, not without reason: the Newcastle Commission, reporting in 1861, cited, for example, a Dr Hodgson's description of these ubiquitous infant teachers—'none are too old, too poor, too ignorant, too feeble, too sickly, too unqualified in any or every way to regard themselves and to be regarded by others as unfit for school-keeping.'[12] Charles Dickens' contemporaneous 'Mr. Wopsle's great aunt' of *Great Expectations* (1861), amply filled this description: 'a ridiculous old woman of limited means and unlimited infirmity, who used to go to sleep from six to seven every evening in the society of youth who paid two pence per week each for the improving opportunity of seeing her do it...'[13] Nevertheless, the women assisted, with their hornbooks and bibles and their sticks or birch, boys and girls to acquire literacy when no other provision was available. William Shenstone (see 'The Schoolmistress', 1737, in this volume) and George Crabbe wrote, to some degree at least, sympathetically of the school dame. Crabbe described her thus:

> A deaf, poor, patient widow sits
> And awes some thirty infants as she knits;
> Infants of humble busy wives who pay
> Some trifling price for freedom through the day.
> At this good matron's hut the children meet,
> Who thus becomes the mother of the street.
> Her room is small, they cannot widely stray,
> With band of yarn she keeps offenders in,
> And to her gown the sturdiest rogue can pin.
>   – *The Borough*, Letter XXIV, 1810[14]

Highly literate and busy parents would entrust their children to a school dame. William Wordsworth and his brothers, the latter destined for careers as eminent scholars, first attended such a school—Anne Birkette's in Penrith, *circa* 1775—before transferring to the Hawkeshead Grammar School. William was then aged nine years. James Boswell, in his *Life of Samuel Johnson, LL.D,* 1791, discusses the first formal teacher, *circa* 1714, of 'Dictionary' (as he was often known) Johnson:

> He was first taught to read English by Dame Oliver, a widow, who kept a school for young children in Litchfield. He told me she could read the black letter, and asked him to borrow for her, from his

father, a Bible in that character. When he was going to Oxford, she came to take leave of him, brought him in the simplicity of her kindness, a present of gingerbread, and said he was the best scholar she ever had. He delighted in mentioning this early compliment: adding, with a smile, "this was as high a proof of his merit as he could conceive".

The 'black letter' is the, not easy to decipher, gothic alphabet—the incident charmingly conjures a fleeting episode in the life of a young child and his school dame. Samuel, then, was sickly and had poor eyesight—one can well imagine, too, the kindly Mrs Oliver plying nineteen year-old Johnson, notoriously careless, with advice on keeping well, as he began the long stagecoach journey from Litchfield to Oxford in the late October of that year.

~~*~*~*~*

Of the many common day schools, for fee paying pupils and usually owned by the master or mistress in charge, Joseph Lancaster (1778–1838) of monitorial school renown (see B.O. Williams' 'Reminiscence of the Lancasterian School in Detroit, USA', *circa* 1818) observed:

> The masters... are often the refuse of superior schools, and too often of society at large... The desks children write at are often badly suited for that purpose, the schoolrooms close and confined, and almost all the accommodations unfit for school purpose. Independent of the bad effects such places produce on the children's health, many having to date the ruin of their constitutions from confinement therein, the drunkenness of the schoolmaster is almost proverbial. Those who mean well are not able to do so: poverty prevents it; and the number of teachers, who are men of liberal minds, are few; yet not being sensible of the incalculable advantages arising from system and order, it is no wonder if it is at a very low ebb among them... The want of system and order is almost uniform in every class of schools within reach of the poor.
> – Joseph Lancaster, *Improvements in Education*, London, 1803

These schools taught reading, writing, arithmetic, penmanship and, sometimes, a little grammar and geography. George Crabbe in *The Borough*, Letter XXIV, 1810, contrasts two such schoolmasters (see 'Reuben Dixon and Leonard' in this volume)—of whom William Cobbett's

opinion of schoolmasters, previously cited, might apply. School memoirs
often recall harsh disciplinary regimes—see, for example, Charles Lamb's
'Christ's Hospital', which he left in 1789, in his *Essays of Elia*, (1823); 'The
Schoolboy', *circa* 1750, in this volume, or Robert Owen's *The Life of Robert
Owen by Himself* (1858), in which he describes his horror on seeing the
wife of his infants' schoolmaster, in the London schoolroom, with a *whip* in
her hand. Charles Kingsley's mother of the recalcitrant Grimes, a good
woman who kept the village school in Vendale, albeit fictional, is contrasted
with the 'regiments and brigades of cruel schoolmasters—more than half
of whom were nasty, dirty, frowzy, grubby, smelly...'[15] Schoolteachers,
whether semi-literate or university educated and thoroughly imbued as they
were with the mores of the period, saw no need to justify their barbarity: a
pupil seeking to question it would be flogged for impertinence. One of Dr
Johnson's schoolmasters, none of whom spared the rod, would say, 'And
this I do to save you from the gallows.'[16] Charles Dickens in his periodical,
Household Words, of 15 November 1851, describes Dr. Laon Blose (lay-
on-blows) of the Royal Free Grammar School of Thistledown (High Barnet),
an endowed school, with inimitable scorn—'It is not he who is an abuse;
he is but one among four thousand men, whose lot is cast among these
rotten places.' Dr. Blose is contrasted with the village schoolmistress:

> By the wayside, there is a cottage with nasturtium and monthly roses
> blooming about its windows, and a woman—not young—neatly
> dressed, leans over the gate, her head upon one hand, and she is
> looking up the lane pleasantly, pensively, her eyes upon the little
> multitude. Very coarse her neat dress is, very refined the look of
> love toward the children... and then, we see, built up against her
> cottage, the clean little school-house with its windows open...

Such a pleasant picture helps to explain fond memories of school. The
master or mistress was not always unsuccessful in creating an
ambience in which happy school memories were held. Wordworth's
'Mathew' poems, for example, celebrate a much loved village
pedagogue—notably in his 'Address to the Scholars of the Village
School of—', 1799, where, long after Mathew's decease:

> His benefits, his gift, we trace...
> Expressed in every eye we meet
> Round this dear Vale, his native place.

P.B. Ballard—a London school inspector—in 'My Old School',
circa 1900, in this volume, is equally certain that the school's most
valuable asset is the master or mistress:

And though the builders of the place
had broken every rule,
And though the trappings scarce were fit
to educate a fool
'Twas all redeemed to me because
the master was the school.

Many memoirs provide endearing portraits of village schoolteachers—
despite, in some, their obvious deficiencies—see, for example in this
volume, Oliver Goldsmith's Thomas Byrne; William Shenstone's Sarah
Lloyd; George Crabbe's Nathaniel Perkin; J. Henri Fabre's and Walter C.
Smith's village schoolmasters; Syed Wajid Ali's guru mahasay; Sir Ernest
Barker's Miss Gregory and his Headmaster, Silas Whipp, and so on.

~~*~*~*

The charity schools[17] (see 'Charity Schools to be Encouraged'), followed
by the Sunday School movement, initiated in 1780 by Robert Raikes
(1735–1811) of Shropshire, were amongst the first attempts to
systematically provide basic literacy for children and young adults. They
were taught the alphabet; they read from the Bible; perhaps did a little
writing, and for the girls in the charity schools, there was needlework.
However: 'The new charity schools and Sunday schools had the merit
of trying to do something for all but they had the demerit of too great
an anxiety to keep the young scholars in their appointed sphere of life
and train up a submissive generation.'[18] Charles Dicken's Noah Claypole
and Uriah Heep were drawn from such charity school products of the
first decades of the nineteenth century. The Sunday schools, in which
the process of teaching and learning was necessarily tedious, may have
reduced public pressure for a better-organized daily school system.
Sunday school, held on the only day of the week when a child had any
time free from work, and the daily three-hour instruction programmes
provided by the Factory Acts, if implemented, were for most working
children, simply an additional burden. The testimony below is from
evidence, taken in 1840, published in the Scriven Report on Child
Labour in the Potteries:[19]

Josiah Bevington, aged 8:
I come at six o'clock, sometimes five, to light fires... I can read and
write a little; can sign my name. I have been at day school at

'National', and go now to Sunday school always. I go Monday nights to write.

Ann Bradley, aged 10:

I cannot read or write. I go to Sunday school, and went a little while to National School, and learnt to sew and knit, and make my own pinafores. I come at seven in the morning and go home at six...

John Reeve, aged 15:

We come to work at six, and leave at eight or nine... I can read but very little, and can write little. I go to Sunday school at the Tabernacle, and went to a day school two or three years...

Ann Baker, aged 19:

I do not read or write; I go at Sunday school to learn to read, and would go Wednesday nights, but my mother goes then to learn to read, and I stay at home to look after the young children; the youngest is four years; none of them can read or write. They are all except the youngest at work...

In the twenty first century, a glance at the school register of Raja Jang village school in Pakistan, reveals similar reasons as those of pre-compulsory attendance England for children dropping out of school: 'Left to work with father' [an agriculturist] (boy, eight years); 'Left to work in factory' (two boys, eight and nine years); 'Left due to her illness' (girl, eight years); 'Left due to mother's illness' (girl, seven years) and so on.

~~*~*~*~*

The next stage in voluntary schools' provision was, in effect, an extension of the Sunday School—the monitorial schools of the National Society for Promoting the Education of the Poor in the Principles of the Established Church (the 'National'), founded in 1811, and the British and Foreign School Society (the 'British'), founded in 1814. The former society was created by the Church of England to compete with the growing popularity of Joseph Lancaster's non-denominational schools. One schoolmaster ran the school with the assistance of selected monitors, each of whom was responsible for some ten other pupils. The great advantage of the monitorial system, and which encouraged its rapid development, lay in it being cheap. It offered the opportunity to attain a level of literacy to children who would otherwise not have had any opportunity. By the 1830s the largest numbers of pupils in school in England were in the National schools, followed by the British schools.

Discipline was maintained by competition and reward. In the British schools, such punishments as the dunce's cap, leg shackles, a log hung around the neck and suspension from the ceiling in a basket were employed—these humiliating measures at least replaced the commonplace brutality in schools.[20] However, the condemnation applied by Lancaster and others to schools 'within reach of the poor' was to apply, in due course, to the monitorial schools. While B.O. Williams painted a positive picture of his monitorial school, in incompetent hands such schools must have been wholly inefficient and, in fact, the government's Newcastle Commission, reporting in 1861, found them to be so.

Constance Battersea provides a mid-nineteenth century village National school example (see 'Ousting the Straw-Plaiting Dames'). Of an 1850s' school in Buckinghamshire, England, she recalled: 'At that time, in the 'fifties, the only day school in Aston Clinton was kept by a drunken schoolmaster, who had about thirty dejected-looking male scholars. This was the National School, under the Rector's sway, and a disgracefully bad one it was.' Equally objectionable was that, while the boys were in school, the girls were taught straw plaiting. The parish priest, in Lady Battersea's account, illustrates the common antipathy of the wealthier classes towards the provision of education for the poor, and especially, towards that of girls' education—an attitude that continued, although decreasingly, much beyond 1870 and even in the decades following the Great War.

The voluntary societies reduced their reliance on monitors, who were in reality, low-cost child workers, as funds, pupil teachers and more trained teachers became available from the 1840s onwards.

~~*~*~*~*

In the Asian subcontinent, there is ample evidence to suggest that British rule discouraged indigenous education to the extent that literacy levels were reduced during this period. M.K. Gandhi thought so, and famously stated in Chatham House, London, in 1931:

I say without fear of my figures being challenged successfully, that today India is more illiterate than it was fifty or a hundred years ago, and so is Burma, because the British administrators, when they came to India, instead of taking hold of things as they were, began to root them out. They scratched the soil and began to look at the root, and left the root like that, and the beautiful tree perished. The village schools were not good enough for the British administrator, so he came out with his programme. Every school must have so much paraphernalia, building, and so forth.

Dr. G.W. Leitner, Principal of Government College, Lahore, 1864–1887, cited the statistical evidence in 1882 in his *History of Indigenous Education in the Punjab*[21] (see 'A Love of Poetry' in this volume). He, early in his history, quotes A.P. Howell's *Education in British India prior to 1854 and in 1870-1871*:

> It is much to be regretted that, as each province fell under our rule, the Government did not take advantage of the time... to make the village school an important feature in the village system that was almost everywhere transmitted to us. Had this been done, and had the numerous village allowances been diverted to this object, and had the Government devoted itself to the improvement of school-books and school-masters, instead of establishing a few new schools of its own, and thereby encouraging the belief that it was for the State and not for the community, to look for education, the work of general improvement would have been substituted for the work of partial construction, and we should now have had in every province a really adequate system of national primary education.[22]

Syed Wajid Ali describes, in this volume, two traditional village schools in Bengal that he attended in the 1890s (see 'The Maktab and the Pathsala'). There was, however, no 'system' in England (Howell's stricture came after the Elementary Education Bill was passed) until the 1870 Elementary Education Act provided a nucleus around which a national system was eventually built. In England, forms of funded and supervised basic education for the poor masses were conceded slowly and resentfully. That for the wealthy was absurdly narrow, irrelevant, and harsh. Dr Bell adapted the National schools' low-cost monitorial system from the system he found in Madras, and in other parts of India, in the 1790s (see, too, Syed Wajid Ali's reminiscence of the way in which the monitorial system was employed in Bengal in the 1890s, in 'The Maktab and the Pathsala'). The principle, too, of levying local taxes for the establishment and maintenance of village schools was an ancient custom in India: '...the instruction of the people is provided for by a certain charge upon the produce of the soil, and by other endowments in favour of the village teachers, who are thereby rendered public servants of the community.'[23]

What then was the official policy of the British in India? In the early decades of the nineteenth century it was to do nothing. Thomas Macaulay's often quoted 1835 'Minute on Indian Education' referred only to higher education and recommended that it should be devoted to western learning. However, if higher education, and therefore government jobs, required English, English would be favoured in school at ever-earlier ages. Then in 1844, by regulation, government service required an English education; at the same time, English was adopted as the language of public business and the courts. Thus the Viceroy, Lord Curzon, was caused to emphatically state at the turn of the century: 'Ever since the cold breath of Macaulay's rhetoric passed over the field of Indian languages and Indian textbooks, the elementary education of the people in their own language has shrivelled and pined.'[24]

A Despatch from the Directors of the East India Company in 1853, to the Governor-General, gave direction on 'the responsibility of the Government towards the toiling millions, and its desire to combat the ignorance of the people, which may be considered the greatest curse of the country.'[25] Departments of Public Instruction were established; grants-in-aid to private institutions were made. It was also decreed that 'English instruction should always be combined with a careful attention to the vernacular languages of the district, and with such general instruction as can be conveyed through that language.'[26] Due in part to the war of independence of 1857–1858, little was done. Syed Ahmed Khan in his *The Causes of the Indian Mutiny* (1873), quoting Sir Alfred Lyall's 'The Old Pindaree' (in this volume), discusses a widespread suspicion of government schools by the people at this period—see, too, for further explanation, 'A Love of Poetry' in this volume.

Elementary education in India received little government support. An official survey of 1904 reported that four out of five villages were without a school and recommended that the state should accept greater responsibility for primary education. This was not forthcoming. State education had officially and popularly by-passed indigenous education but was unable to meet its obligations. The voluntary societies and private enterprise, although encouraged by government, were unable to fill the enormous gaps, while indigenous education resembled no longer 'the beautiful tree' of Gandhi's description, but more that of a shrivelled plant.

~~*~*~*

In the UK, the Newcastle Commission, to which we have referred, reporting in 1861 on the state of elementary education in England and how to extend 'sound and cheap' elementary instruction, provided a major impetus towards, albeit low cost, national provision of elementary education. The commission stated bluntly that, for the poor, elementary education was 'inefficient, superficial, or of a kind not calculated to be helpful to the recipients'. They further declared: '...it is quite possible to teach a child soundly... all that is necessary for him in the shape of intellectual attainment by the time that he is ten years old.'[27] Robert Lowe (1811–1892) appointed, in 1859, Vice-President of the newly formed Education Department, agreed, and responded accordingly. As parliamentary representative of the Department with the President sitting in the Lords, he was, effectively, the Minister of Education. The gulf, however, between the 'two nations' was not, in principle, diminished by his tenure:

> I do not think it is any part of the duty of the Government to prescribe what people should learn, except in the case of the poor where time is so limited that we must fix upon a few elementary subjects... the lower classes ought to be educated to discharge the duties cast upon them. They should also be educated that they may appreciate and defer to a higher cultivation when they meet it, and the higher classes ought to be educated in a very different manner, in order that they may exhibit to the lower classes that higher education to which, if it were shown to them, they would bow down...[28]

Thus to ensure that the three Rs were not neglected, Lowe devised the 'payments by results' scheme, of which the impact on the curriculum and its delivery continued until the late 1890s. The system raised the standards of the many bad schools, but narrowed the curriculum for all schools to the few examined subjects upon which the school grant (with attendance) was now dependent. Many children perceived school as mechanical and boring, and for the school Head and his or her staff, the most important event of the year became that of the visit by the school inspector—see, for example, 'A Village School Inspection', 1871—from a school inspector's perspective, and from the pupil's perspective, 'A Visit by Her Majesty's Inspector', 1880s, and 'My Village School', 1880–1886, in this volume. Voices were raised against such limited horizons, including that of Sir John Lubbock for example (see 'A Discourse on Curriculum in Village Schools', in this volume).

The annual parliamentary grant to education began in 1833, and although always inadequate, rose steadily. However, by 1865, Robert Lowe's revised code considerably reduced the expenditure. His view was that '...those for whom this system is designed are the children of persons who are unable to pay for their teaching. We do not profess to give these children an education which will raise them above their station and business in life—that is not our object.'[29] Lowe was clearly not concerned with his popularity with the voteless masses. He was appointed Chancellor of the Exchequer in 1868 and W.E. Forster introduced the Elementary Education Bill in the following year.

****

In England and Wales, the Elementary Education Act of 1870 created 2500 School Boards elected by the ratepayers. They were able to build, improve and maintain schools out of the rates to ensure a school place for each child in their district. In rural areas the Boards could be niggardly, even illiterate, and in the complete control of the Clerk or Chairman. E.M. Sneyd-Kynnersley recalled one such example:

> "When does the board meet?" I asked.
> "Oh, we don't meet: I get what is wanted and then on market-day I go to the town, where I am sure to find the members; they are all farmers. I say to [them], 'The Inspector was here last week; wants some more desks; always asking for something; suppose you agree?'"[30]

It was proposed in one parish to raise the salary of the Headmistress. "Why", said one member, "thet there young woman is getting a matter of saxteen shellin a week: look what thet is for a young woman as hasn't only herself tu keep." (An agricultural worker at this time earned ten shillings a week.) The country schools were, according to the inspector, usually very small, and sometimes very bad:

> A very green girl, fresh from the training college, would take a school, and at the end of the year would get a poor report. In her second year she would work with more vigour and more skill, and would get a Report sufficiently good to earn her Parchment Certificate. Then she would take another school, or a husband, and the education of the village would relapse...[31]

Nevertheless, of the first Board School teachers, Sneyd-Kynnersley declaimed in 1908:

> It was a hard life for the pioneers in the backwoods of Arcady in the early 'seventies. You laboured, and other men have entered into your labours. Ill-paid, often ill-housed; worried by inspectors; worried by managers and managers' wives; worried by parents, and worried by children, who came to school as a personal favour, and, if affronted, stayed away for a week, you served your generation... as I look through these books I see the names of many whom all men honoured, and who reaped a full reward in the affectionate gratitude of the children...[32]

'Arcady' was rural Norfolk. Philip Snowden (1864–1937), Chancellor of the Exchequer in the first Labour Government in 1924, was a pupil in Cowling village school in Yorkshire in 1870. His father, an 1840s' chartist, was a weaver. Snowden's recollections of the changes brought about by the newly formed School Board were very positive:

> Steps were taken at once to build new school premises. A trained master was appointed, and a new era in child education in the village was opened up. I was between ten and eleven years old when this change took place. It brought me into a new world of learning. We were taught in a new schoolroom, which by comparison with the dingy old place we left seemed like a palace to us. The walls were covered with maps and pictures. Our curriculum was extended to include grammar, geography, history, elementary mathematics, and the simple sciences...
>
> – Philip Snowden, *An Autobiography*, 1934[33]

****

In France, (see 'A Village School in the Rouergue', 1827, in this volume), contemporary French reports described rural school premises in the 1830s, to the following effect:

> Of 20,000 communes provided with schools, scarcely one-half had school buildings of their own; in the other half the school was held in a barn, in a cellar, in a stable, in the church porch, in the open air, in the room which served at the same time as the dwelling place of the schoolmaster and his family, where his meals were cooked and his children were born. Where school premises existed, they were often no better than their less-pretentious substitutes; they were often hovels, dilapidated, windowless, fireless, reeking with damp.[34]

This description, too, applied to the premises used for school purposes in rural England until the voluntary societies, government grants and, after 1870, the local rates and building rules, made their impact. Rural schools, even after 1870, were often financed and maintained from a relatively small income. The voluntary societies were in an even more difficult position than the rate-assisted School Boards. Sneyd-Kynnersley, for example, noted in the 1870s: '...on Wednesday I drove ten miles to a country village, where the whole 45 lambs of the flock were collected in what an esteemed inspector called "a third class waiting-room and jam cupboard." '[35] In Hyde in Hampshire in 1885, the National Society replaced its very dilapidated mud-wall building with a new school of a very simple and cheap design—the resources of the voluntary societies had been much stretched everywhere since 1870.

All schools until the later Victorian period, including the grammar and public schools, accommodated their pupils within one schoolroom where the principal teacher with his ushers or, from the 1840s, his pupil teachers, would work. With the introduction of the 'Standards', or attainment levels, of the revised code of 1862, the system of classroom organization developed, initially by building rooms adjacent to the schoolroom. This created difficulties in the supervision of pupil teachers, aged thirteen years and above, but made the teaching of such subjects as science more practicable. The basic design of the rural school, however, remained that of the single schoolroom with possibly a separate room or apportioned off section for the infants (or 'babies' as they were affectionately known), with a raised platform for the Headmaster or Headmistress.

The Newcastle Commissioners found the single schoolroom to be '...the only arrangement sufficiently general to require distinct notice...', and the rural school retained this plan to the modern era. E.M. Sneyd-Kynnersley described a typical village school in Wales, in 1871, in the following terms:

> We find a long, rather low building with a thatched roof: the windows are somewhat low and narrow, and filled with diamond panes; and inside the light is scanty. There is a tiled floor; there are desks for the upper standards only; the other children sit on benches with no back-rails: both desks and benches are evidently the work of the carpenter on the estate. There is no cloak-room, and the damp clothes of the children are hung around the walls, sending out a gentle steam, as if it were washing day next door, and the water were not very clean. About a quarter of the room at one end is occupied by a platform, which is found convenient for village entertainments; and a narrow passage by its side leads to a small class-room, "contrived a double-debt to pay": it holds the small Infant Class and it serves as a Green Room for the performers at the aforesaid entertainments.[36]

Sir Ernest Barker (see 'My Village School')—from his 1880s' pupil's perspective—recalled:

I suppose I must have crossed the passage from the infants room to the main school by the time that I was seven or perhaps even earlier. But here also is a cloud. I see a big single room, narrower at one end (the end nearest the infants' room) and broader at the other. Different 'standards' occupied the different parts, and I must have moved from standard to standard, year by year, during the five or six years I sat in the room.[37]

Similarly, Flora Thompson described her school of the 1880s, for forty-five pupils within one schoolroom, as follows:

...though it would seem a hovel compared to a modern council school, it must at that time have been fairly up-to-date. It had a lobby with pegs for clothes, boys' and girls' earth-closets, and backyard with fixed wash basins, although there was no water laid on. The water supply was contained in a small bucket, filled every morning by the old woman who cleaned the schoolroom, and every morning she grumbled because the children had been so extravagant that she had to "fill'un again."[38]

W.H. Perkins, of Manchester Victoria University, described a similar school building in 1927, erected seventy years before (see 'Clogs and Cinders: A Typical Village School').[39] The sole alteration, since 1857, was the adaptation of the porch into cloakrooms—one for the boys and one for the girls. (With the promulgation of the Education Department's building rules, particularly those of 1889 and 1895, one Tory MP attacked 'the fad of having a peg for each child to hang up his hat and coat'.)[40] Of basic-design rural schools still in use in 1959, inspectors noted that: 'The infants in an old and small rural school sometimes suffer grave disadvantages. In buildings not yet renovated they may still be in the ancient "baby room" small and often dark. Sanitary fittings may still be primitive, and there may be scant provision of the materials that the children need for their play and work and almost no space to store such materials. There is to be sure in these rooms a comforting sense of intimacy, but this can scarcely compensate for the disadvantages...'[41]

~~*~*~*~*

The curriculum in England and Wales until the late 1890s was controlled, as we have seen, strictly by government grant payable 'upon rapid examination of every child above seven years of age who had attended 250 times in the school year [out of a total of 440 half-days]... There was a grant of 8 shillings (or 10 shillings if the teacher was certificated) if they were present...'[42] 'It was seldom that the examination of the elder children went beyond the three elementary subjects commonly known as the Three Rs... although an extra grant was payable for success in geography, grammar and history.'[43] As Sir John Lubbock pointed out: if the 1876 rules for Standards II to VI state that the children must 'pass a creditable examination in grammar, history, political geography, and plain needlework, or in any two of these subjects, it is obvious that if two subjects are made compulsory all others are practically excluded.'[44] He discusses the demerits of these subjects and promotes the merits of science in elementary schools. Flora Thompson says of her school's curriculum in the 1880s: 'Reading, writing and arithmetic were the principal subjects with a Scripture lesson every morning and needlework every afternoon for the girls.'[45]

Mathew Arnold, in his capacity of London school inspector, with reference to the curriculum, stated in his report for 1878: 'As regards sewing, calculating, writing, spelling, this is self-evident. They are necessary, they have utility, they are not formative.'[46] He may have been thinking of such children as Flora Thompson once was:

At needlework in the afternoon she [Flora] was no better. The girls around her in the class were making pinafores for themselves, putting in tiny stitches and biting off their cotton like grown women, while she was still struggling with her first hemming strip. And a dingy crumpled strip it was before she had done with it, punctuated throughout its length with blood spots where she had pricked her fingers.[47]

When the Squire's wife paid her visits to the school to inspect the work, the girls trembled, knowing that their sewing 'would never pass that eagle eye without stern criticism...' E.M. Sneyd-Kynnersley agreed:

In country schools there was not much fear of neglect, for Mrs. Squire and Mrs. Rector kept vigilant eyes on this branch of education, and the subscribers to the school funds often got back part of the value of their money by sending their household sewing to be done in school. It was no unusual thing to find five afternoons a week devoted to sewing. "They tell me," said one Lady Bountiful, "that the girls in Standard VI learn DECIMALS! Not that I know what decimals are. I think they should learn to sew, don't you?"[48]

By the early 1920s, brightly coloured fabrics, large needles and coarse threads were in use.

With a curriculum principally of the three Rs, Flora Thompson and countless children since the 1870s escaped the otherwise dull daily routines by taking refuge in the popular *Royal Readers* or their later competitors, such as *Chambers's Stepping Stones to Literature*, 1927, or *Blackies English Study Series, circa* 1925. In the USA, Hamlin Garland (see 'School Life', 1871, in this volume) found in the *McGuffey Readers* (first published in the USA in 1836 and used in schools until the 1920s), his first introductions to great authors. The content of British and North American readers was often robust. They described aspects of travel, adventure and wars. They provided models of excellence in writing. They were mines of information and they contained uplifting and moral tales to encourage a variety of attributes, including, for example, and promulgated over eight verses, honesty and acceptance of one's place in society:

> The rich man's son inherits lands,
> And piles of brick and stone and gold;
> And he inherits soft white hands,
> And tender flesh that fears the cold,
> Nor dares to wear a garment old;—
> A heritage, it seems to me,
> One scarce would wish to hold in fee.
> – *The New Royal Readers*, No.VI, Thomas Nelson: London, 1948[49]

There was little in the readers' content specifically included for girls: that which there was was usually didactic. For example, on seeing three pretty young girls tripping into town, an old owl portends:

> And soon, so soon, three white haired dames
> Will totter into the town.
> Gone then for aye the raven locks,
> The golden hair, the brown;
> And she will fairest be, whose face
> Has never worn a frown!
> – *Royal Crown Readers*, Third Book, Thomas Nelson: London,
> 1890

Importance was placed, for the older pupils, on elocution, or reading 'with expression'. The readers provided passages for recitation, an exercise fondly recalled by Flora Thompson and Hamlin Garland, but most pupils, as Flora points out, did not enjoy such 'dry old stuff'. Ralph Connor (1860-1937), in his popular tale of a one-teacher school in the forests of Ontario, Canada (*Glengarry Schooldays*, 1902), described how 'Marco Bozzaris' was tackled by every pupil—"The master shivered inwardly as he thought of the possibility of Thomas Finch, with his stolidly monotonous voice, being called upon to read the thrilling lines recording the panic-stricken death cry of the Turk: 'To arms! They come! The Greek! The Greek!" ' (See, also, Hamlin Garland's account of his recitation of this poem in 'School Life', 1875). Timmy Large, George Hewins' harassed teacher (see 'The National School', 1880s), and George himself, would certainly have felt the same inner shivering (and yet George, a builder, once participated in plays at the Royal Shakespeare Theatre, Stratford-upon-Avon).[50] Lord Boyd Orr (see 'Pupil and Pupil Teacher', 1885–1898) admitted to the popular preference, in the 1890s, of *Panther Paul the Prairie Pirate* and other blood-and-thunder stories to higher forms of literature.

When, by the turn of the nineteenth century, school grants were no longer dependent upon examinations of pupils in the three Rs, more time was allocated to the teaching of geography, history and science. Science usually took the form of 'nature study' for the younger pupils, a subject popular with generations of school children until the reorganization of the curriculum following the Education Reform Act, 1988 (see, in this volume, 'From Castle Camps to Linton Village College', 1930–1939, and for another view, 'Change in the Village', 1912). Geography textbooks produced in the 1900s were described by their publishers as 'readers' and were charming, illustrated, narrative descriptions of long journeys in the British Isles and the Empire, with occasional excursions to exotic, faraway, places such as Siam or, for example, the Chinese Empire. The chapters of Nelson's *The World and its People: The British Isles* (1904), for example, include 'Our Father Thames'; 'London, "The Mother of Cities" '; 'A Bicycle Ride through North Wales'; 'The Rivers of the Wash'; 'Yorkshire Hives of Industry'— in total, the representation of a golden Edwardian age—with merely passing references to the appalling poverty in which lived most of the inhabitants of these wonderful places. History textbooks enjoyed such titles as *Gateways to History: Wardens of Empire* (Edward Arnold: London, 1930) or *A Survey of the British Empire* (Blackie and Son, Ltd.: London and Glasgow, 1927), which combined the history with the geography of the countries visited. The textbooks are interesting now as historical artifacts: the teaching and learning of these subjects has developed in inverse proportion to the dissolution of the empire.

Penmanship was an important, carefully taught, skill. Children progressed from the slate or, as used in the monitorial schools, the sand tray and slate, to the copybook. Copperplate script, so named from the engraved plates from which the copybooks were printed, was in use until, in some schools, the second half of the twentieth century. The maxim of the copybooks was 'Lightly on the up-strokes, heavy on the down'. Steel pen nibs, which required these variations in muscular pressure, replaced quills when Birmingham factories began producing them in large quantities from the 1830s. Thomas Hood (1799–1845) in his 'Ode to Perry, the inventor of the Patent Perryan Pen', noted that Perryan Pens:

> True to their M's and N's,
> Do not with a whizzing zig-zag split,
> Straddle, turn up their noses, sulk and spit,
> Or drop large dots,
> Huge full stop blots,
> Where even semicolons were unfit.
> They will not frizzle-up or, broom-like, drudge
> In sable sludge —...[51]

Where English is taught in the village schools of the Punjab of Pakistan, one can occasionally see, painted on boards nailed to the walls, nineteenth century exhortations to good conduct. They are in copperplate script and are sometimes used, as they were in England, for writing practice:

> We'll go to our places
> With clean hands and faces,
> And at home and in school we will do as we're told:
> And so we shall ever.
> Be happy and clever,
> For learning is better than silver or gold.

In the subcontinent, the popular writing materials were, and remain for young children, the *qalam* (bamboo pen), the *davat* (inkpot), and the *takhti* (wooden writing board). The *qalam* has the strength and springiness of a chubby steel nib, and the writing board, once the smeared clay has dried, is the child's desk (see '*Takhties*, to start with...' 1998, in this volume). Elsewhere, traditionally, boys were taught to draw letters and figures on the sand with their fingers, or to chalk them on the floor. They then progressed to writing on palm leaves (which can be washed and reused), then banana leaves, and finally, paper. Boys went to school every morning carrying their rush mats or *pattaries* (about three feet long and two feet wide, around which their belongings would be arranged). Books, reed pen and other articles, were rolled into a neat bundle called the *daftar*. The palm leaves were tucked into the rolled-up *pattaries* and an earthen inkpot was swung by a little string tied to a finger (see Syed Wajid Ali, 'The Maktab and the Pathsala', 1890s, in this volume).

****

Transitions in school curriculum in Gujarat, India, are discernible in the official biography of Samaldas Parmananddas (1828–1884) — a Maharaja's *Dewan* or Prime Minister.[52] The grandfather, Ranchhoddas (1723–c. 1796), '...received his education at an indigenous school at Gogha where he was taught reading, writing and the old Indian system of accounts and book-keeping, which was all that was then required to qualify a boy for his occupation in life and also served to protect him against unfair dealings.' His son, Samaldas' father, Parmananddas (1794–1850) received a similar education, and besides, studied Persian privately. Of his education, the biographer, the *Naib-Dewan*, or Deputy Prime Minister, of Bhavanagar, wistfully recalled:

> ...if the instruction imparted did not include the English language and modern literature or science, it certainly taught boys their duties in the positions in life to which they were born. It made the boys good men of business both in the administrative and mercantile spheres. It made them good calligraphists and accountants. Students at these schools generally attained great proficiency in doing sums in arithmetic without the use of slate or paper. The education thus imparted was extremely useful for all practical requirements in those days.[53]

Samaldas, too, received a similar education in the three Rs, Persian, and the indigenous system of accounts. The author observed, '...such an education consisted less in what it did for a young mind than in what it did not do. Its positive contents were, judged by our modern standards, inconsiderable; but it did not crush the tender shoot under a load of examinations and it left plenty of room for one's native talent to develop.' The son of Samaldas, Vithaldas (b. 1846), was educated at the Anglo-Vernacular School established in 1852. He distinguished himself for his proficiency in English Literature and Mathematics. Vithaldas' sons and grandsons were the first to continue from the new High School in Bhavanagar to Bombay University.

Thus can be seen transitions in curriculum for the Hindu writer-mercantile caste.

G.W. Leitner, in his *Indigenous Education in the Punjab*, noted:

> If a boy learns arithmetic in our schools [i.e. the government schools], he is of little use for the shop, because he finds there a different system of accounts, and the meanest Banya can cost up the intricacies of grain-trade accounts by a mental process far more rapidly than if he had taken honours in Mathematics at the Calcutta University.[54]

While Board school pupils in England were doing their bills of parcels, some of their Indian contemporaries were in vocational schools with a curriculum relevant to father's and, therefore, their own future occupation.[55] Leither considered that '...indigenous schools provide education for its own sake or preparation for the work of life; that of [the British Indian] Government schools is examination and employment under Government.'[56]

The competition between indigenous schools and government schools led, as earlier discussed, to the virtual demise of indigenous schools. Clearly, despite whatever may be said in extenuation of this circumstance, a great cultural loss transpired as a result.

Such administrators as F.L. Brayne did their best for the betterment of government village schools (see Brayne's *The Remaking of Village India*, OUP, 1929, and *Better Villages*, OUP, 1937. 'The Punjab Village Schoolmaster', 1920s, in this volume, is taken from the former). He wanted the village school curriculum to meet the needs of the village rather than it leave pupils dissatisfied with village life:

> Reading and writing must be taught, books must be read and sums must be done, but the school games and the school farm and garden and the teaching of a clean and regular and orderly manner of living are probably the most important parts of the village child's education, and it is for the examinations to accommodate themselves to such a curriculum rather than for the curriculum to be sacrificed for the examinations.[57]

Such appeals were never heeded and examinations have been the most important influence on the village school curriculum ever since.

~~*~*~*~*

In the industrialized countries the teaching of agricultural and horticultural skills in rural schools was reduced in proportion to the realization that a rural child must be as equally well equipped as the urban child to compete for occupations in the towns and cities (see 'From Castle Camps to Linton Village College', for example). The intended provision of equal educational opportunity—culminating in the UK with the Education Reform Act of 1988—ensures that a standard curriculum is in place in all schools. Urban children may compete for the skilled occupations of the countryside, as do the rural children for those of the city. The popular 'Young Farmers' Club' of the country school thankfully remains, however. A school must provide equal educational opportunity while reflecting the culture and needs of the community whom it serves.

This introduction allows only brief references to comparative curricula and their breadth and depth and, too, to the influences upon systems of formal village education and its organization. The following accounts by contemporary observers, whether as past pupils, teachers, inspectors, or as observers in other capacities, that form the greater part of this book, will assist in providing a coherent overview. More importantly, as we have stated in the Preface, they enable the reader to 'hear the people talking'.

~~*~*~*~*

In compiling this anthology, the editor has been guided by certain criteria, the first of which is that each account must represent as closely as possible the author's actual experience and not a 'fictionalized experience'—hence the exclusion of Mark Twain's school experiences in Hannibal on the Mississippi river in the 1840s, Ralph Connor's early experiences in the Ontario wilderness of the 1860s, and also, for example, George Eliot's sympathetic description in *Adam Bede*, 1859, of a village schoolroom in the English midlands and of the schoolmaster with his rural labourer pupils, whom he nightly taught in the early 1800s. Thomas Hood's 'The Irish Schoolmaster', *circa* 1830, inspired by William Shenstone's 'The Schoolmistress', is excluded for the same reason, although some lines from this long poem are included in the introduction to 'Temple Grove'. Similarly Hamlin Garland's (1860–1940) reminiscences of the 1870s (see 'School Life'), replete with frozen lunches and the school's chilblains, are preferred to Laura Ingalls Wilder's (1866–1957) story-form autobiographical accounts of her school and school teaching days during the same pioneering period in the mid-west of the USA, although the student of educational systems will find them most rewarding.

While no two schools are ever the same, even when sharing the same values and curriculum, a further selection criterion is that, to achieve a continuous 'verbal' history of rural elementary education, each chapter must represent a different category, or type, of school—and throughout the long period with which this anthology is concerned, there have been considerable differences in forms of rural schools.

The original spelling, grammar and punctuation have been retained in each chapter except where absolute necessity required change.

~~*~*~*~*

While the great challenges of isolation, poverty and of reactionary feudal societies, that delayed the development of rural education in parts of the western world, have largely been removed, they remain in the developing world (see, for example, 'A Reminiscence of Bhera School', 1902; 'An Adult Education Project in the Solomon Islands', 1960s; 'The School Is Our Own', 1974; 'Takhties, to start with ... 1998').

At the present time, polarity increases between rural education in the developed and the developing worlds. In poor countries, the present concerns are that child labour be eradicated and that the quality of educational provision, to which we have referred, where it exists, be enhanced. Between the urban and rural areas significant gaps in school enrolment rates persist:

These gaps are the product of inequality in the distribution of resources, lower quality of learning material, higher teacher absenteeism, existence of ghost schools [i.e. schools that exist 'on paper' only], lack of access and higher opportunity cost for parents in rural areas. There are many reasons for the high dropout rate. Apart from socio-economic constraints and the dearth of adequate resources and schooling facilities, many youngsters find themselves squeezed into crowded, dilapidated classrooms, lacking even basic writing materials, while the teachers drill lessons by rote...[58]

M. Athar Tahir movingly describes in his short story *The Inspector of Schools* (1992), how a conscientious rural schoolmaster copes without a school building. Based on his own experiences as a school inspector, he relates how, on the occasion of the inspector's visit, the school is sited in a field from which the master and his boys were first obliged to cut the sugar beet, a very wearying crop to harvest even for adult villagers. As an example of ongoing investment in infrastructure needs in a developing country, the statistics for a school buildings' construction programme for shelterless and new schools in the Sindh province of Pakistan are given in the notes.[59]

~~*~*~*~*

In the United Kingdom, a small school is usually defined as one with less than one hundred pupils. There is much evidence to show that such schools can produce significantly better outcomes than larger schools:

> The strong, usually pro-active leadership of the headteacher, who usually also has some class-teaching responsibility, remains highly significant. In small schools, under the influence of a small closely-knit team, there is some effective 'domestication' of national learning initiatives by employing eclectic teaching methods and pupil groupings with a genuine 'fit for purpose' character. There is a greater use of apprenticeship learning, with children teaching other children...[60]

Of the many strengths of modern small schools, the UK's National Small Schools Forum include the following:

> Within an atmosphere close to the natural experience of home and family, children in small schools are secure, work hard, co-operate effectively, are happy to accept responsibility, have self-esteem, positive attitudes and behave very well. Small schools, with their humanity of scale, offer ideal conditions for children's learning.[61]

The same remarks may well be applied by a school inspector, journeying in distance and time, to Syed Wajid Ali's maktab and pathsala in the rural Bengal of the 1890s and, indeed, to many of the village schools in this volume.

Sue Thomas (see 'Frittenden CE Primary School', 1997) would agree. Perhaps the poet, Laurie Lee, would have agreed, at least when the Slad village school pupils were within sight of their patient teacher, Miss Wardley:

> ...we moved together out of the clutch of the Fates, inhabitors of a world without doom; with a scratching, licking and chewing of pens, a whisper and passing of jokes, a litter of tickling, a grumble of labour, a vague stare at the wall in a dream...[62]

NOTES

1. Estimates of nineteenth century UK literacy have usually depended upon ascertaining percentages of populations able to sign their names. In the early decades, evidence comes from parish registers and marriage licences; from 1837, copies of births, deaths and marriages were deposited with the Registrar-General's office, and from 1841, census returns were made. The ability to sign one's name clearly does not indicate a literacy level, or, indeed, whether one is literate at all (see note 3, below). This, and other information pertaining to literacy levels in the UK is taken from: J.L. Dobson, 'The interpretation of statistical data on the levels of literacy in nineteenth-century England and Wales', in G. Brooks and A.K. Pugh (eds.) *Studies in the History of Reading*, Reading University and UKRA: Reading, 1984, pp. 40–47.

2. The Elementary Education Act, 1870, established the Board School era. In 1902, the management of the schools was taken over by the newly established local education authorities (LEAs). In 1870, 11,000 parishes were without voluntary schools.

3. Definitions of literacy vary. A working child's reading attainment usually declines rapidly on leaving school. In Pakistan, the various census definitions of a literate person range from, in 1951: 'One who can read a clear print in any [one] language' to, in 1981: 'One who can read a newspaper and write a simple letter.' Dame schools and Sunday schools in England usually taught reading but not writing. However, as M.K. Gandhi pointed out: 'Literacy is not the end of education nor even the beginning. It is only one of the means whereby man and woman can be educated. Literacy in itself is no education.' See: J.C. Kumarappa, *Why the Village Movement?* The Hindu Publishing Co., Ltd.: Rajahmundry, 1939, pp. 103–104.

4. The first UK state survey of elementary schools was made in 1816—parish clergy supplied information. An enquiry into education in England and Wales was conducted as part of the 1851 ecclesiastical census. A Royal Commission was appointed in 1858 '...to inquire into the present state of popular education in England.' The Report of the Commission, chaired by the Duke of Newcastle, was issued in 1861. The combination of the recommendations of the Newcastle Commission and of Robert Lowe, Vice-President of the Education Department, led to payment by results, with government grant dependent upon average attendance and examination performance. A parliamentary investigation into the state of elementary education in Liverpool, Manchester, Leeds, and Birmingham was conducted in 1869. The following year W.E. Forster's Elementary Education Bill was passed.

5. The population in England and Wales rose from 8.9 million in 1801 to 32.5 million in 1901. In Scotland it rose from 1.6 million in 1801 to 4.5 million in 1901. While the percentage of children in school rose slowly, pupil numbers rose rapidly. The Board schools provided school places where industrial development created huge gaps in provision (see for example, 'Childhood Days', 1889–1894, in this volume).

6. Eric Hobsbawm, *The Age of Revolution 1789–1848*, Weidenfeld and Nicholson Ltd: London, 1962; Abacus reprint: London, 2002, p. 169.

7. W. Cunningham, *The Growth of English Industry and Commerce in Modern Times*, Cambridge University Press: Cambridge, 1917, pp. 628–629.

8. Phil Mason, *Nothing Good Will Ever Come Of It: A History of Parliamentary Misgivings, Misjudgements and Misguided Predictions*, Warner Books: London, 1993, p. 50.

9. Ibid., p. 51.

10. The 1901 Census Report recorded that, while the regular employment of children less than ten years of age had practically been abolished, nearly 900,000 children aged ten to fifteen were at work. Traditionally too, urban children would be employed seasonally, with their parents, in rural tasks, for example, in hop and apple picking in southern England.

11. George Ewart Evans, *The Crooked Scythe. An anthology of oral history*, Faber and Faber: London, 1993, pp. 22–23.

12. www.gober.net/victorian/reports/schools.htm

13. Charles Dickens, *Great Expectations*, 1861, chpt. 7. According to his biographer, Dickens had a vague memory of attending, in Chatham, a preparatory day school: '...it had been over a dyer's shop; that he went up steps to it; that he had frequently grazed his knees in doing so; and that in trying to scrape the mud off a very unsteady little shoe, he generally got his leg over the scraper.' (John Forster, *The Life of Dickens*, Cecil Palmer: London, 1874, p. 6.)

14. See also, for example, *When I was a Child* by Charles Shaw. Writing of the time, c. 1839, when he was seven years old, Shaw said: 'The course of education given by the old lady was very simple, and graded with almost scientific precision. There was an alphabet with rude pictures for beginners, though she never taught writing, her scholars were generally noted for ability to read while very young. I know I could read my Bible with remarkable ease when I left her school, when seven years old. Betty's next grade, after the alphabet, was the reading made easy book... The next stage was spelling, and reading of the Bible. George Smith of Coalville, who became famous in getting legislation carried to relieve the children employed on brickyards, was one of old Betty's scholars at this time...'
See: *Background to Education in the Potteries* at: www.netcentral.co.uk/steveb/focus/001.htm (11.02.05)

15. Charles Kingsley, *The Water Babies*, 1863, chpt. 5.

16. James Boswell, *The Life of Samuel Johnson, LL.D.*, [1791], Macmillan: London, 1914, p. 8 ff. Despite Locke (1632–1704), Rousseau (1712–1778), Pestalozzi (1746–1827), Froeble (1782–1852), Owen (1771–1858) and many others, there was, generally, little understanding of child psychology in the nineteenth century—even less of how to apply it in the schoolroom later in the century. This was, perhaps, due to a general belief, in western societies, of an inherent wickedness in children. A human tendency to pass on to the next generation the forms of upbringing employed on the present, is sometimes, if required, a hard cycle to break. This may also explain the brutality in English schools throughout, at least, the first two centuries with which this anthology is concerned.

17. G.M. Trevelyan, *English Social History*, Longmans, Green and Co.: London, 2nd ed., 1946, p. 361: 'Methodism in one form or another inspired much of the philanthropic work of the century that ended with Wilberforce. Methodism was seen to advantage in the strict, beneficent life of the charming lady Elizabeth Hastings (1662–1739), immortalized by Steele's epigram, "to love her was a liberal education"; she devoted her great wealth to charity, in particular to well devised schemes for the schooling and university education of poor scholars.'

18. M.G. Jones, *The Charity School Movement; a study of eighteenth-century Puritanism in action*, Cambridge University Press: Cambridge, 1938, p. 27.
19. Scriven Report, *Child Labour in the Potteries*, 1840.
20. Joseph Lancaster, *Improvements in Education as it Respects the Industrious Classes of the Community*, London, 1803 at: www.constitution.org/lanc/improv–1803.htm (11.02.05)
21. G.W. Leitner, LL.D., *History of Indigenous Education in the Punjab since Annexation and in 1882*, [1882], Republican Books: Lahore, 1991.
22. Ibid., p. 21.
23. Ibid.
24. Quoted by G. Anderson, *British Administration in India*, Macmillan: London, 1930, p. 144.
25. See: Despatch No. 49, dated the 19th July, 1854; Project South Asia: www.mssc. edu/Projectsouthasia/history/Primarydocs/education/Educational_Despatch_of 1854. htm (12.02.05)
26. Ibid., para. 14.
27. W. Kenneth Richmond, *Education in England*, Penguin Books: Harmonsworth, 1945, p. 72.
28. Robert Lowe, *Primary and Classical Education*, quoted by Richmond, ibid., p. 73.
29. Ibid.
30. E.M. Sneyd-Kynnersley, *H.M.I. Some Passages in the Life of one of H.M. Inspectors of Schools*, Macmillan: London, 1908, pp. 135–136.
31. Ibid., pp. 64–65.
32. Ibid., p. 71.
33. Philip Snowden, *An Autobiography*, 1934: online at *The National Archives Learning Curve*: www.spartacus.schoolnet.co.uk/REsnowden.htm (11.02.05)
34. From contemporary reports quoted by *The New Popular Encyclopedia*, vol. XII, The Gresham Publishing Company: London and Glasgow, 1902, p. 373. A rigorous law of 1833, which made compulsory what was previously optional for the communes, laid the foundations for a national system of primary education in France.
35. Sneyd-Kynnersley, op.cit., p. 108.
36. Ibid., p. 45.
37. Sir Ernest Barker, *Age And Youth*, OUP: London, 1953, pp. 249–250.
38. Flora Thompson, *From Lark Rise to Candleford*, OUP: Oxford, 1945, pp. 166–167.
39. W.H. Perkins, 'The Problem of the Village School' in *Education at Work. Studies in Contemporary Education*, ed. H. Bompas Smith, MUP: Manchester, 1927, pp. 47–75.
40. Quoted by Seaborne and Lowe, *The English School: its architecture and organization*, vol. II, 1870–1970, Routledge and Kegan Paul: London, 1977, p. 11.
41. 'Infants in old, small rural schools' in *Primary Education*, HMSO: London, 1959, pp. 51–52.
42. Sneyd-Kynnersley, op.cit., p. 43.
43. Ibid., p. 44.

44. Sir John Lubbock, 'Elementary Education' in *The Contemporary Review*, London, 1876; abridged in this volume as 'A Discourse on Curriculum in Village Schools', 1876.
45. Flora Thompson, op.cit., p. 178.
46. *Primary Education*, op. cit., 1959, p. 239.
47. Flora Thompson, op.cit., p. 178.
48. Sneyd-Kynnersley, op.cit., p. 2
49. From 'The Heritage' by J.R. Lowell (1819–1891) in *The New Royal Readers*, No. VI, Thomas Nelson: London, 1948, pp. 28 ff.
50. Angela Hewins, *A Stratford Story*, Oxford University Press: Oxford, 1994, pp. 165 ff.
51. Thomas Hood, *The Serious Poems of Thomas Hood*, Ward, Lock, & Co.: London, 1876, p. 427.
52. Harilal Savailal, *Samaldas Parmananddas, Scholar and Statesman. A Biographical Sketch*, B. H. Shinde: Bombay, 1912.
53. Ibid., p. 9.
54. G.W. Leitner, *History of Indigenous Education in the Punjab*, op.cit., Part III, p. 13.
55. This is not to suggest that English arithmetic was less onerous. In 1909, for example, one pound sterling consisted of the following denominations: 2 half-sovereigns; 4 crowns; 8 half-crowns; 10 florins; 20 shillings; 40 sixpences; 240 pence; 480 halfpence; 960 farthings—all of which were duly added to, subtracted from or multiplied and divided by subdivisions of one pound or multiples of one pound and its subdivisions. The editor forbears to list the contemporary weights and measures that were similarly treated.
56. G.W. Leitner, ibid.
57. F.L. Brayne, *Better Villages*, OUP: Oxford, 1937, p. 167.
58. *The News*: Lahore, 12 June 2002
59. For example, the targets and achievements of the Sindh Primary Education Department's construction programme, in the period 1990–1995,were:

i) Construction of shelterless schools:	Target	Achieved
2 roomed schools	2838	1863
5 roomed schools	355	106
ii) Construction of new schools:		
2 roomed schools	2412	1885
5 roomed schools	65	64
iii) Addition of classrooms in mosques	4000	1864
iv) Sanitation/water supply	2100	632
v) Boundary walls	2400	604

60. A speaker at a seminar entitled 'The Truth about Small Schools' held at the House of Commons on 25 June 2002. Human Scale Education, the National Association of Small Schools and the National Small School Forum organized the seminar. See: http://www.nssf.co.uk
61. National Association of Small Schools, ibid.
62. Laurie Lee, *Cider with Rosie*, The Hogarth Press: London, 1959, p. 63.

2

CHARITY SCHOOLS TO BE ENCOURAGED, 1712

London
Sir Richard Steele

Philanthropic individuals in all communities, past and present, in which literacy is recognized as a necessary skill, have seen reasons and purpose for the establishment of schools by endowment or other means. All schools in the county of Somerset, until the year 1800, for example, were established by such means. The charity school movement, as it is known, was a first attempt, following the founding, in 1698, of the Society for the Propagation of Christian Knowledge, or SPCK, at organizing the widespread provision of schools.

In a letter to the Archbishops in 1711, Queen Anne announced that '...it hath been very acceptable to us to hear that... many charity Schools are now created throughout this Kingdom by the liberal Contributions of our good subjects; We do therefore earnestly recommend you by all Proper Ways to encourage and promote so excellent a work.' The history of organized rural elementary education, despite the distinctive challenges in its provision, is hardly separable from the history of urban education in terms of national initiatives at voluntary and governmental level. It is appropriate, therefore, to begin this anthology and history of rural elementary education in London. It returns to London in the 1870s for the measured opinion of Sir John Lubbock on contemporary developments in rural elementary education.

The poverty of the people, their utter ignorance and a common indifference to their needs, and especially to those of poor children, were the incentives to the founders of charity schools. By the middle of the eighteenth century, it is estimated that the SPCK had established more than two thousand schools, attended by more than fifty thousand

The Spectator, no. 430, Monday, 14 July 1712, F.C. and J. Rivington: London, 1822

pupils. Children received not only free instruction, but also free food and clothing. The girls were prepared for domestic service and the boys for trades; they were, therefore, to a considerable degree, vocational schools. However, while school dames and country clergy maintained schools (the latter through subscription or their own means), many villages and country towns remained without a teacher of any kind. Sir Richard Steele (1672–1729), in *The Spectator*, supported the charity school movement, although he found it necessary to remind readers of the equally pressing needs of other impoverished people.

SIR,

'I was last Sunday highly transported at our parish-church; the gentleman in the pulpit pleaded movingly in behalf of the poor children, and they for themselves much more forcibly by singing a hymn; and I had the happiness of being a contributor to this little religious institution of innocents, and am sure I never disposed of money more to my satisfaction and advantage. The inward joy I find in myself and the good-will I bear to mankind, make me heartily wish these pious works may be encouraged, that the present promoters may reap the delight, and posterity the benefit of them. But whilst we are building this beautiful edifice, let not the old ruins remain in view to sully the prospect. Whilst we are cultivating and improving this young hopeful offspring, let not the ancient and helpless creatures be shamefully neglected. The crowds of poor, or pretended poor, in every place, are a great reproach to us, and eclipse the glory of all other charity. It is the utmost reproach to society that there should be a poor man unrelieved, or a poor rogue unpunished. I hope you will think no part of human life out of your consideration, but will, at your leisure, give us the history of plenty and want, and the natural gradations towards them, calculated for the cities of London and Westminster.

I am SIR, your most humble servant,
'T.D.'

3

THE SCHOOLMASTER, 1730s[*]

Lissoy, Westmeath, Ireland
Oliver Goldsmith

Oliver Goldsmith (1728–1774) was born at Pallas, Fernoy, in county Longford, Ireland, the son of a poor parish priest. His mother was the daughter of the Headmaster of the church school at nearby Elphin. According to the historian, Thomas Macaulay, Goldsmith was first taught the alphabet by the family maidservant. His first schoolmaster, Thomas Byrne, in Lissoy, provided a model for the village schoolmaster of this poem, of whom the unaccredited note, *circa* 1885, below, provides some biographical information.

Oliver—destined to earn his future livelihood in a merchant's office—was accordingly sent to a kind of hedge school in the parish, where he was taught reading, writing, and arithmetic, by the village schoolmaster; an old soldier who had been quarter-master in the army in Queen Anne's days, and had fought in Spain during the wars of the Spanish Succession,[1] under the chivalrous and romantic Earl of Peterborough. Often, when lessons were over, this singular pedagogue entertained his young pupils with stories of those days of wild adventure and heroic daring. Oliver's vivid imagination kindled at these recitals; and the love of adventure and excitement thus instilled into his childish mind tinged all his after life. Doubtless, pleasant memories of his first teacher inspired the charmingly playful description of the schoolmaster in the "Deserted Village". At the age of seven or eight years, Oliver attempted to write poetry, and would scribble verses which he afterward burnt; but his mother

---

Oliver Goldsmith, *The Deserted Village*, 1770
*Editorial note: Where there is a difference, the year refers to the period the author describes and not to the year of composition.

detected in them the germ of his future powers, and pleaded hard
that he might receive better instruction...[2]

The Schoolmaster

Beside yon straggling fence that skirts the way,
With blossom'd furze unprofitably gay,
There, in his noisy mansion, skill'd to rule,
The village master taught his little school;
A man severe he was, and stern to view;
I knew him well, and every truant knew:
Well had the boding tremblers learn'd to trace
The day's disasters in his morning face;
Full well they laugh'd, with counterfeited glee,
At all his jokes, for many a joke had he;
Full well the busy whisper, circling round,
Convey'd the dismal tidings when he frown'd;
Yet he was kind; or if severe in aught,
The love he bore to learning was in fault;
The village all declar'd how much he knew;
'Twas certain he could write, and cipher[3] too;
Lands he could measure, terms and tides[4] presage,
And e'en the story ran that he could gauge.[5]
In arguing too, the parson own'd his skill,
For e'en though vanquish'd, he could argue still;
While words of learned length and thund'ring sound
Amaz'd the gazing rustics rang'd around,
And still they gaz'd, and still the wonder grew
That one small head could carry all he knew.

~~*~*~*~*

But past is all his fame. The very spot
Where many a time he triumph'd is forgot.

NOTES

1. They took place from 1701 to 1714. The Earl of Peterborough, Richard Mordaunt, arrived in Lisbon in June 1705 with 5000 Dutch and English soldiers. Thomas Byrne, to be appointed to his responsible role, in addition to his literacy and numeracy skills, clearly required some maturity. Perhaps he was born, therefore, about 1680—he would then be aged fifty or so, when Oliver entered his school. While later scholarship suggests Peterborough fabricated many adventures, Macaulay considered him to be 'the most extraordinary character of the age... his virtues and vices those of the Round Table.' Perhaps Byrne knew, too, that the flamboyant Earl 'loved to dictate six or seven letters at once', which would have amused the infant Goldsmith. See Thomas Macaulay, 'War of the Succession in Spain', [1833] in *Critical and Historical Essays,* vol. ii, J.M. Dent: London, 1907.
2. *The Poems and Plays of Oliver Goldsmith,* F. Warne and Co.: London, n.d. (c. 1885), pp. v-vi. Thomas Macaulay (see *Lord Macaulay's Miscellaneous Writings,* vol. II, Longman, Green, Longman and Roberts: London, 1860, p. 245) adds that Thomas Byrne was 'of the Protestant religion; but he was of the aboriginal race, and not only spoke the Irish language, but could pour forth unpremeditated Irish verses.' Washington Irving states in his biography of Goldsmith, that Goldsmith was sent first to the village dame, Mistress Elizabeth Dewlap, but that he 'did not profit by it'; nevertheless, it was Mistress Dewlap's 'pride and boast that she had first put a book (doubtless a hornbook) into Goldsmith's hands.' Irving adds that 'Paddy' Byrne, as he was known, believed implicitly in the fairy superstitions of Ireland and 'under his tuition Goldsmith soon became almost as proficient in fairy lore.' See Project Gutenberg's *The Life of Oliver Goldsmith* by Washington Irving at http://etext.library.adelaide.edu.au/i/irving/washington/goldsmith/chapter1.htm/ (12.02.05).
3. cipher: simple arithmetic.
4. terms: probably the dates when the legal terms begin and end; tides: the future dates of the various church festivals, e.g., Shrovetide, Eastertide.
5. gauge: calculate areas and quantities.

4

THE SCHOOLMISTRESS, 1737

- Some excerpts

Halesowen, Shropshire (now Worcestershire), England
William Shenstone

In his gossipy *Curiosities of Literature* (1784), the learned Isaac D'Israeli (Benjamin's father), observes that 'The inimitable "Schoolmistress" of William Shenstone, is one of the felicities of genius; but the purpose of this poem has been entirely misconceived.' It is not, D'Israeli argues, a 'moral work' as designated by Shenstone's first editor, Roger Dodsley: 'It is a portrait of Shenstone's old school-dame, Sarah Lloyd... a refined species of ludicrous poetry, which is comic yet tender, lusory yet elegant, and with such a blending of the serious and the facetious, that the result of such a poem may often, amongst its other pleasures, produce a sort of ambiguity; so that we do not always know whether the writer is laughing at his subject or whether he is to be laughed at... "The Schoolmistress" of Shenstone has been admired for its simplicity and tenderness, not for its exquisitely ludicrous turn...'

William Shenstone added in the first edition of the poem, in 1737, a 'ludicrous index'—a list of humorous subtitles 'to show fools that I am in jest'. Dodsley, apparently on his own initiative, D'Israeli informs his readers, removed these in the revised edition of 1764. Since then, as far as the present editor is aware, the 'ludicrous index', we presume incorrectly, has not been published with the poem. Shenstone's 'ludicrous index' has therefore been restored to the poem before each relevant stanza or stanzas.[1]

William Shenstone (1714–1763) was educated at Pembroke College, Oxford. He was born in and inherited the country estate, the Leasowes,

---

William Shenstone, *Works in verse and prose*, R. and J. Dodsley: London, 1764

in which Sarah Lloyd's school was held. The Leasowes was renowned, under Shenstone's direction, for its landscape gardening. Of William Shenstone's early education, Dr Samuel Johnson, in his *Life of William Shenstone* (1779), says:

> He learned to read of an old dame, whom his poem of the School-mistress has delivered to posterity; and soon received such delight from books, that he was always calling for fresh entertainment, and expected that when any of the family went to market a new book should be brought him, which when it came, was in fondness carried to bed and laid by him. It is said, that when his request had been neglected, his mother wrapped up a piece of wood of the same form, and pacified him for the night. As he grew older, he went for a while to the Grammar-school in Hales-Owen, and was placed afterwards with Mr. Crumpton, an eminent school-master at Solihul, where he distinguished himself by the quickness of his progress.[2]

Introduction

Ah me! full sorely is my heart forlorn,
    To think how modest worth neglected lies,
    While partial Fame doth with her blasts adorn
    Such deeds alone as pride and pomp disguise;
    Deeds of ill sort, and mischievous emprize;
    Lend me thy clarion, Goddess! Let me try
    To sound the praise of merit ere it dies;
    Such as I oft have to espy,
    Lost in the dreary shades of dull obscurity.

The subject proposed

    In every village mark'd with little spire,
    Embower'd in trees, and hardly known to fame,
    There dwells, in lowly shed, and mean attire,
    A matron old, whom we school-mistress name;
    Who boasts unruly brats with birch to tame;
    They grieven sore, in piteous durance pent,
    Awed by the power of this relentless dame;
    And oft-times, on vagaries idly bent,
    For unkempt hair, or task unconn'd, are sorely shent.[3]

A circumstance in the situation of the mansion of early discipline, discovering the surprising influence of the connexion of ideas

And all in sight doth rise a birchen tree,
Which Learning near her little dome did stow,
Whilom a twig of small regard to see,
Though now so wide its waving branches flow,
And work the simple vassals mickle woe;
For not a wind might curl the leaves that blew,
But their limbs shudder'd, and their pulse beat low,
And as they look'd, they found their horror grew,
And shaped it into rods, and tingled at the view.

Some peculiarities indicative of a country school, with a short sketch of the sovereign presiding over it

Near to this dome is found a patch so green,
On which the tribe their gambols do display.
And at the door imprisoning board is seen,
Lest weakly wights of smaller size should stray,
Eager, perdie,[4] to bask in sunny day!
The noises intermix'd, which thence resound,
Do Learning's little tenement betray;
Where sits the dame, disguised in look profound,
And eyes her fairy throng, and turns her wheel around.

Some account of her nightcap, apron, and a tremendous description of her birchen sceptre

Her cap, far whiter than the driven snow,
Emblem right meet of decency does yield;
Her apron dyed in grain, as blue, I trow,
As is the harebell that adorns the field;
And in her hand, for sceptre, she does wield
Tway birchen sprays; with anxious fear entwined,
With dark distrust, and sad repentance fill'd;
And steadfast hate, and sharp affliction join'd,
And fury uncontroll'd, and chastisement unkind.

Her gown

A russet stole was o'er her shoulders thrown,
  A russet kirtle fenced the nipping air;
  'Twas simple russet, but it was her own;
  'Twas her own country bred the flock so fair;
  'Twas her own labour did the fleece prepare;
  And, sooth to say, her pupils ranged around,
  Through pious awe, did term it passing rare;
  For they in gaping wonderment abound,
  And think, no doubt, she been the greatest wight on ground.

Her titles, and punctilious nicety in the ceremonious assertion of
them

  Albeit ne flattery did corrupt her truth,
  Ne pompous title did debauch her ear;
  Goody, good woman, gossip, n'aunt, forsooth,
  Or dame, the sole additions she did hear;
  Yet these she challenged, these she held right dear;
  Ne would esteem him act as mought behove,
  Who should not honour'd eld with these revere;
  For never title yet so mean could prove,
  But there was eke a mind which did that title love.

A digression concerning her hen's presumptuous behaviour, with a
circumstance tending to give the cautious reader a more accurate
idea of the officious diligence and economy of the old woman

  One ancient hen she took delight to feed,
  The plodding pattern of the busy dame,
  Which, ever and anon, impell'd by need,
  Into her school, begirt with chickens, came;
  Such favour did her past deportment claim;
  And, if neglect had lavish'd on the ground
  Fragment of bread, she would collect the same;
  For well she knew, and quaintly could expound,
  What sin it were to waste the smallest crumb she found.

A view of this rural potentate as seated in her chair of state, conferring honours, distributing bounties, and dispersing proclamations

In elbow-chair, like that of Scottish stem
By the sharp tooth of cankering Eld defaced,
In which, when he receives his diadem,
Our sovereign prince and liefest liege is placed,
The matron sate; and some with rank she graced,
(The source of children's and of courtiers' pride!)
Redress'd affronts, for vile affronts there pass'd,
And warn'd them not the fretful to deride,
But love each other dear, whatever them betide.

Right well she knew each temper to descry,
To thwart the proud, and the submiss to raise;
Some with vile copper prize exalt on high,
And some entice with pittance small of praise;
And other some with baleful sprig she 'frays:
Even absent, she the reins of power doth hold,
While with quaint arts the giddy crowd she sways;
Forewarn'd, if little bird their pranks behold,
'Twill whisper in her ear, and all the scene unfold.

The action of the poem commences with a general summons; follows a particular description of the artful structure, decoration, and fortifications of an horn-bible[5]

Lo! now with state she utters her command;
Eftsoons the urchins to their tasks repair;
Their books of stature small they take in hand,
Which with pellucid horn secured are,
To save from finger wet the letters fair;
The work so gay, that on their back is seen,
St. George's high achievements does declare,
On which thilk wight that has y-gazing been,
Kens the forthcoming rod, unpleasing sight, I ween![6]

In the highest posts and reputation[7]

Yet nursed with skill, what dazzling fruits appear!
Even now sagacious foresight points to show
A little bench of heedless bishops here,
And there a chancellour in embryo,
Or bard sublime, if bard may e'er be so,
As Milton, Shakespeare, names that ne'er shall die!
Though now he crawl along the ground so low,
Nor weeting how the Muse should soar on high,
Wisheth, poor starveling elf! his paper kite may fly.

But now Dan Phoebus gains the middle sky,
And liberty unbars her prison door,
And like a rushing torrent out they fly,
And now the grassy cirque han cover'd o'er
With boisterous revel rout and wild uproar;
A thousand ways in wanton rings they run,
Heaven shield their short-lived pastimes I implore!
For well may Freedom erst so dearly won,
Appear to British elf more gladsome than the sun.

Enjoy, poor imps! enjoy your sportive trade,
And chase gay flies, and cull the fairest flowers,
For when my bones in grass-green sods are laid,
O never may ye taste more careless hours
In knightly castles or in ladies' bowers.
O vain to seek delight in earthly thing!
But most in courts, where proud Ambition towers;
Deluded wight! who weens fair peace can spring
Beneath the pompous dome of kesar or of king.

A deviation to a huckster's shop

See in each sprite some various bent appear!
These rudely carol most incondite lay:
Those sauntering on the green, with jocund leer
Salute the stranger passing on his way;
Some builden fragile tenements of clay;
Some to the standing lake their courses bend,

With pebbles smooth at duck and drake to play;
Thilk to the huxter's savoury cottage tend,
In pastry kings and queens the allotted mite to spend.

NOTES

1. The editor acknowledges the Shropshire County Council Library Services' website *West Midlands Literary Heritage* for the text and the Project Leader for restoring (albeit as a footnote) the 'ludicrous index' (12.02.05<http://www3.shropshire-cc.gov. uk/etexts/E000370.htm#X1232). The selections from Shenstone's thirty-five stanzas are the editor's.

2. Johnson, Samuel. *The Life of William Shenstone.* The Penn State Archive of Samuel Johnson's *Lives of the Poets.* K.N. Kemmerer (ed.), 1.07.04. <www.hn.psu.edu/ faculty/kkemmerer/poets/shenstone/default.html

3. shent: blamed.

4. perdie: by God—from *par adieu.*

5. The horn-bible, or hornbook as it is more usually known, was a sheet of paper fastened to a board on which were written the letters of the alphabet, and often, the ten digits and the Lord's Prayer. A thin plate of cow's horn protected the paper from, as Shenstone says, wet fingers. William Cowper (1731–1800) described the hornbook in his poem 'Tirocinium; Or, A Review of Schools' (c. 1785), as follows:

> Neatly secured from being soiled or torn
> Beneath a pane of thin translucent horn,
> A book (to please us at a tender age
> 'Tis called a book, though but a single page)
> Presents the prayer the Saviour deigned to teach,
> Which children use and Parsons —when they preach.
> Lisping our syllables we scramble next
> Through moral narrative, or sacred text,
> And learn with wonder how this world began...

6. Nine stanzas follow which describe the brutal beating of the boy, the fear and response of his sister and class fellows and Sarah Lloyd's unsuccessful attempt at reconciliation with the boy. The poet reflects on the destruction of innate ability by such means:

> Beware, ye dames! with nice discernment see
> Ye quench not, too, the sparks of nobler fires...

7. D'Israeli suggested that the poet Thomas Gray had drawn his inspiration for 'Elegy written in a country churchyard', 1751, from this stanza. See also Syed Wajid Ali's reflections on Gray's Elegy in 'The Maktab and the Pathsala', in this volume.

5

THE SCHOOLBOY, c. 1750

England

Thomas Fullor (1608–1661), in his essay 'The Good Schoolmaster', advocated 'moderation in inflicting deserved correction... No wonder if his scholars hate the muses, being presented unto them in the shapes of fiends and furies...' The poem below, of which the provenance is unknown, is taken from *The Young Dragon Book of Verse*, Oxford University Press: Oxford, 1993.

Hey! hey! by this day!
What availeth it me though I say nay?

I would fain be a clerk,
But yet it is a strange work;
The birchen twigs be so sharp,
It maketh me have a faint heart.
What availeth it me though I say nay?

On Monday in the morning when I shall rise
At six of the clock, it is the guise
To go to school without advice—
I would rather go twenty miles twice!
What availeth it me though I say nay?

My master looketh as he were mad:
"Where hast thou been, thou sorry lad?"
"Milking ducks, as my mother bade":
It was no marvel that I were sad.
What availeth it me though I say nay?

Anonymous

My master peppered my tail with good speed,
It was worse than fennel seed,
He would not leave till it did bleed.
Much sorrow have he for his deed!
What availeth it me though I say nay?

I would my master were a hare,
And all his books greyhounds were,
And I myself a jolly hunter;
To blow my horn I would not spare,
For if he were dead I would not care!
What availeth it me though I say nay?

6

MICKLEY SCHOOL, c. 1760

Cherryburn, Northumberland, England
Thomas Bewick

Thomas Bewick (1753–1822), the celebrated engraver in wood of animals, birds and scenes of the Northumberland countryside, was born at Cherryburn on the river Tyne, near Newcastle. His father was the tenant of an eight-acre farm and adjacent colliery. Bewick's most important works include his *General History of Quadrupeds* (1790); *Birds* - the first volume of which came out in 1797 and the second in 1804 - and *Aesop's Fables* (1818).

In the extract, below, from his unfinished memoir (published forty years after his death), Bewick describes his experience of Mickley village school. He was afterwards sent to the nearby Vicar of Ovingham who taught him Latin—the study of which Bewick enlivened by filling 'every space of spare and blank paper...with various kinds of devices and scenes I had met with...but as I soon filled all the blank spaces in my books, I had recourse at all spare times to the grave stones and the floor of the church porch, with a bit of chalk...' It was not uncommon, even into the twentieth century, for university educated parish priests, on small stipends, to tutor pupils (usually no more than two) to the level required for enrolment in Oxford and Cambridge Universities.

In August 1753 I was born and was mostly intrusted to the care of my Aunt Hannah (my mother's sister) and my grandmother Agnes Bewick, and the first thing I can remember was that the latter indulged me in every thing I had a wish for, or in other words made me a great *Pet*. I was not to be snubbed (as it was called) do what I would and in consequence of my being thus suffered to have my own way, I was often scalded and burnt, or put in danger of breaking my bones by falls from heights I had clambered up to.

Thomas Bewick, *My Life*, [1862] The Folio Society: London, 1981

The next circumstance, which I well remember, was that of my being put to Mickley school, when very young, and this was not done so much with a view to my learning, as it was to keep me out of *'harm's way'*. I was sometime at this school without making much progress in learning my letters and spelling small words. The master perhaps was instructed not to keep me very close at my book, but in the process of time he began to be very severe upon me, and I see clearly at this day, that he frequently beat me when faultless, and also for not learning what it was not in my power to comprehend. Others suffered in the same way, for he was looked upon as a severe or cross man and did not spare his rod. His name I do not recollect but he was nicknamed *Shabby Rowns*. He was a tall thin man, and with a countenance severe and grim he walked about the school room with the taws or a switch in his hand, and he no doubt thought he was keeping the boys to their lessons; while the gabbering and noise they made was enough to stun any one, and impressed the people passing by with the idea that Bedlam was let loose. How long he went on in this way I do not recollect, but like many others of his profession, who were at that time appointed to fulfill that most important of all offices, no pains was taken to enquire into the requisite qualifications befitting them for it,—and this teacher was one of that stamp. He went on with a senseless system of severity, where ignorance and arrogance were equally conspicuous. Conduct like this sours the minds of some boys, renders others stupid and serves to make all more or less disgusted with learning.

Upon some occasion or other, he ordered me to be flogged—and this was to be done by what was called hugging, that is by mounting me upon the back of a stout boy, who kept hold of my hands over his shoulders, while the posteriors was laid bare, and where he supposed he could do the business freely; in this instance however he was mistaken for, with a most indignant rage I sprawled, kickt and flung, and as I was told, bit the innocent boy on the neck, when be instantly roared out and flung me down, and on my being seized again by the old man, I rebelled and broke his shins with my iron hooped cloggs and ran off. By this time, the boy's mother, who was a spirited woman, and lived close by, attracted by the ferment that was raized, flew (I understood) into the school room, when a fierce scold ensued between the master and her. After this I went no more to his school, but played the truant every day, and amused myself by making dams and swimming boats in a small bourne which ran through a place then called the 'Colliers-close-Wood', 'till the evening, when I returned home with my more fortunate or more obedient school fellows. How long it was before my absence from school was discovered I know not, but I got many severe beatings from my father and mother, in the interval between my utterly leaving the school and the old master's death. As soon as another schoolmaster (James Burne) was appointed, I was quite happy, and learned as fast as any other of the boys and with as great pleasure. After the death this much respected young man, who lived only a very few years after his being appointed schoolmaster, my learning any more at Mickley School was at an end.

Sometime after this, my father put me to school under the care of the Reverend C. Gregson of Ovingham, and well do I remember the conversation that passed between them on the occasion. It was little to my credit, for my father begun by telling him that I was so very unguideable that he could not do it, and begged of my new master that he would undertake that task, and they both agreed that 'to spare the rod was to spoil the child' and this system was I think too severely acted upon, sometimes upon trivial occasions, and sometimes otherwise.

7

EARLY RECOLLECTIONS, 1770s

Newtown, Montgomeryshire, Wales
Robert Owen

Robert Owen, (1771–1858), a Welshman and the son of a saddler, created model social organizations for his factory workers in Manchester, and then, from 1797, in New Lanark, Glasgow. He was a creative educationist and a leading advocate of reducing the working hours of children. He established model infant schools for his workers' children of one year and above, and included, in their enlightened curriculum, not only the three Rs but also much play, singing, dancing and nursery care. In order that no harsh words or actions might hurt the child's development, he selected as schoolmaster, one James Buchanan, who had been, Owen stated in his autobiography, 'previously trained by his wife to perfect submission to her will.'

I was the youngest but one of a family of seven,—two of whom died young. The survivors,—William, Anne, and John, were older, and Richard was younger than myself. The principal adjacent estate was Newtown Hall, at the period of my birth and for a few years afterwards the property and residence of Sir John Powell Price, Bart.;—and my first recollection is of Sir John opening a glass door which divided my father's shop from the dwelling part of the house, and setting a bird flying towards us, saying there was something for the children's amusement, and they must take care of it.

This must have been shortly before he left his estate, I suppose from being in debt, for it soon passed into other hands. My next recollection is being in school in apartments in the mansion of this estate, and a Mr. Thickness, or some such name, was the schoolmaster. I must have been sent young to school,—probably at

Robert Owen, *The Life of Robert Owen—by Himself*, [1857] G. Bell: London, 1920

between four and five years of age,—for I cannot remember first going there. But I recollect being very anxious to be first in school and first home, and the boys had always a race from the school to the town, and, being a fast runner, I was usually at home the first, and almost always the first at school in the morning. On one occasion my haste nearly cost me my life. I used to have for breakfast a basin of flummery,—a food prepared in Wales from flour, and eaten with milk, and which is usually given to children as the Scotch use oatmeal porridge. It is pleasant and nutritious, and is generally liked by young persons. I requested that this breakfast might be always ready when I returned from school, so that I might eat it speedily, in order to be the first back again to school. One morning, when about five years old, I ran home as usual from school, found my basin of flummery ready, and as I supposed sufficiently cooled for eating, for no heat appeared to arise from it. It had skinned over as when quite cold; but on my hastily taking a spoonful of it, I found it was quite scalding hot, the body of it retaining all its heat. The consequence was an instant fainting, from the stomach being scalded. In that state I remained so long, that my parents thought life was extinct. However, after a considerable period I revived; but from that day my stomach became incapable of digesting food, except the most simple and in small quantity at a time.

This made me attend to the effects of different qualities of food on my changed constitution, and gave me the habit of close observation and of continual reflection; and I have always thought that this accident had a great influence in forming my character.

In schools in these small towns it was considered a good education if one could read fluently, write a legible hand, and understand the four first rules of arithmetic. And this I have reason to believe was the extent of Mr. Thickness's qualification for a schoolmaster,—because when I had acquired these small rudiments of learning at the age of seven, he applied to my father for permission that I should become his assistant and usher, as from that time I was called while I remained in school. And thenceforward my schooling was to be repaid by my ushership. As I remained at school about two years longer, those two years were lost to me, except that I thus early acquired the habit of teaching others what I knew.

But at this period I was fond of and had a strong passion for reading everything which fell in my way. As I was known to and knew every family in the town, I had the libraries of the clergyman, physician, and lawyer—the learned men of the town—thrown open to me, with permission to take home any volume which I liked, and I made full use of the liberty given to me. Among the books which I selected at this period were *Robinson Crusoe, Philip Quarle, Pilgrim's Progress, Paradise Lost*, Harvey's *Meditations among the Tombs, Young's Night Thoughts*, Richardson's, and all other standard novels. I believed every word of them to be true, and was therefore deeply interested; and I generally finished a volume daily. Then I read Cook's and all the circumnavigators' voyages—*The History of the World*,—Rollin's *Ancient History*,—and all the lives I could meet with of the philosophers and great men.

At this period, probably when I was between eight and nine years of age, three maiden ladies became intimate in our family, and they were Methodists. They took a great fancy to me, and gave me many of their books to read. As I was religiously inclined, they were very desirous to convert me to their peculiar faith. I read and studied the books they gave me with great attention; but as I read religious works of all parties, I became surprised, first at the opposition between the different sects of Christians, afterwards at the deadly hatred between the Jews, Christians, Mohammedans, Hindus, Chinese, etc, and between these and what they called Pagans and Infidels. The study of these contending faiths, and their deadly hatred to each other, began to create doubts in my mind respecting the truth of any one of these divisions. While studying and thinking with great earnestness upon these subjects, I wrote three sermons, and I was called the little parson. These sermons I kept until I met with Sterne's works, in which I found among his sermons three so much like them in idea and turn of mind, that it occurred to me as I read them that I should be considered a plagiarist, and with out thought, as I could not bear any such suspicion, I hastily threw them into the fire; which I often after regretted, as I should like to know now how I then thought and expressed myself on such subjects.

But certain it is that my reading religious works, combined with my other readings, compelled me to feel strongly at ten years of age that there must be something fundamentally wrong in all religions, as they had been taught up to that period.

8

SILFORD VILLAGE SCHOOL, 1800s

Suffolk, England
George Crabbe

George Crabbe (1754–1832) was born in Aldeburgh, Suffolk. His father was a collector of customs duties. Crabbe attended schools in Suffolk— in Bungay, 1762–1766, and in Stowmarket, 1766–1768. In such poems as 'The Village', 1783, an excerpt from which is given in the Introduction to this volume, and 'The Borough', 1810, Crabbe described, realistically, and therefore contrarily to the contemporary romantic school of poetry, the living conditions of working people. The excerpt, below, from 'Silford Hall; or The Happy Day' forms the introduction to a poem of 737 lines.

Village schoolmasters, such as Nathaniel Perkin in Crabbe's poem or J. Henri Fabre's schoolmaster (see 'A Village School in the Rouergue', 1827, in this volume) often supplemented meagre fee incomes with a variety of forms of employment. This practice prevails today in many rural areas of the world where the village school does not form part of a state-run education system. Sometimes, in rural schools, where land is attached to the mosque, church or temple as part of the endowment, it is worked by the schoolmaster himself (see also 'A Love of Poetry' in this volume). Some rural schoolmasters, either because money is not available or in preference to it, depend upon gifts of provisions. In Syed Wajid Ali's 'Pathsala', in this volume, the guru mahasay's chief income was in writing deeds and other documents '... as more or less an unlicensed lawyer and as such he fills an important place in the economy.' This is a not uncommon practice in rural communities even today.

George Crabbe, 'Silford Hall; or The Happy Day' in *Posthumous Tales*, 1834.

Within a village, many a mile from town,
A place of small resort and no renown;—
Save that it form'd a way, and gave a name
To Silford Hall, it made no claim to fame;—
It was the gain of some, the pride of all,
That travellers stopt to ask for Silford Hall,
    Small as it was, the place could boast a School,
In which Nathaniel Perkin bore the rule.
Not mark'd for learning deep, or talents rare,
But for his varying tasks and ceaseless care;
Some forty boys, the sons of thrifty men,
He taught to read, and part to use the pen;
While, by more studious care, a favourite few
Increased his pride—for if the Scholar knew
Enough for praise, say what the Teacher's due?—
These to his presence, slates in hand, moved on,
And a grim smile their feats in figures won.
This Man of Letters woo'd in early life
The Vicar's maiden, whom he made his wife.
She too can read, as by her song she proves—
The song Nathaniel made about their loves:
Five rosy girls, and one fair boy, increased
The Father's care, whose labours seldom ceased.
No day of rest was his. If, now and then,
His boys for play laid by the book and pen,
For Lawyer Slow there was some deed to write,
Or some young farmer's letter to indite,
Or land to measure, or, with legal skill,
To frame some yeoman's widow's peevish will;
And on the Sabbath,—when his neighbours drest,
To hear their duties, and to take their rest—
Then, when the Vicar's periods ceased to flow,
Was heard Nathaniel, in his seat below.
    Such were his labours; but the time is come
When his son Peter clears the hours of gloom,
And brings him aid: though yet a boy, he shares
In staid Nathaniel's multifarious cares.
A king his father, he, a prince, has rule—
The first of subjects, viceroy of the school:
But though a prince within that realm he reigns,

Hard is the part his duteous soul sustains.
He with his Father, o'er the furrow'd land,
Draws the long chain in his uneasy hand,
And neatly forms at home, what there they rudely plann'd.
Content, for all his labour, if he gains
Some words of praise, and sixpence for his pains.
Thus many a hungry day the Boy has fared,
And would have ask'd a dinner, had he dared.
When boys are playing, he, for hours of school
Has sums to set, and copy-books to rule;
When all are met, for some sad dunce afraid,
He, by allowance, lends his timely aid—
Taught at the student's failings to connive,
Yet keep his Father's dignity alive:
For ev'n Nathaniel fears, and might offend,
If too severe, the farmer, now his friend;
Or her, that farmer's lady, who well knows
Her boy is bright, and needs nor threats nor blows.
This seem'd to Peter hard; and he was loth,
T'obey and rule, and have the cares of both—
To miss the master's dignity, and yet,
No portion of the school-boy's play to get.

9

REUBEN DIXON AND LEONARD, 1800

Aldeburgh, Suffolk, England
George Crabbe

Common day schools often formed the next stage for pupils who continued in full-time education after dame school. They were independent, fee paying schools that taught reading, writing (and the essential penmanship), arithmetic, and possibly, for a small extra fee, such additional subjects as geography and grammar. The schools were self-sufficient. Their systems of teaching, no matter how inefficient, were not open to question or improvement. In developing countries today, many similar establishments exist by reason of the vacuum left by inadequate state school systems.

> Poor *Reuben Dixon* has the noisiest school
> Of ragged lads, who ever bow'd to rule;
> Low in his price—the men who heave our coals
> And clean our causeways, send him boys in shoals;
> To see poor Reuben, with his fry beside,—
> Their half-check'd rudeness, and his half-scorned pride,—
> Their room, the sty in which th' assembly meet,
> In the close lane behind the Northgate street;[1]
> T'observe his vain attempts to keep the peace,
> Till tolls the bell, and strife and troubles cease,—
> Calls for our praise; his labour praise deserves,
> But not our pity; Reuben has no nerves:
> 'Mid noise and dirt, and stench, and play, and prate
> He calmly cuts the pen or views the slate.

George Crabbe, *The Borough*, Letter XXIV, 1810

But *Leonard!*—yes, for Leonard's fate I grieve,
Who loathes the station which he dares not leave:
He cannot dig, he will not beg his bread,
All his dependence rests upon his head;
And deeply skill'd in sciences and arts
On vulgar lads he wastes superior parts.

Alas! What grief that feeling mind sustains,
In guiding hands, and stirring torpid brains;
He whose proud mind from pole to pole will move,
And view the wonders of the worlds above;
Who thinks and reasons strongly:—hard his fate,
Confined for ever to the pen and slate:
True, he submits, and when the long dull day
Has slowly passed, in weary tasks away,
To other worlds with cheerful view he looks
And parts the night between repose and books.

Amid his labours, he has sometimes tried
To turn a little from his cares aside;
Pope, Milton, Dryden, with delight has seized,
His soul engaged, and of his trouble eased;
When, with a heavy eye and ill-done sum,
No part conceived, a stupid boy will come;
Then Leonard first subdues the rising frown,
And bids the blockhead lay his blunders down;
O'er which disgusted he will turn his eye;
To his sad duty his sound mind apply,
And, vex'd in spirit, throw his pleasures by.

NOTE

1. While commentators agree that Aldeburgh and its environs provide the
    setting for *The Borough* - and there were several schools in Aldeburgh in
    the early nineteenth century (including the dame school to which Crabbe
    had sent his own sons) - the town has no 'Northgate Street'. There are,
    however, Northgate Streets in Ipswich, Norwich, Gt. Yarmouth, Bury St.
    Edmunds, and Leicester - all towns and cities with which Crabbe was
    familiar. Possibly Crabbe both obscured the identity of Reuben's school
    while indicating the generality of schools of this sort.

10

THE SCHOOL BELL, c. 1813

Yorkshire, England
George Borrow

George Henry Borrow (1803–1881) was a philologist, an eccentric and a humorist. His father was a captain and, latterly, a recruiting officer, in the army. The family followed the regiment—as a result Borrow attended many schools. The autobiographical *Lavengro* (not well received on its publication in 1851) and its sequel *Romany Rye*, 1857, told of his colourful early travels and adventures. His other works include *The Bible in Spain*, 1843, a contemporarily highly acclaimed account of his adventures as an agent of the Bible Society in Spain.

The school Borrow describes, below, was a private day school that included the teaching of Latin in its curriculum. *Lilly's Latin Grammar*, the study of which Borrow first recalls, was used, at Henry VIII's insistence, in Eton in 1540. It continued to be used there for at least the next two hundred years, and possibly, too, at the time of which George Borrow writes.

My father, who did not understand the classical languages, received with respect the advice of his old friend, and from that moment conceived the highest opinion of *Lilly's Latin Grammar*. During three years I studied *Lilly's Latin Grammar* under the tuition of various schoolmasters, for I travelled with the regiment, and in every town in which we were stationary I was invariably (God bless my father!) sent to the classical academy of the place. It chanced, by good fortune, that in the generality of these schools the grammar of *Lilly* was in use; when, however, that was not the case, it made no difference in my educational course, my father always stipulating with the masters that I should be daily examined in *Lilly*. At the end

George Borrow, *Lavengro—The Gypsy, The Scholar, The Priest*, [1851] Oxford University Press: London, 1907

of the three years I had the whole by heart; you had only to repeat the first two or three words of any sentence in any part of the book, and forthwith I would open cry, commencing without blundering and hesitation, and continue till you were glad to beg me to leave off, with many expressions of admiration at my proficiency in the Latin language. Sometimes, however, to convince you how well I merited these encomiums, I would follow you to the bottom of the stair, and even into the street, repeating in a kind of sing-song measure the sonorous lines of the golden schoolmaster. If I am here asked whether I understood anything of what I had got by heart, I reply: "Never mind, I understand it all now, and believe that no one ever yet got *Lilly's Latin Grammar* by heart when young, who repented of the feat at a mature age." And when my father saw that I had accomplished my task, he opened his mouth, and said: "Truly, this is more than I expected. I did not think that there had been so much in you, either of application or capacity; you have now learnt all that is necessary, if my friend Dr B ___'s opinion was sterling, as I have no doubt it was. You are still a child, however, and must yet go to school, in order that you may be kept out of evil company. Perhaps you may still contrive, now you have exhausted the barn, to pick up a grain or two in the barnyard. You are still ignorant of figures, I believe—not that I would mention figures in the same day with *Lilly's Grammar*."

These words were uttered in a place called ___, in the north, or in the road to the north, to which, for some time past, our corps had been slowly advancing. I was sent to the school of the place, which chanced to be a day-school. It was a somewhat extraordinary one, and a somewhat extraordinary event occurred to me within its walls.

It occupied part of the farther end of a small plain, or square, at the outskirts of the town, close to some extensive bleaching fields. It was a long low building of one room, with no upper story; on the top was a kind of wooden box, or sconce, which I at first mistook for a pigeon-house, but which in reality contained a bell, to which was attached a rope, which, passing through the ceiling, hung dangling in the middle of the school-room. I am the more particular in mentioning this appurtenance, as I had soon occasion to scrape acquaintance with it in a manner not very agreeable to my feelings. The master was very proud of his bell, if I might judge from the fact of his eyes being frequently turned to that part of the ceiling from which the rope depended. Twice every day, namely, after the morning and evening tasks had been gone through, were the boys rung out of school by the monotonous jingle of this bell. This ringing out was rather a lengthy affair, for, as the master was a man of order and method, the boys were only permitted to go out of the room one by one; and as they were rather numerous, amounting, at least to one hundred, and were taught to move at a pace of suitable decorum, at least a quarter of an hour elapsed from the commencement of the march before the last boy could make his exit. The office of bell-ringer was performed by every boy successively; and it so happened that, the very first day of my attendance at the school, the turn to ring the bell had, by order of succession, arrived at the place which had been allotted to me; for the master, as I have already observed, was a man of method and order, and every boy had a particular seat, to which he became a fixture as long as he continued at the school.

So, upon this day when the tasks were done and completed, and the boys sat with their hats and caps in their hands, anxiously expecting the moment of dismissal, it was suddenly notified to me, by the urchins who sat nearest to me, that I must get up and ring the bell. Now, as this was the first time that I had been at the school, I was totally unacquainted with the process, which I had never seen, and, indeed, had never heard of till that moment. I therefore sat still, not imagining it possible that any such duty could be required of me. But now, with not a little confusion, I perceived that the eyes of all the boys in the school were fixed upon me. Presently there were nods and winks in the direction of the bell-rope; and, as these produced no effect, uncouth visages were made, like those of monkeys when enraged; teeth were gnashed, tongues thrust out, and even fists were bent at me. The master, who stood at the end of the room, with a huge ferule under his arm, bent full upon me a look of stern appeal; and the ushers, of whom there were four, glared upon me, each from his own particular corner, as I vainly turned, in one direction and another, in search of one reassuring look.

But now, probably in obedience to a sign from the master, the boys in my immediate neighborhood began to maltreat me. Some pinched me with their fingers, some buffeted me, whilst others pricked me with pins, or the points of compasses. These arguments were not without effect. I sprang from my seat, and endeavoured to escape along a double line of benches, thronged with boys of all ages, from the urchin of six or seven, to the nondescript of sixteen or seventeen. It was like running the gauntlet; every one, great or small, pinching, kicking, or otherwise maltreating me as I passed by.

Goaded on in this manner, I at length reached the middle of the room, where dangled the bell-rope, the cause of all my sufferings. I should have passed it—for my confusion was so great, that I was quite at a loss to comprehend what all this could mean, and almost believed myself under the influence of an ugly dream—but now the boys, who were seated in advance in the row, arose with one accord, and barred my farther progress; and one, doubtless more sensible than the rest, seizing the rope, thrust it into my hand. I now began to perceive that the dismissal of the school, and my own release from torment, depended upon this selfsame rope. I therefore, in a fit of desperation, pulled it once or twice, and then left off, naturally supposing that I had done quite enough. The boys who sat next the door, no sooner heard the bell, than rising from their seats, they moved out at the door. The bell, however, had no sooner ceased to jingle, than they stopped short, and, turning round, stared at the master, as much as to say, "What are we to do now?" This was too much for the patience of the man of method, which my previous stupidity had already nearly exhausted. Dashing forward into the middle of the room, he struck me violently on the shoulders with his ferule and, snatching the rope out of my hand, exclaimed, with a stentorian voice, and genuine Yorkshire accent, 'Prodigy of ignorance! Dost not even know how to ring a bell? Must I myself instruct thee?' He then commenced pulling at the bell with such violence, that long before half the school was dismissed the rope broke, and the rest of the boys had to depart without their accustomed music.

11

REMINISCENCE OF A LANCASTERIAN SCHOOL, c. 1818

Detroit, Michigan, USA
B.O. Williams

Joseph Lancaster (1778–1838), a Quaker, opened his first monitorial school in the Borough Road, Southwark, in 1798. The British and Foreign School Society was formed in 1814 (succeeding the Royal Lancasterian Society of 1808) to continue his work. Dr Andrew Bell (1753–1832), similarly devised and implemented in competition, a more-widespread system on behalf of the National Society, founded in 1811; by 1851 there were 17,000 National schools. The two societies were therefore responsible for the dissenting 'British' and the established church 'National' schools. In their various stages of internal organization, they were a familiar sight in the towns and villages of the nineteenth and twentieth centuries.

The monitorial system was cheap, simple, and as it depended upon the older children teaching the younger, it provided a solution to the teacher shortage. From a modern perspective, the schools are easy to criticize; they depended solely upon a repetitious learning of facts, for example—and the average standard achieved was very low. Dr Bell, about 1820, said that: 'It is not proposed that the children of the poor be educated in an expensive way, or even be taught to write or cipher.' However it can be seen from Joseph Lancaster's 1803 description of the often dreadfully low quality common day schools, given in the Introduction, combined with its perceived advantages, why the monitorial system grew so rapidly.

B.O. Williams, 'My Recollections of the Early Schools of Detroit That I Attended From the Year 1816 to 1819', in *Pioneer Collections: Report of the Pioneer Society of the State of Michigan*, V. 5 (Lansing, 1884), pp. 549–550: www.constitution.org/lanc/lanc_detroit.htm (14.02.05)

Government inspectors, by the 1840s, found monitorial schools ineffective. Dr James Kay Shuttleworth's pupil teacher scheme began to provide at the same time teachers in ever-greater numbers, thus aiding the decline of the monitorial system. Lancasterian schools were generally absorbed into the Board school system after 1870 while the 'National' remained in the voluntary sector. A tragic outcome of the rivalry of the two societies was that, in England and Wales, educational development was greatly hindered until the Elementary Education Act was finally passed in 1870.

In the USA, from 1806, the Lancasterian system developed rapidly, perhaps demonstrated by it being found so far west as Detroit as early as 1818. The numerous charitable societies formed in the USA in the first two decades of the nineteenth century to extend elementary education to the poor, clearly appreciated its effective use, at low cost, for large numbers of children. Contrarily to the commonly found, one-room, one teacher, ungraded school, the societies were impressed by the Lancasterian schools promotion of the use of apparatus, the grading of pupils, discipline and hygienic premises. Lancaster, in 1818, apparently disheartened by sectarian malice, went penniless to the USA to promote his school system.

See also, in this volume, 'Ousting the Straw-Plaiting Dames'; 'An Oxfordshire Village School', and 'A National School'.

My next and last attendance, at a Detroit school, was the then celebrated and much prized Lancasterian, under the direction of Mr. Lemuel Shattuck, who came from Concord, Mass. It was opened in the new two-story brick building, and was probably the first school-house built in Detroit, after the great fire of 1805, if not the first ever erected exclusively for school purposes, in which the English language was taught... it had two distinct departments, one comprising the common English branches, on the ground floor, the room divided in the centre, like church pews. The sexes on separate sides, and seated in classes of ten or twelve, facing each other at a double desk. Beginning with the sand scratchers, each class presided over by a scholar taken from a higher class seated at the end of the desks to preserve order and give instruction for the day or week.

There were broad aisles on the outsides, in which, around half circles, the classes recited their lessons to the instructor, standing within the circle with a pointer. The lessons for the juveniles, on placards upon the wall; all the classes reciting at the same time, being a school graded into classes. At the entrance end, between the doors, upon a raised platform, were seated two monitors, a young gentleman and lady from the high school, with desks and chairs, overlooking the whole room, keeping order, giving instruction, and receiving reports from those presiding over classes, and probably receiving pay. The principal, Mr. Shattuck, over all; quietly entering the room, passing around, giving instructions, sometimes carrying a small rattan, or raw-hide, but seldom used, except to tap a pupil on the shoulder when found playing or dozing.

There was very little corporal punishment. A system of rewards and fines in representatives of federal currency was used, mills, cents, half dimes, dimes, dollars and eagles. Probably few ever gained a dollar, and fewer an eagle (which was said to be of gold), the mills, cents, and half dimes were round bits of tin stamped L.S. for mills, the cents figure 1 and C, half dimes, 5c, the higher values on fine cards with principal's name written. Rewards for good scholarship, and fines for delinquencies, were given and exacted, at the end of the week.

Promotions — Any scholar standing at the head of the class three nights in succession, having been put back to the foot of the class each day, was allowed to graduate to the foot of the next higher class; and for any serious misconduct was sometimes put back a class, and compelled to climb up again, thus offering a double incentive for progress in studies and for good behaviour.

The languages were, with mathematics and the higher branches of English, taught in the upper room, where Mr. Shattuck presided, and of its mysteries I knew nothing. That school was of more importance to me than all the others I ever attended for study, as it allowed the pupils to advance according to their industry and application to their studies, and were not held back by duller scholars, a fault I greatly fear often the case under our present school system, and which has a tendency to level down too much for the general good, if no improvement can ever be effected, by those having our schools in charge.

I must now refer briefly to a subject that perhaps the least said the better, but as it was probably among the first, if not the first, attempt at counterfeiting or issuing of bogus currency in the territory, ought to be preserved. The cupidity, or the temptation to do wrong, so often found among scholars, caused the counterfeiting of the tin mills and cents, and I believe tin half dimes. Some blacksmith had imitated very closely the genuine stamp or dies used, and large issues were put in circulation about the time or shortly before we removed from Detroit. The bogus coin although of same size and fineness of metal, had somewhat larger letters, and was readily detected when closely examined, and caused quite a sensation, which I believe led to a radical change in the system of reward and fines, as I afterwards heard that it was feared by the patrons of the school, that its tendency was to develop very undesirable passions and genius.

12

A VILLAGE SCHOOL IN THE ROUERGUE, 1827

St. Leon, Guyenne, France
Jean Henri Fabre & Eleanor Doorly

Jean Henri Fabre (1823–1915), a distinguished French entomologist and author, demonstrated the importance of instinct among insects. It was said that he '...almost lived with the beetle and the spider, the bee, the wasp and the caterpillar.' Fabre famously once said: 'Human knowledge will be erased from the world's archives ere we know the last word concerning the gnat.' He taught until 1870 and thereafter devoted himself to entomological studies. Fabre worked almost exclusively from nature, his literary style bringing him as much renown as his observations. His principal work is *Souvenirs Entomologiques* (10 vol., 1879–1907). English translations of selections from this work include *The Life of the Spider*, 1912; *The Marvels of the Insect World*, 1938; and *The Insect World of J. Henri Fabre*, 1949. His books were read in every country in the world—selections from his works were often, too, included in school readers in England until the 1950s.

In 1833, in France, a comprehensive system of state elementary education was established—it becoming free in 1881, and compulsory for children aged six to thirteen years, in 1882. An extract from a French contemporary report of rural school premises in the 1830s is quoted in the Introduction.

The Insect Man is a delightful account for young readers of the life of the renowned French naturalist. It is described by its author, Eleanor Doorly, as 'A tale of how the Yew Tree children went to France to hear the story of Jean Henri Fabre in the places where he lived and to see the homes of some of the insects whose life-story he has written.' In the first part of this extract from *The Insect Man*, Eleanor Doorly has taken Fabre's description of his St. Leon village school, which he

Eleanor Doorly, *The Insect Man*, Heinemann Educational Books: London, 1936.

attended from 1827, from 'Tale of the School' in *Souvenirs Entomologiques* (Series VI, Chapter IV).

Eleanor Doorly also wrote *Radium Woman*, the Carnegie Medal winner of 1939.

"What shall I call the room in which I was to make the acquaintance of the alphabet? It would not be possible to find a name for it, for it served for everything. It was at once school, kitchen, bedroom, refectory and even henhouse and pigsty. In those days, people didn't use palaces for schools, a miserable hut sufficed.

"From that room, a ladder led to the one above; under the ladder, there was a big shed in a wooden alcove. What was there above?

"I never really found out. From time to time I saw the master bring down an armful of hay for the ass or a basket of apples that the housekeeper poured into the pot, where piggie pie boiled...those two rooms were the whole house. Let us come back to the lower one. To the south was the window, the only one in the house and so small that your head touched the top and your shoulders the sides at the same time. That sunny opening was the only gay point in the dwelling; it looked out upon nearly the whole village and in its recess stood the master's table.

"There was a niche in the opposite wall where a copper pail glittered full of water. From that the thirsty drank whenever they wished, by means of a cup which was always within reach. At the top of the niche, on some shelves, shone the pewter dishes, plates and goblets that were taken down from their sanctuary only on feast days.

"Here and there, wherever a little light came in, highly-coloured pictures were stuck on the wall. Among them 'Our Lady of Seven Sorrows,' the divine mother of grief, half opening her blue cloak to show her seven-times-pierced heart.

"Between the sun and moon, like two big eyes staring at you, was the Father Eternal, whose robes seemed blown into a balloon by the wind.

"To the right of the window we had 'The Wandering Jew' in a three-cornered hat, a white leather apron, iron-nailed shoes, and a stout stick in his hand. 'Never was seen a man with beard so long' was printed around him, and the painter had not forgotten that detail, for the old man's beard was spread in a snowy avalanche over his apron and down to his knees.

"To the left was 'Genevieve de Brabant and the Fawn'. In the thickets fierce Golo lurked, a dagger in his hand. Above was 'The Death of Monsieur Credit', killed by his debtors on the threshold of his inn, and so on, a collection of varied subjects on the four walls.

"If the museum of halfpenny pictures delighted me all the year round, I had another joy in winter at the time of the great cold when the snow lay long on the ground. Against the wall was the fireplace, a really huge fireplace like my Grandfather's. Its overhanging ledge took up the whole width of the room. In the middle of it was the fire; but to right and left opened two little nooks made half of wood and half of masonry. Each held a bed with a mattress of wheat husks. Two sliding panels served as curtains and shut the box if the sleeper wished to be alone.

"This sleeping place in the chimney corner served as dormitory for the privileged—the two school boarders. It must have been comfortable in there at night with the panels closed when the north wind whistled at the entrance of the narrow valley making eddies in the snow."

******

Look at that neat, stone, twentieth-century village school, said Penelope, so prim and clean; and picture that other, where nevertheless a great man had his first lessons.

In that older schoolroom there were three-legged stools and benches; certainly not such a thing as a desk. The rest of the furniture consisted of a heavy shovel, that needed two hands to use, a pair of bellows, a salt box hanging on the wall, because the dinner was cooking on the fire; three big pots full to the brim, which all lesson-time gave out little jets of steam and the gentle pouf! which is the usual conversation of boiling pots. Sometimes a bold lad would, when the master's back was turned, dip in a fork and take out a potato to add to his own bread. For the matter of that, the boys ate all lesson time, cracking nuts or munching crusts. They had also unexpected amusement; for if anyone left the door open, and open they left it as often as possible—in would come a family of piglets, trooping, trotting, grunting, with fine tails nicely curled. And when the pigs had gone, came mother hen with her yellow, fluffy, downy brood. Henri loved to stroke the soft things as they pecked around.

And the schoolmaster? He seems to have been very patient and to have used no severer weapon against the intruders than a wave of his pocket-handkerchief. He was a busy man and many things besides a schoolmaster. First and foremost he managed the affairs of the absentee landlord of the castle.

All the children turned and looked up at the square solid grey mass with its four pointed turrets, which even in Fabre's day were used as dovecotes.

"But it must be very empty now," said Geraldine. "I haven't seen a single dove or pigeon. What else did the schoolmaster do except chase the pigs and manage the castle?"

Managing the castle meant that he had to oversee the hay and the harvest, the plum gathering and the milking; so that nearly all the summer and well into autumn the schoolmaster and elder scholars were out of school and the younger did lessons in the hay or substituted for lessons, when their master happened to want them, catching snails, or cleaning the dovecote.

Then the schoolmaster was also the village barber and the village bell ringer, so that a wedding or a christening stopped lessons. So did dark clouds, for the bell had to be rung to ward off hail and lightning. He was leader of the choir and, of course, they had services on saints' days as well as Sundays. He regulated the church clock, not probably the present church clock but certainly one in the same place. As there were no other clocks near, he set it by the sun.

"You've forgotten, Penél," said Giles, "to mention anything about lessons."

The schoolmaster had to teach all ages at once. The little ones sat on a bench, an alphabet in their hands, little grey books with a pigeon on the outside and inside ba be bi bo bu. The elders sat at table learning to write. Henri studied the pigeon, and sometimes asked a neighbour's help with his letters, but they knew little more than he. But he knew the pigeon off by heart, its one bright eye and its feathers.

Arithmetic consisted of addition, subtraction and tables up to twelve times; for in those days France did not have decimals.

"Shame she ever began!" exclaimed Giles, "did she invent the horrid things?"

On a Saturday, went on Penél, they always ended with tables. One boy would get up and recite twice one are two, up to twice twelve, and then the whole class would stand and shout that table all together with so much noise that the pigs and chickens took flight; and so on to twelve times. They really knew their tables, but they never used them.

For reading, they read nothing but Bible stories in French and their prayers in Latin. No one there had ever heard of geography or history.

"Or nature study?" asked Margaret.

No, laughed Penelope, nothing of that kind.

13

TEMPLE GROVE, 1834

East Sheen, Surrey, England
Henry J. Coke

The poor clearly lost little in not having schools such as Temple Grove and its many cousins. Such institutions blunted sensitivity, thus ensuring their perpetuation for future generations. The school's sole objective was to instill in its pupils a good knowledge of the writings of selected Greek and Latin authors. Few boys were capable of attaining it. The philosophy of Thomas Hood's (1799–1845) 'The Irish Schoolmaster' is apt:

> For some are meant to right illegal wrongs,
> And some for Doctors of Divinitie,
> Whom he doth teach to murder the dead tongues,
> And soe win academical degree;
> But some are bred for service of the sea,
> Howbeit, their store of learning is but small,
> For mickle waste he counteth it would be
> To stock a head with bookish wares at all,
> Only to be knocked off by ruthless cannon ball.

Henry J. Coke (1827–1916), a grandson of 'Coke of Norfolk', the renowned agriculturalist and MP of Holkam, joined the Royal Navy as a cadet aged eleven years. He saw active service in China during the first Opium War, 1839–42. Temple Grove was established in 1810. It flourishes today, now at the edge of the Ashdown Forest, as a modern and popular prep school.

Henry J. Coke, *Tracks of a Rolling Stone*, [2nd ed., 1905] Project Gutenberg: www.gutenberg.org

Soon after I was seven years old, I went to what was then, and is still, one of the most favoured of preparatory schools—Temple Grove—at East Sheen, then kept by Dr. Pinkney. I was taken thither from Holkham by a great friend of my father's, General Sir Ronald Ferguson, whose statue now adorns one of the niches in the façade of Wellington College.

The school contained about 120 boys; but I cannot name any one of the lot who afterwards achieved distinction. There were three Macaulays there, nephews of the historian—Aulay, Kenneth, and Hector. But I have lost sight of all.

Temple Grove was a typical private school of that period. The type is familiar to everyone in its photograph as Dotheboys Hall. The progress of the last century in many directions is great indeed; but in few is it greater than in the comfort and the cleanliness of our modern schools. The luxury enjoyed by the present boy is a constant source of astonishment to us grandfathers. We were half starved, we were exceedingly dirty, we were systematically bullied, and we were flogged and caned as though the master's pleasure was in inverse ratio to ours. The inscription on the threshold should have been 'Cave canem'.[1]

We began our day as at Dotheboys Hall with two large spoonfuls of sulphur and treacle. After an hour's lessons we breakfasted on one bowl of milk—'Skyblue' we called it—and one hunch of buttered bread, unbuttered at discretion.

Our dinner began with pudding—generally rice—to save the butcher's bill. Then mutton—which was quite capable of taking care of itself. Our only other meal was a basin of 'Skyblue' and bread as before. As to cleanliness, I never had a bath, never bathed (at the school) during the two years I was there. On Saturday nights, before bed, our feet were washed by the housemaids, in tubs round which half a dozen of us sat at a time. Woe to the last comers! for the water was never changed. How we survived the food, or rather the want of it, is a marvel.

Fortunately for me, I used to discover, when I got into bed, a thickly buttered crust under my pillow. I believed, I never quite made sure, (for the act was not admissible), that my good fairy was a fiery-haired lassie (we called her 'Carrots', though I had my doubts as to this being her Christian name) who hailed from Norfolk. I see her now: her jolly, round, shining face, her extensive mouth, her ample person. I recall, with more pleasure than I then endured, the cordial hugs she surreptitiously bestowed upon me when we met by accident in the passages. Kind, affectionate 'Carrots'! Thy heart was as bounteous as thy bosom. May the tenderness of both have met with their earthly deserts; and mayest thou have shared to the full the pleasures thou wast ever ready to impart!

There were no railways in those times. It amuses me to see people nowadays travelling by coach, for pleasure. How many lives must have been shortened by long winter journeys in those horrible coaches. The inside passengers were hardly better off than the outside. The corpulent and heavy occupied the scanty space allotted to the weak and small—crushed them, slept on them, snored over them, and monopolized the straw which was supposed to keep their feet warm.

A pachydermatous old lady would insist upon an open window. A wheezy consumptive invalid would insist on a closed one. Everybody's legs were in their own, and in every other body's, way. So that when the distance was great and time precious, people avoided coaching, and remained where they were. For this reason, if a short holiday was given—less than a week say—Norfolk was too far off; and I was not permitted to spend it at Holkham. I generally went to Charles Fox's at Addison Road, or to Holland House. Lord Holland was a great friend of my father's; but, if Creevey is to be trusted—which, as a rule, my recollection of him would permit me to doubt, though perhaps not in this instance— Lord Holland did not go to Holkham because of my father's dislike to Lady Holland.

NOTE

1. Cave canem ('Beware of the dog') was the mosaic inscription, with graphic illustration, found in the entrance to a building in ancient Pompeii.

14

COLHARES VILLAGE SCHOOL, 1835

Near Cintra, Estremadura, Portugal
George Borrow

Shortly after his arrival in Lisbon in November 1835, on his mission to distribute Bibles, George Borrow set out to ascertain the level of literacy in the region. In the course of his research he is first teased by a learned Jesuit priest before visiting Colhares village in the Estremadura.

Until 1759 the Jesuit teaching order dominated education in Portugal. The reforms of 1750–1777 were an attempt to develop a system of public and secular primary and secondary schools. These and later reform initiatives were severely impeded by the Peninsular War and by intermittent revolutions and civil wars. In the 1830s, the literacy level was a little above two per cent. Until the early 1990s, Portugal had, mainly among older people, an illiteracy rate of 20 per cent. Illiteracy has hampered Portugal's development until modern times. The high dropout rate from secondary school, especially in Portugal's rural areas, continues to be a serious problem today.

After praising the beauty of the surrounding scenery, I made some inquiry as to the state of education amongst the people under his [the Jesuit's] care. He answered that he was sorry to say that they were in a state of great ignorance, very few of the common people being able either to read or write; that with respect to schools, there was but one in the place, where four or five children were taught the alphabet, but that even this was at present closed. He informed

---

George Borrow, *The Bible in Spain*, [1842] John Murray: London, 1912

me, however, that there was a school at Colhares, about a league distant.

Amongst other things, he said that nothing more surprised him than to see Englishmen, the most learned and intelligent people in the world, visiting a place like Cintra, where there was no literature, science, nor anything of utility (*coisa que presta*). I suspect that there was some covert satire in the last speech of the worthy priest; I was, however, Jesuit enough to appear to receive it as a high compliment, and, taking off my hat, departed with an infinity of bows.

That same day I visited Colhares, a romantic village on the side of the mountain of Cintra, to the northwest. Seeing some peasants collected round a smithy, I enquired about the school, whereupon one of the men instantly conducted me thither. I went upstairs into a small apartment where I found the master with about a dozen pupils standing in a row; I saw but one stool in the room, and to that, after having embraced me, he conducted me with great civility. After some discourse, he showed me the books which he used for the instruction of the children; they were spelling books, much of the same kind as those used in the village schools in England.[1] Upon my asking him whether it was his practice to place the Scriptures in the hands of the children, he informed me that long before they had acquired sufficient intelligence to understand them they were removed by their parents, in order that they might assist in the labours of the field, and that the parents in general were by no means solicitous that their children should learn anything, as they considered the time occupied in learning as so much squandered away. He said that, though the schools were nominally supported by the government, it was rarely that the schoolmasters could obtain their salaries, on which account many had of late resigned their employments.

NOTE

1. 'Spelling-book', 'speller', 'primer', and, later, 'reader', were used to describe a first reading book. The pupils next step may have been to identify letters and small words from the Bible and so build up a reading vocabulary (see, also, note 14 in Introduction). It seems from Borrow's description of the schoolroom that writing was not taught, although 'ciphering', or number work, may well have been.

15

A VISIT TO A FREE SCHOOL, 1842

Cincinnati, Ohio, USA
Charles Dickens

The passage below is a journal-like account by Dickens (1812–1870) of his visit to a free school during the course of his first visit to the USA in 1842. 'It is a part of the record of impressions I received from day to day during my hasty travels in America, and sometimes (but not always) of the conclusions to which they and after-reflection have led me...' His impressions were published as American Notes in the same year.

Pennsylvania in 1834 was the first state in the USA to introduce a Free School Act. Free Schools, established in rural and urban areas, were funded by local and county taxes with some additional help from the state. (See also, Hamlin Garland's 'School Life', 1871, in this volume.) Of Cincinnati, Dickens said: 'Cincinnati is only fifty years old but is a very beautiful city: I think the prettiest place I have seen here, except Boston. It has arisen out of the forest like an Arabian-night city; is well-laid out; ornamented in the suburbs with pretty villas; and above all, for this is a rare feature in America, has smooth turf plots and well-kept gardens.'[1]

Cincinnati is honourably famous for its free-schools, of which it has so many that no person's child among its population can, by possibility, want the means of education, which are extended, upon an average, to four thousand pupils, annually. I was only present in one of these establishments during the hours of instruction. In the boys' department, which was full of little urchins (varying in their ages, I should say, from six years old to ten or twelve), the master offered to institute an extemporary examination of the pupils in algebra; a proposal, which, as I was by no means confident of my

Charles Dickens, American Notes [1842] Macmillan and Co., Ltd.: London, 1903.

ability to detect mistakes in that science, I declined with some alarm. In the girls' school, reading was proposed; and as I felt tolerably equal to that art, I expressed my willingness to hear a class. Books were distributed accordingly, and some half-dozen girls relieved each other in reading paragraphs from English History. But it was a dry compilation, infinitely above their powers; and when they had blundered through three or four dreary passages concerning the Treaty of Amiens, and other thrilling topics of the same nature (obviously without comprehending ten words), I expressed myself quite satisfied. It is very possible that they only mounted to this exalted stave in the Ladder of Learning for the astonishment of a visitor; and that at other times they keep upon its lower rounds; but I should have been much better pleased and satisfied if I had heard them exercised in simpler lessons, which they understood.

NOTE

1. John Forster, *The Life of Dickens*, Cecil Palmer: London, 1874, p. 162.

16

OUSTING THE STRAW-PLAITING DAMES, 1850s

Aston Clinton, Buckinghamshire, England
Lady Constance Battersea

Lady Constance Battersea (1843–1922) was the great-granddaughter of M.A. Rothschilde, the founder of the international financial house. Her family's country residence, from 1853, was near Aston Clinton, a village with a population then of less than 1000, and five miles from the county town of Aylesbury. It was there, at the age of eleven (Connie's sister, Annie, was then nine), that Constance began her life-long devotion to philanthropic causes.

This extract illustrates a common antipathy to the education of girls. In some rural areas of southern England learning a craft was a first priority—for example, in Devon, Bedfordshire, Northamptonshire and Buckinghamshire it was lace making; in parts of Bedfordshire and in Buckinghamshire, Essex, Hertfordshire and Suffolk, it was glove making or straw-plaiting. In Constance Battersea's village, it was straw-plaiting. Girls, from four years of age, were usually taught plaiting at home. They went to the 'plait school' to make plait for their parents to sell to the specialists in making finished articles, which included bonnets, hats and baskets. Professor G.E. Mingay in his *Rural Life in Victorian England* (Heinemann, 1977) notes:

> In the trade's heyday straw-plaiters could make as much or more money as did farm labourers, and the farmers of the area grew a special type of wheat which produced a straw suitable for the work. When mother and children were all occupied in making as much plait as possible, home comforts were often neglected. The trade enabled young workers to gain an early financial independence and leave home, and it was no doubt a combination of these things

Constance Battersea, *Reminiscences*, Macmillan: London, 1922.

which accounted for the high rate of illegitimate births prevalent in straw-plaiting villages. The children's education was sadly neglected, and before 1870 the parents could not be induced to send their children to school unless plaiting was made part of the curriculum. Even after that date the trade was a cause of irregular attendance, especially among girls, and the employment of very young girls remained a feature of the plaiting trade. Cheap foreign plait and changes in fashion ultimately caused a rapid decline in the trade.

At the time, in the 'fifties, the only day-school in Aston Clinton was kept by a drunken schoolmaster, who had about thirty miserable dejected-looking male scholars. This was the National School, under the Rector's sway, and a disgracefully bad one it was.

During those years straw-plaiting was the staple industry and main feature of the county. Schools for teaching children to plait were held by a few old women in the village. One of these schools at Aston Clinton was presided over by a little cripple, deformed and unable to stand or walk. She was carried into her chair, and managed her classes like a queen from her throne. She could only use two of her fingers, but would grasp a little stick or birch, with which she threatened any lazy pupils. She also succeeded in working some very wonderful samplers. The atmosphere was asphyxiating.

At the early age of eleven I developed a passion for teaching, and, my sister obediently conforming to my wishes, we both resolved, if permitted, to introduce some measure of education into the school of our friend the dame. We explained our wishes and designs to the accommodating dame, and, armed with some lesson-books, we proceeded to instruct the little "plaiters". They were delightfully ignorant, and we enjoyed ourselves extremely, and were even encouraged to go further afield to another school of the same sort in our village.

On one damp, warm afternoon in autumn our mother found us immersed in this, our favourite occupation, and was so horrified at the atmosphere she encountered upon entering the room that she forbade us to continue our self-imposed work. Great distress resulted on our part, but we were not to be beaten.

The boys did not attend their school on Saturdays; why not beg for the use of their building for our purposes? No sooner said than done. We appealed to the Rector of the day, and he, although an anti-educationist, granted us this favour, and we boldly issued invitations to the girls frequenting the dame's school to attend our classes on the following Saturday afternoon. It was a bold venture, but when my mother came to inspect us in our new and airy premises, she found us surrounded by a number of very eager pupils, who were being taught reading and writing by my sister and myself, and arithmetic by our competent German companion, Miss Morck. Our mother soon felt that our youthful attempts at instruction should give place to some method of real education, so my kind and ever-generous father, obedient to her desire, built a beautiful girls' school for the village of Aston Clinton. Never has the building of any edifice been so carefully and affectionately watched as this was by our young selves. I even tested the growth of the walls by going each day to jump over them, until my efforts were out-distanced by the masons' work. In an early diary of that date I find: "The wish of my heart is now granted, we have a school of our own at Aston Clinton." Then we canvassed the village most diligently to secure pupils for the opening day, and proudly counted fifteen girls whose parents were anxious to see their children properly educated.

The Rector was most discouraging. He feared that in time many would be lured away from the plaiting schools, which would ruin the old dames, and he would not even be pacified by my mother's assurance that the old dames should be pensioned for the rest of their lives. He did not see the use of education for girls, and thought the Sunday School (which was a very bad one) gave them all the teaching they required. We listened, but inwardly triumphed. Education was at a low ebb in the 'fifties in England, but we can now congratulate ourselves that Aston Clinton led the way to a better state of things, at all events in Buckinghamshire. We really loved that little school, and some of the happiest hours of our lives were spent there. When a few years later it had become too small for the number of scholars, my dear father enlarged it, and later again he was faced by the fact that it could not contain the Infants—boys and girls—who were then becoming eligible for school attendance.

It was about that time that, my father asking me what I should like to have for a birthday present, I boldly answered, "An Infants' School". My request was granted, and I was allowed to lay the first stone of the new building. I must add that the capital teaching in this school, with the songs and recitations of infants, greatly entertained my dear father for many years. It is not a little interesting to record here that Mathew Arnold was our first Inspector, and became one of our greatest friends.

17

THE VILLAGE PHILOSOPHER, c. 1855

Milnathort, Perth and Kinross, Scotland
Walter C. Smith

Walter Chalmers Smith (1824–1908) was the author of the popular 'Immortal, Invisible, God Only Wise' and other hymns. The humour of 'The Village Philosopher' compares well with Goldsmith's description of his village pedagogue, and as a portrait of a village schoolmaster, the poem provides a social history snapshot of interest. Samuel Butler's (1612–1680) 'The Astrologer' in his 'Hudibras' was a forerunner in style to both of these poems.

Walter C. Smith was ordained pastor in Islington, London, in 1850. Then from 1853 to 1858, he was the Free Church minister in Milnathort, a village situated at the foot of the Ochil Hills. In the nineteenth century, woollen and spinning mills were established in the village. Smith was elected Moderator of the Free Church of Scotland in 1893.

Although England and Scotland were united in 1707 with one parliament, Scotland retained a separate education system. In 1696 an Act for the 'settling of Schools' ordained that there should be a school and a schoolmaster in every parish. Scotland subsequently had one of the highest literacy rates in Europe in the eighteenth and early nineteenth centuries. However, when city populations increased in the nineteenth century, voluntary effort could not keep pace with school requirements and, as in England, thousands of children were without schools. In addition, where parishes were particularly extensive, as in the remote and mountainous areas, sufficient schools could not be provided. The Education Act of 1872, provided School Boards where required, as did that of 1870 in England. However, in Scotland, education was made compulsory between five and thirteen years, thus considerably anticipating England.

Walter C. Smith, *North Country Folk*, James Maclehose: Glasgow, 1883

See also, 'Pupil and Pupil Teacher', 1885–1898, and 'Childhood Days',
1889–1894.

He kept the village school—some score
Of boys and girls, with little primers;
Their fathers he had taught before,
Had called their mothers "idle limmers":[1]
For well he liked to give hard names,
But still in blandest accent spoken;
They never spoilt the children's games,
Nor yet by them their heads were broken.

He had been village 'merchant' once,
But had not prospered in that calling;
A trade, he said, for any dunce,
To be a ledger overhauling:
A silly, mindless business, he
Was heard in very scorn to mutter,
To barter cloth and combs and tea
And spades and rakes for eggs and butter!

For he was a philosopher,
And such with trade make no alliance;
They said that even the minister
Was puzzled with his views of science:
He knew the hour of the Eclipse,
He made the Kirk a ventilator,
And could have sailed the biggest ships
Across the line of the Equator.

Before the school door he had reared
A pillar-stone and true sun-dial;
And in the window there appeared
For weather glass a wondrous phial,
Its neck was partly ground, and then
'Twas hung, mouth-downward, filled with water;
And if it dropped, there would be rain,
But if it shrunk, the clouds would scatter.

He had a glass that showed the moon
Whose mountains looked like inky blotches,
He had a box that played a tune,
When rightly touched at certain notches;
He had a round electric wheel
Could give a shock to all the village,
That made their elbows ache, and feel
As tired as with a hard day's tillage.

He beat the smith—until he drank—
At working cures on sickly cattle;
For when he came to byre or fank,
The sight of him was half the battle:
In very fear the ewes grew well
The moment that they smelt his potions,
And cows to healthy sweating fell
To see his poultices and lotions.

So blandly as he pinched his snuff
When he did horse or bullock handle;
So careful as he mixed the stuff
By light of flaring lamp or candle;
So wisely as he could discourse
Of Pleuro, Foot-and-Mouth, or Staggers,
And if the stubborn brutes grew worse,
He glared at them with looks like daggers.

O little village-world that hast
Thy prophets, watched with faith and wonder,
Stoutly believed in to the last
In spite of failure, loss and blunder,
What art thou but the world in small?
And what its prophets more than thine are?
Perhaps an inch or two more tall,
But hardly even a shade diviner.

NOTE

1. limmers: rascals.

18

THE OLD PINDAREE, 1866

Nerbada River, Gujarat, India
Sir Alfred Lyall

Sir Alfred Lyall (1835–1911), a distinguished administrator of the British raj, became India's Home Secretary and Foreign Secretary and, finally, a member of the India Council in London. Lyallapur, a new planned town or 'canal colony' of the Punjab, now renamed Faisalabad and the second largest city in Pakistan, was first named, in the 1890s, in his honour. The Pindaris are described in *Indian History for Matriculation*[1] 1933, as follows:

The Pindaris were lawless marauders of all castes and classes, originally loosely attached to the Maratha armies (e.g., of Scindia and Holkar), who developed into a terrible scourge of India. Under their leaders, Chitu, Wasil Muhammad, and Karim Khan, they swept over India, killing, burning, devastating, and committing the most atrocious outrages upon the people. In 1812 they attacked Mirzapur and Bihar; in 1816, the Northern Sarkars. The hunt of the Pindaris became merged in the Third Maratha War and struck the final death-knell of the Maratha power. Lord Hastings extirpated the Pindaris in 1818. Chitu fled into the jungles and was devoured by a tiger. Karim Khan submitted and was given Gorakhpur. Amir Khan had already been made Amir of Tonk.

In his *The Causes of the Indian Revolt*, 1873, Syed Ahmed Khan, the founder of Aligarh Muslim College, cited the development of government schools and, in particular, the common fear that the schools will subvert

Alfred Lyall, *Verses Written in India*, Kegan Paul, Trench, Trubner and Co., Ltd.: London, 1890

their children from Islam, as a major factor in determining Muslims
to revolt against the British in 1857. Syed Ahmed included 'The Old
Pindaree' in *Causes*. The English text differs from Lyall's original text in
that it was translated into Urdu by Syed Ahmed and then into English,
without reference to the original.
The Nerbada river flows through Gujarat state.

(From verse 3)

There goes my lord the Feringhee, who talks
so civil and bland,
Till he raves like a soul in Jehannum if I
don't quite understand;
He begins by calling me Sahib, and ends by
calling me Fool;
He has taken my old sword from me, and
tells me to set up a school;

Set up a school in the village! "and my
wishes are," says he,
"That you make the boys learn reg'lar, or
you'll get a lesson from me;"
Well Ramlal the oilman spites me, and
pounded my cow last rains;
He's got three greasy young urchins; I'll see
that *they* take pains.

Then comes a Settlement Hakim, to teach
us to plough and to weed,
(I sowed the cotton he gave me, but first I
boiled the seed).
He likes us humble farmers, and speaks so
gracious and wise
As he asks of our manners and customs; I
tell him a parcel of lies.

"Look," says the school Feringhee, "what a
silly old man you be,
"You can't read, write, nor cipher, and your
grandsons do all three;

"They'll total the shopman's figures, and
reckon the tenant's corn,
"And read good books about London and
the world before you were born."

Well, I may be old and foolish, for I've
seventy years well told,
And the Franks have ruled me forty, so my
heart and my hand's got cold;
Good boys they are, my grandsons, I know,
but they'll never be men,
Such as I was at twenty-five when the sword
was king of the pen...

NOTE

1. K. P. Mitra, *Indian History for Matriculation*, Macmillan: Calcutta, 1933, p. 255.

19

SCHOOL LIFE, 1871

Osage, Iowa, USA
Hamlin Garland

Hamlin Garland (1860–1940) began writing in the 1890s. In 1917, he published *A Son of the Middle Border*, possibly the best of his autobiographical books portraying pioneering life on the farms of Wisconsin, Iowa and Dakota. The extract below is taken from this book. Osage is a small town in northeastern Iowa, near which the Garland farm was situated.

Iowa Territory, created in 1838, became a state in 1846. As in traditional rural communities, the sense of interdependence was strong amongst pioneer families. Schools were early established, usually in log houses—in 1861, for example, there were 893 such schools in use, while by 1875 only 121 had not yet improved their premises. In 1870, the Iowa legislature reorganized its education system into independent school districts based on the 1785 Land Ordinance, whereby land was to be divided into townships made up of 36 sections, each six miles square, one section of which was to support public schools.

Our first winter had been without much wind but our second taught us the meaning of the word 'blizzard' which we had just begun to hear about. The winds of Wisconsin were 'gentle zephyrs' compared to the blasts, which now swept down over the plain to hammer upon our desolate little cabin and pile the drifts around our sheds and granaries, and even my pioneer father was forced to admit that the hills of Green's Coulee had their uses after all.

One such storm which leaped upon us at the close of a warm and beautiful day in February lasted for two days and three nights, making life on the open prairie impossible even to the strongest

Hamlin Garland, *Son of the Middle Border*, The Macmillan Company: New York, 1917

man. The thermometer fell to thirty degrees below zero and the snow-laden air moving at a rate of eighty miles an hour pressed upon the walls of our house with giant power. The sky of noon was darkened, so that we moved in a pallid half-light, and the windows thick with frost shut us in as if with grey shrouds.

Hour after hour those winds and snows in furious battle, howled and roared and whistled around our frail shelter, slashing at the windows and piping on the chimney, till it seemed as if the Lord Sun had been wholly blotted out and that the world would never again be warm. Twice each day my father made a desperate sally toward the stable to feed the imprisoned cows and horses or to replenish our fuel—for the remainder of the long pallid day he sat beside the fire with gloomy face. Even his indomitable spirit was awed by the fury of that storm.

So long and so continuously did those immitigable winds howl in our ears that their tumult persisted, in imagination, when on the third morning, we thawed holes in the thickened rime of the window panes and looked forth on a world silent as a marble sea and flaming with sunlight. My own relief was mingled with surprise—surprise to find the landscape so unchanged. True, the yard was piled high with drifts and the barns were almost lost to view but the far fields and the dark lines of Burr Oak Grove remained unchanged.

We met our schoolmates that day, like survivors of shipwreck, and for many days we listened to gruesome stories of disaster, tales of stages frozen deep in snow with all their passengers sitting in their seats, and of herders with their silent flocks around them, lying stark as granite among the hazel bushes in which they had sought shelter. It was long before we shook off the awe with which this tempest filled our hearts.

The schoolhouse which stood at the corner of our new farm was less than half a mile away, and yet on many of the winter days which followed, we found it quite far enough. Hattie was now thirteen, Frank nine and I a little past eleven, but nothing, except a blizzard such as I have described, could keep us away from school. Facing the cutting wind, wallowing through the drifts, battling like small intrepid animals, we often arrived at the door moaning with pain yet unsubdued, our ears frosted, our toes numb in our boots, to meet others in similar case around the roaring hot stove.

Often after we reached the schoolhouse another form of suffering overtook us in the 'thawing out' process. Our fingers and toes, swollen with blood, ached and itched, and our ears burned. Nearly all of us carried sloughing ears and scaling noses. Some of the pupils came two miles against these winds.

The natural result of all this exposure was, of course, chilblains! Every foot in the school was more or less touched with this disease, to which our elders alluded as if it were an amusing trifle, but to us it was no joke.

After getting thoroughly warmed up, along about the middle of the forenoon, there came into our feet a most intense itching and burning and aching, a sensation so acute that keeping still was impossible, and all over the room an uneasy shuffling and drumming arose as we pounded our throbbing heels against the floor or scraped our itching toes against the edge of our benches. The teacher understood and was kind enough to overlook this disorder.

The wonder is that any of us lived through that winter, for at recess, no matter what the weather might be, we flung ourselves out of doors to play 'fox and geese' or 'dare goal' until, damp with perspiration, we responded to the teacher's bell, and came pouring back into the entryways to lay aside our wraps for another hour's study.

Our readers were almost the only counterchecks to the current of vulgarity and baseness which ran through the talk of the older boys, and I wish to acknowledge my deep obligation to Professor McGuffey,[1] whoever he may have been, for the dignity and literary grace of his selection! From the pages of his readers I learned to know and love the poems of Scott, Byron, Southey, Wordsworth and a long line of the English masters. I got my first taste of Shakespeare from the selected scenes which I read in these books.

With terror as well as delight I rose to read 'Lochiel's Warning,' 'The Battle of Waterloo' or 'The Roman Captive.' 'Marco Bozzaris' and 'William Tell' were alike glorious to me. I soon knew not only my own reader, the fourth, but also all the selections in the fifth and sixth as well. I could follow almost word for word the recitations of the older pupils and at such times I forgot my squat little body and my mop of hair, and became imaginatively a page in the train of Ivanhoe, or a bowman in the army of Richard the Lionheart, battling the Saracen in the Holy Land.

With a high ideal of the way in which these grand selections should be read, I was scared almost voiceless when it came my turn to read them before the class. "STRIKE FOR YOUR ALTARS AND

YOUR FIRES. STRIKE FOR THE GREEN GRAVES OF YOUR
SIRES—GOD AND YOUR NATIVE LAND,"[2] always reduced me
to a trembling breathlessness. The sight of the emphatic print was a
call to the best that was in me and yet I could not meet the test.
Excess of desire to do it just right often brought a ludicrous gasp
and I often fell back into my seat in disgrace, the titter of the girls
adding to my pain. Then there was the famous passage, "Did ye not
hear it?" and the careless answer, "No, it was but the wind or the
car rattling o'er the stony street."[3] —I knew exactly how those
opposing emotions should be expressed but to do it after I rose to
my feet was impossible. Burton was even more terrified than I.
Stricken blind as well as dumb he usually ended by helplessly
staring at the words, which, I conceive, had suddenly become a blur
to him.

No matter, we were taught to feel the force of these poems and
to reverence the genius that produced them, and that was worthwhile.
Falstaff and Prince Hal, Henry and his wooing of Kate, Wolsey and
his downfall, Shylock and his pound of flesh all became a part of
our thinking and helped us to measure the large figures of our own
literature, for Whittier, Bryant and Longfellow also had place in
these volumes. It is probable that Professor McGuffey, being a
southern man, did not value New England writers as highly as my
grandmother did, nevertheless 'Thanatopsis'[4] was there and 'The
Village Blacksmith',[5] and extracts from *The Deer Slayer* and *The
Pilot* gave us a notion that in Cooper we had a novelist of weight
and importance, one to put beside Scott and Dickens.

A by-product of my acquaintance with one of the older boys was
a stack of copies of the *New York Weekly*, a paper filled with stories
of noble life in England and hairbreadth escapes on the plain, a
shrewd mixture, designed to meet the needs of the entire membership
of a prairie household. The pleasure I took in these tales should fill
me with shame, but it doesn't—I rejoice in the memory of it.

I soon began, also, to purchase and trade Beadle's Dime Novels
and, to tell the truth, I took an exquisite delight in *Old Sleuth and
Jack Harkaway*. My taste was catholic. I ranged from *Lady
Gwendolin to Buckskin Bill* and so far as I can now distinguish one
was quite as enthralling as the other. It is impossible for any print
to be as magical to any boy these days as those weeklies were to
me in 1871.

One day a singular test was made of us all. Through some agency now lost to me my father was brought to subscribe for *The Hearth and Home* or some such paper for the farmer, and in this I read my first chronicle of everyday life.

In the midst of my dreams of lords and ladies, queens and dukes, I found myself deeply concerned with backwoods farming, spelling schools, protracted meetings, and the like familiar homely scenes. This serial (which involved my sister and myself in many a spat as to who should read it first) was *The Hoosier Schoolmaster*, by Edward Eggleston, and a perfectly successful attempt to interest western readers in a story of the middle border.

To us 'Mandy' and 'Bud Means', 'Ralph Hartsook', the teacher, 'Little Shocky', and sweet patient 'Hannah', were as real as Cyrus Button and Daddy Fairbanks. We could hardly wait for the next number of the paper, so concerned were we about 'Hannah' and 'Ralph'. We quoted old lady Means and we made bets on 'Bud' in his fight with the villainous drover. I hardly knew where Indiana was in those days, but Eggleston's characters were near neighbours.

The illustrations were dreadful, even in my eyes, but the artist contrived to give a slight virginal charm to Hannah and a certain childish sweetness to Shocky, so that we accepted the more than mortal ugliness of old man Means and his daughter Mirandy (who simpered over her book at us as she did at Ralph), as a just interpretation of their worthlessness.

This book is milestone in my literary progress as it is in the development of distinctive western fiction, and years afterward I was glad to say so to the aged author, who lived a long and honored life as a teacher and writer of fiction.

It was always too hot or too cold in our schoolroom and on certain days when a savage wind beat and clamoured at the loose windows, the girls, humped and shivering, sat upon their feet to keep them warm, and the younger children with shawls over their shoulders sought permission to gather close about the stove. Our dinner pails (stored in the entry way) were often frozen solid and it was necessary to thaw out our mince pie as well as our bread and butter by putting it on the stove. I recall, vividly, gnawing, doglike, at the mollified outside of a doughnut while still its frosty heart made my teeth ache.

Happily all days were not like this. There were afternoons when the sun streamed warmly into the room, when long icicles formed on the eaves, adding a touch of grace to the desolate building, moments when the jingling bells of passing wood-sleighs expressed the natural cheer and buoyancy of our youthful hearts.

NOTES

1. William Holmes McGuffey (1800–1873) was brought up in Ohio. He taught in rural, frontier schools and, thereafter, followed a distinguished university career in Ohio, where he also assisted in organizing the public school system. He published his first *McGuffey Eclectic Readers* in 1836. By the 1920s more than 122 million Readers, of various editions, had been sold. In the USA and Canada, they were the first popular, wholly American, elementary reading books. They were primarily concerned with imparting moral values and didactic information, as were the British *Royal Readers* (see the Introduction and Flora Thompson's reminiscences of them in the 1880s in 'An Oxfordshire Village School and A Visit by Her Majesty's Inspector' in this volume).

2. From 'Marco Bozzaris' by the American poet Fitz-Green Halleck (1795–1867). Marco Bozzaris (1790–1823) was a hero of the Greek war of independence.

3. This is from Byron's *Childe Harold's Pilgrimage*, 'The Eve of Quatre Bras', 1815:

   Did ye not hear it? No: 'twas but the wind,
   Or the car rattling o' er the stony street:
   On with the dance! Let joy be unconfined:
   No sleep till morn, when Youth and Pleasure meet
   To chase the glowing Hours with flying feet.
   But hark! That heavy sound breaks in once more,
   As if the clouds its echo would repeat;
   And nearer, cleaner, deadlier than before!
   Arm! Arm! It is—it is—the cannon's opening roar!

4. William Gullen Bryant (1794–1878) published 'Thanatopsis' in 1815. The poem reflects on death:

   ...As the long train
   Of ages glide away, the sons of men,
   The youth in life's green spring, and he who goes
   In the full strength of years, matron and maid,
   The speechless babe, and the gray-headed man—
   Shall one by one be gathered to thy side
   By those who in their turn shall follow them...

5. Henry Wadsworth Longfellow (1807-1882).

20

A VILLAGE SCHOOL INSPECTION, 1871

'Llangastanau', Carnarvonshire (now Gwynedd), Wales
E.M. Sneyd-Kynnersley

Edmund Mackenzie Sneyd-Kynnersley (b. 1842), in his retirement as HMI NW Division, and at the request of his former colleagues, described aspects of his life as one of the first Board School inspectors. In 1870, he was 'a briefless barrister' when appointed Inspector of Returns as a first step towards an appointment as H.M. Inspector of Schools. From 1854 (on completion of his own elementary education) until 1871, he was not, he said:

...interested in elementary education, though after leaving Oxford I took some part in Classical teaching... The storms of Mr. Lowe's Revised Code passed over my head: and the Elementary Education Bill of 1870 was fought in Parliament while I was sailing home from Australia. The School Board elections of November, 1870, caused some excitement in the large towns, but the Franco-German war was raging, and the siege of Paris was of more general interest. To the supporters of the Government the New Education Act appeared to be an admirable measure; the Opposition maintained the contrary opinion; but, as is usually the case, the great majority of the people adopted one or the other side without tedious enquiry into details. I think that was my case.

E.M. Sneyd-Kynnersley, *H.M.I.: Some passages in the life of one of H.M. Inspectors of Schools*, Macmillan: London, 1908

Flora Thompson (see 'An Oxfordshire Village School and A Visit by Her
Majesty's Inspector', 1880s,) provides the pupils' perspective of a
school inspection. The payment by results' system, as discussed in the
Introduction (see, also, 'A Discourse on Curriculum in Village Schools',
1875), was introduced in England and Wales in 1861 and finally
abolished by 1898. 1861 also saw the compulsory maintenance of log
books for all elementary school Heads.

Conceive, oh ye inhabitants of towns, of a condition of existence so
devoid of incident that the annual inspection of the village school
is the event of the year. The Bishop holds no Confirmation here, and
the Eisteddfod keeps afar off. To these people October is the first of
months, because of the 'Xaminashun'. September is the long vigil,
during which, in spite of late harvest, truants are hunted up, cajoled,
threatened, bribed to complete their tale of 250 attendances. Rising
early, and so late taking rest, the teachers struggle with their little
flock. The third week comes, and the post is watched with keenest
anxiety. Has the day been fixed? Surely he won't come on the First!
Suppose it rains! Suppose they get the measles! "Suppose there is
an earthquake," says the Rector cheerfully.

The children do not look so far ahead, but when the actual day
is fixed they catch the infection, and weary their mothers with
speculations of probable success, possible failure. The eve of the
awful day brings a half-holiday, on which the school floor has its
annual wash: but the children hang about the playground and the
school gate; for even blackberrying has lost its charm today. Do they
lie awake at night? I doubt it, but I have no knowledge. Certainly
they rise early, and clamour for early breakfast. Do they, like
Falkland at Newbury, "put on a clean shirt to be killed in"? There,
again, I have no information; but I know that it is a day of best
frocks, of ribbons, above all of BOOTS.

And the Inspector? The children, nay, possibly the youngest
teachers, think (like Poor Peter Peebles), "I have not been able to
sleep for a week for thinking of it, and, I dare to say, neither has the
Lord President himself." Alas! At Llangastanau the inspector wants
yet ten years to teach him the most needful lesson, that what to him
is "Wednesday's job" is the day of the year to them. He sleeps a
solid eight hours' sleep, and dreams that he is playing football with
Harry and the Druid.

In 1871 school inspection was, as a science, still in its infancy.
The chief function of H.M. Inspector was to assess the amount

which the Treasury should pay; and this was done by rapid examination of every child above seven years of age who had attended 250 times in the school year. Those who had made less than the specified number usually came to school to see the stranger; but in most cases they were rewarded for their habitual truancy by being sent home as soon as the great man arrived. Whereby they got a holiday, with the additional relish of thinking that the good children were on the rack.

The children under seven were, and are, called infants. There was a grant of 8 shillings (or 10 shillings if the teacher was certificated) for these sucklings, *if they were present*. If the weather was so bad that they could not come, or if they got measles, whooping cough, chicken-pox, scarlet fever, or any other of the dreadful list, and were unable to appear, the grant for the absentees was lost. The principal function of the Inspector in an Infant School was to call over the names of the children on the Schedule. He might go on to hear them sing; and, if he were an enthusiast, he might carry his enquiries to any length. The instructions issued by the Department advised that "every fourth child in the first class should be called out and strictly examined". But even in my greenest days I cannot remember that I was so green as to obey that recommendation. A little experience taught me that infants should be left in the hands of their own teachers, and that the inspectors should look on. My Lords had not discovered this in May, 1871, when they issued Circular 11.

It was seldom that the examination of the elder children went beyond the three elementary subjects commonly known as the Three Rs. (What philosopher was it who first found out that reading, writing, and arithmetic all begin with R? Think of him as a time-saver!) But a town school might hunt up a few boys, who in Oxford parlance *ambiebant honores* in geography, grammar, history, or mathematics. There was an extra grant for a child who "passed" in one of these luxuries, but Circular 18 safeguarded the public purse by requiring that the examination should be on paper. To express themselves intelligibly on paper was far beyond the powers of these mute inglorious Miltons.

As for investigation of methods of teaching, or of causes of weakness in any subject, such refinements were but just beginning to be known. The great aim of inspector, teacher, and children was to finish by 12.30 at the latest.

Our plan of campaign was delightfully simple. Most of the children were in the two lowest standards. These were supplied with slates, pencils, and a reading-book, and ere drawn up in two long lines down the middle of the room. They stood back-to-back, to prevent copying, and did dictation, and arithmetic, sometimes dropping their slates, sometimes their pencils, sometimes their books, not infrequently all three, with a crash on the floor. When we had marked the results on the Examination Schedule, all these children were sent home, and the atmosphere was immensely improved. Then we proceeded to examine the rest, the aristocracy, who worked their sums on paper. As a rule, if we began about 10 we finished about 11.45. If the master was a good fellow, and trustworthy, we looked over the few papers in dictation and arithmetic, marked the Examination Schedule, and showed him the whole result before we left. Then he calculated his "percentage of passes", his grant, and his resulting income; and went to dinner with what appetite he might. But if the man were cross-grained, and likely to complain that the exercises were too hard, the standard of marking too high, and so on, he would be left in merciful ignorance of details. Half an hour in the evening sufficed for making up the Annual Report, and the incident was closed. Think of the simplicity of it!

We breakfast early at the Rectory. The Rector is a little uneasy and rather silent: at 7.30 the weather was rather bad, and if the children are kept away by rain—some of them having long distances to walk over the bleak country—not only will the grant suffer, but the teachers will be grievously disappointed. Happily the clouds lift and hope returns.

Soon after nine we visit the stables to arrange about sending me to the station in the afternoon, and the groom touches his cap to me, gazing with a wistful eye. He expresses an ardent wish that it may be a fine day for the school children, and as we make our way to the school the Rector informs me that there is a young person teaching there, to whom the groom is much attached; in fact he believes there is an engagement.

We find a long, rather low building with a thatched roof: the windows are somewhat low and narrow, and filled with diamond panes; and inside the light is scanty. There is a tiled floor; there are desks for the upper standards only; the other children sit on benches with no back-rails: both desks and benches are evidently the work of the carpenter on the estate. There is no cloak-room, and the damp clothes of the children are hung round the walls, sending out a gentle steam, as if it were washing-day next door, and the water were not very clean. About a quarter of the room at one end is occupied by a platform, which is found convenient for village entertainments; and a narrow passage by its side leads to a small class-room, "contrived a double debt to pay":[1] it holds the small Infant Class and it serves as a Green Room for the performers at the aforesaid entertainments.

The children greet us with effusion, and I am introduced to the teachers. Mr. Evans receives me with a smile, but does not presume unduly. There is Mrs. Evans, who takes the Infant Class, and also teaches the girls to sew for four afternoons a week, during which time a big girl "minds" the infants: an admirable woman, Mrs. Evans, but getting rather middle-aged for the little ones; always motherly, but not always fresh and gamesome.

And there is pretty Myfanwy Roberts, formerly a Pupil Teacher here, now Assistant Mistress, "till she can save a bit". Clearly this is "the young person", and I admire the groom's taste. Myfanwy is trembling with excitement in her Celtic manner, and Evans himself is uneasy, for he does not know my ways, and I may frighten the children. If I insist on giving out the Dictation, my deplorable English accent will be fatal; and if I laugh at the children's efforts to talk English, they will close up like tulips in a shower.

The children are for the most part either black-haired and dark eyed, or red-haired, freckled, and snub-nosed: but some are pure Saxon.

All wear their best clothes, and ribbons, and the maidens know it. They too are uneasy, and they discuss my appearance in their own tongue, which leaves me neither elated nor depressed: as when a Venetian gondolier scathingly delineates his passenger in local patois to another boatman: but the passenger's withers are unwrung. Only when I venture into the Infants' room I hear a murmur from a four-year-old, which the Rector intercepts and translates to me. It was, if I remember rightly, "Welwch-'i-farf-o", "look at his beard". I admit that in those days I had a beard which reached to the third button of my waistcoat: it had an extraordinary fascination for infants.

I call over the names of the fifteen infants, and find great difficulty in distinguishing between Mary Jones, Ty-gwyn; Mary

Jones, Hendre; and Mary Jones The Red Lion. One of them is absent, and her name must be struck off: Mrs. Evans will not admit that it is immaterial which name is cancelled, so long as she gets sixteen shillings for the two survivors: if John Jones, The Red Lion, heard that his Mary was wrongfully marked absent, there would be letters in the paper, and a meeting at Capel Carmel. Yes, sure! Mary Ty-gwyn is sacrificed on the altar of expediency.

Then I lose my heart to Gwen, aged four, and thereby win Mrs. Evans' heart. It was Gwen I find, who commented on my beard, and she is still so wholly absorbed in contemplation of it, that my addresses are unheeded. As I stoop down to press my suit in a language that she does not in the least understand—but the language of Love is universal—she makes a sudden grab at the object of her admiration, to see whether it is real. The other babes hold their breath in terror; but finding that Gwen does not swell up and die, that no she-bears appear, and that I am laughing, they break into a long ripple of choking mirth, in the midst of which I escape.

I return to the main-room, where the fifty "elder scholars" await me. "Will I hear a song?" Certainly I will. Is it the 'Men of Harlech'? It is: and it is rendered with a vigour that leaves nothing to be desired. Mr. Evans volunteers another of a more plaintive character, and we have a native lament in a minor key, which leads me hastily to assure him that the grant is now secure.

We proceed with the examination. I begin with Standards I and II. They find the sums a little trying, though they count most carefully on their fingers. When you have a slate in your arms, it is hard to carry the reckoning across from one hand to the other without dropping the slate. I suggest to Mr. Evans that counting on fingers is not practised in the best circles of mathematicians. He is so much surprised by this novel theory, that he gasps; then, recovering himself, he says, "Well, indeed, why did Providence give them ten fingers for whatever?"

Angharad Davis, a charming maid of seven, to whom I transfer the affection which Gwen scorned, gets one sum right (out of three), and one that is not without merit. She has "borrowed" and omitted to "pay back". I have known grown-ups to do the same thing. I ask her what she makes of four fours: she looks at me with tearful eyes and mutters something in Welsh. "What does she say, Myfanwy?"

"She says 'nid wn i ddim,' and that is, 'I don't know.'"

I think Angharad may pass for her frankness, combined with good looks.

The Squire arrives with the school accounts; and brings Mrs. Trevor, who announces that she is particularly interested in the sewing, and wants to have my opinion as an expert. Horror! Meanwhile Standards III, IV, and V are struggling with sums, and at intervals, with Dictation, given out by the master in a convincing accent. Then they read with a fluency that in those early days used to amaze me, knowing, as I did, that they knew very little English; till I found by greater experience that they knew the two books by heart, and could go on equally well if the book fell on the ground. All the work is done—Geography, Grammar, History, Needlework— done before the Inspector's eyes—all these must wait till October, 1875:[2] the children go home with undisguised joy, and I proceed to mark the papers. Evans has passed 92 per cent; great rejoicings follow, and I am classed above the last inspector, who drew the line at 88. I fear the Consolidated Fund loses by my inexperience, but I hold my tongue.

Mrs. Trevor insists that I shall report on the sewing. There is a table covered with female garments in unbleached calico (which smells like hot glue), linen, and flannel; and I am expected to look as if I knew one stitch from another. By great good luck I drive away both Mrs. Squire and Mrs. Evans by picking up, in my ignorance, a garment so shocking to the modest eye that my critics turn hastily away, and are speechless. I hold it to the light; comment on the backstitching (which I now have reason to believe was hemming); pull at the seams; and find that my lay assessors have fled. Rather abashed I also go, and find the Druid at the door. He has had a wedding, and he has left the loud bassoon and its moaning that he may explain to me about those hamlets with the cacophonous names.

"Good-bye, Mr. Evans: 92 per cent is excellent. Good-bye, Mrs. Evans: love to Gwen. Ffarwel, Myfanwy."

"Beg pardon, sir," interposes Evans, nervously; "but you haven't signed the Log Book, or seen the Accounts; and you have left Form IX and the Schedule behind, and here they are." This dims the glory of my departure, and I return to sign the Log Book, a custom of those days. The Squire comes with me, and as I open the cash-book, and wonder which is Income and which Expenditure, he remarks quite casually to the master: "By-the-bye, Mr. Evans, I have arranged with the architect and the builder to carry out the improvements in the premises recommended by H.M. Inspector last year, if this gentleman approves."

I, of course, intimate that I should not presume to have an opinion contrary to my chief's: and the Squire continues: "The windows will be enlarged; the diamond panes will be taken out; the floor will be boarded; and I have ordered some new desks. If we can manage to get three weeks' holiday without frost at Christmas, we can do all the work then."

Evans was radiant with joy, and we started for the street. Just by the gate I again hear a soft murmur from infant lips; this time as a soliloquy: "welwch-'i-farf-o!" It is Gwen. Ffarwel, Gwen bach.

"Now, Mr. Inspector," says the pertinacious Druid, "from here you can see my parish. On the hill-side is Llanfair-castanwydd-uwch-y-mynydd-uchaf..."

"Look here, Mr. Morgan," the Squire says hurriedly, "come up to the Hall with the Inspector; the Rector is coming... Give him a rest now."

NOTES

1. Oliver Goldsmith, *A Deserted Village*, line 227:
   ...The chest contriv'd a double debt to pay, -
   A bed by night, a chest of drawers by day.
2. Note by E.M. S.-K.: These and other subjects were introduced by the Code of 1875.

21

A DISCOURSE ON CURRICULUM IN VILLAGE SCHOOLS, 1876

House of Commons, London
Sir John Lubbock

The Revised Code of 1861 introduced an improved system of payment by results but was open to the objection that it recognised proficiency in the three Rs only and thus tended to discourage the teaching of other subjects. The revision of 1875 allowed two other subjects from geography, grammar, history, or needlework to be included for a grant. E.M. Sneyd-Kynnersley noted in *H.M.I.*, 1908, (see 'A Village School Inspection'), that the 1875 'Circular 18 safeguarded the public purse by requiring that the examination should be on paper...a town school might hunt up a few boys...[but] to express themselves intelligibly on paper was far beyond the powers of these mute inglorious Miltons.' In the following abridged article, taken from *The Contemporary Review* of 1876, Lubbock analyses the elementary school curriculum, particularly, here, with regard to its implementation in rural schools. He advocates the teaching of domestic economy for boys; questions the value of teaching grammar in elementary schools and says that dialect should not be underestimated. He is scathing on the history curriculum. He provides a strong case for the teaching of science in elementary schools using certain village schools as his examples. He deprecates centralized curriculum planning.

Sir John Lubbock (1834-1913), created Lord Avebury in 1900, was a pallbearer at Darwin's funeral in Westminster Abbey. He was a banker, statesman and naturalist. As a Member of Parliament from 1870, he introduced many reform bills, especially in banking, including legislation establishing bank holidays. His scientific studies were in entomology and anthropology. He published *Prehistoric Times*, 1865, *Ants, Bees and Wasps*, 1882, and *The Pleasures of Life*, 1887–89.

Sir John Lubbock, 'Elementary Education' in *The Contemporary Review*, London, 1876

The present code is, it seems to me, open to the grave objection that it regulates too minutely the system of education, thus weakening the school boards and committees, and greatly checking those improvements which experience would suggest, and which, beginning in a few schools, would gradually become general. Thus, by article 19c, it is provided that the classes from which the children are examined in Standards II—VI should "pass a creditable examination in grammar, history, political geography, and plain needlework, or in any two of these subjects." Now it is obvious that if two subjects are thus made compulsory all others are practically excluded. We have already seen that out of all England only 26,474 children passed last year in two subjects, and we may be sure that the number who will pass in three must be quite insignificant. It cannot, I think, be denied that by making history, political geography, and grammar, or to speak more correctly, two of them, compulsory subjects, all others are practically excluded, and the managers of schools deprived of the power of selection which they previously exercised.

Nothing, however, but the most absolute unanimity of opinion amongst those qualified to judge, could justify such a course, which moreover would, under such circumstances, be unnecessary. So far, however, from this being the case, there is still so much difference as to the best system of education, that it is very undesirable to lay down cast-iron rules of this kind, and thus to stereotype a system which, after all, may prove to be by no means the best.

No doubt the great majority of schools have selected history,[1] geography, or grammar; but some on the other hand have made a different choice. The Committee of Council,[2] indeed, say that "a fair proportion of scholars take up other branches of study." Well then, if they themselves admit that the school boards have acted with judgment, that in their opinion the different subjects have been judiciously chosen, why take away a power which has been so wisely exercised?

I am anxious at the outset to deny that I wish to render the school examinations any more difficult, or to introduce profound subjects, above the comprehension of children. The very reverse is the case, and one of my main objections to our present system is that it is above the children in many respects, and that there is no sufficient element of reality in it—it has no connection with their everyday life, or the common objects around them.

One of the so-called specific subjects is domestic economy. This is defined as follows: "Food and its preparation. Clothing and materials. The dwelling; warming, cleaning, and ventilation. Rules for health; the management of sickness. Cottage income, expenditure, and savings." Surely this is all very sensible and appropriate, but it can only be taken up after history, geography, and grammar, or two of them; and even then is restricted to girls. Why should not boys, also, be allowed to learn about food and clothing? Are not cleanliness and ventilation as necessary for men as for women? Are boys never ill? Improvident? Surely there might be advantage, and could be no evil, in allowing boys, as well as girls, to be instructed in these humble, yet most important subjects.

Why should so decided a preference be given to grammar? English grammar, as it is ordinarily taught in elementary schools, seems to me of very doubtful value. Moreover, the power of speaking grammatically is more a matter of practice and tact, than of tuition. I do not wish to undervalue grammar, with reference to language, but would say in the words of George Herbert:—

"Who cannot dress it well want wit, not words."

Savages, indeed, often possess a very complicated grammar that they use most correctly; and what we call the bad grammar of the less well-educated classes, is often a matter not so much of ignorance, as of local idiom. Moreover, grammar is not generally interesting to children, and this is a point, the importance of which we are, it seems to me, very far from appreciating. In venturing, however, to express these doubts regarding grammar, it will of course be understood that I am only speaking with reference to elementary schools.

As regards history, again, though it is doubtless one of the most important branches of human knowledge, still, as generally taught with a view to the government grant, it seems to combine the respective disadvantages of the multiplication table and the Newgate Calendar, being little better than a list of dates and battles, enlivened by murders and other crimes, with a sprinkling of entertaining stories, most of which are now no longer regarded as authentic, and which we are taught first to believe and afterwards to disbelieve.

We have all heard the proverb, "Happy the nation which has no history." And if this proverb is not equally true of the child who has no history to learn this at least may be said, that ordinary history is misleading in this respect—that it dwells on periods of war and bloodshed, passing over almost without comment that peaceful progress which brings about the development of nations; for the real condition of a people depends more upon their wisdom in peace than on their success in war.

Let us take the case of Scotch children. The younger and by far the more numerous classes have, under the present code, to study the period from the time of Robert the Bruce to the union of the two crowns. The history of Scotland during this period, as treated in any of the condensed histories, consists mainly of the long and bloody struggle with England, varied by feuds between the great Scotch clans and nobles. Of course wars and battles cannot be omitted; it would be as base and ungrateful, as it would be impossible, to exclude Wallace and Bruce from Scotch history. English children, as well as Scotch, thrill with interest as they follow the adventures of Bruce, and burn at the melancholy end of Wallace. It is only when wars and dates are made almost the sole constituents of history, and when history itself is used to exclude other not less important branches of education, that some protest seems to be necessary.

The air of unreality which pervades our whole system is one of its greatest drawbacks. So far from preparing the children for the great battle of life, our schools seem calculated to carry them into another, a dimmer and a duller world: not indeed a fairy-land by any means, but one crowded by difficult abstractions and vague shadows; where the mind is wearied by dates and tables; the conscience seared by crime none the less objectionable because it is gilded by rank; and where the imagination has no more energetic stimulant than the dates of rulers who are mere names, and the names of distant countries to them almost as shadowy as clouds.[3]

If, however, amongst those best qualified to judge, there were a general opinion that history, geography, and grammar were not only the best, but also the only suitable subjects, the case would be very different. But this is not so. There are still great differences on the subject. Perhaps there have never been more successful village schools than those of Dean Dawes and Mr. Henslow. In Mr. Henslow's hands botany proved a most excellent subject. This would be no sufficient reason for insisting on its general adoption; but it shows how greatly the interest of a subject depends upon the teacher.

Dean Dawes's school at King's Somborne[4] was the subject of a special report to the Education Department by Mr. Moseley, and to what does Mr. Moseley principally attribute the excellence of the school?

"That feature," he says, "in the Kings's Somborne school, which constitutes probably its greatest excellence, and to which Mr. Dawes attributes chiefly its influence with the agricultural population around him, is the union of instruction in a few simple principles of natural science, applicable to things familiar to the children's daily observation—with everything else usually taught in a National School."

Dean Dawes himself, in his excellent 'Suggestive Hints on Secular Instruction in Schools', dwells most forcibly on the great value of elementary science as a means of education.

"In no way," he says, "can the teachers in our higher class of elementary schools give such a character of usefulness to their instruction, as by qualifying themselves to teach in these subjects; introducing simple and easy experiments, which illustrate the things happening before their eyes every day, and convey convictions with them the moment they are seen and explained. It is a great mistake to suppose that boys of twelve and thirteen years of age cannot understand elementary knowledge of this kind, when brought before them by experiment."

As regards Mr. Henslow's school, and the botanical instruction so successfully carried on there, Dr. Hooker gave some very interesting evidence before the Public School Commission. Lord Clarendon asked him as to Mr. Henslow's method of instruction: —

"Invariably," said Dr. Hooker, "he made it practical. He made it an objective study. The children were taught to know the plants and to pull them to pieces, and to give their proper names to those parts, to indicate the relation of those parts to one another, and to find out the relation of one plant to another by the knowledge thus obtained." Lord Clarendon continued—

"Those were children, you say, generally from eight to twelve?— Yes, and up to fourteen.

"And they learnt it readily?—Readily and voluntarily, entirely.

"And were interested in it?—Extremely interested in it. They were exceedingly fond of it.

"Do you happen to know whether Professor Henslow thought that the study of botany developed the faculties of the mind, and that it taught these boys to think; and do you know whether he perceived

any improvement in their mental faculties from that?—Yes; he used
to think it was the most important agent that could be employed, for
cultivating their faculties of observation, and for strengthening their
reasoning powers.

"He really thought that he had arrived at a practical result?—
Undoubtedly, and so did every one who visited the school or the
parish.

"These were children of quite the lower class?—The labouring
agricultural class.

"So that the intellectual success of this objective study was
beyond question?—Beyond question."

Dr. Hooker went on to say that a child might very well begin
natural history at eight or nine years old.

On the same subject Professor Faraday gave also some striking
evidence:—

"At my juvenile lectures at Christmas times, I have never found
a child too young to understand intelligently what I told him. I never
yet found a boy who was not able to understand a simple explanation,
and to enjoy the point of an experiment." And (speaking, however,
mainly with reference to Public Schools) he adds—"That the natural
knowledge, which has been given to the world in such abundance
during the last fifty years, I may say, should remain untouched, and
that no sufficient attempt should be made to convey it to the young
mind growing up and obtaining its first views of these things, is to
me a matter so strange that I find it difficult to understand."

In the year 1868, the House of Commons appointed a committee
to consider the present state of scientific instruction in this country.
This committee, after taking a great deal of evidence, reported that
the opportunities of acquiring a knowledge of elementary science in
the National Schools on the Continent are far greater than in this
country; and added that the witnesses they examined concurred in
considering 'that nothing less will suffice here if we are to maintain
our position in the van of industrial nations.' They recommended
therefore, that elementary instruction "in the phenomena of nature"
should be introduced into our National Schools.

Again, the Royal Commission, so ably presided over by the Duke
of Devonshire, have reported that in their opinion instruction in the
elements of natural science should be made an essential part of the
course of instruction in elementary schools. Such lessons, they add,
should be devoid of technicality, and confined to such facts as can

be a brought under the direct observation of the children, the principal object being to give the children an intelligent idea of the more prominent natural phenomena by which they are surrounded.

For the present purpose no evidence can, however, be more important than that of the school inspectors themselves. Now without going beyond last year's Education Report, it will be seen that they have very great doubts—to say no more—on the subject. As regards grammar, for instance, Mr. Blakiston says, "Grammar, as usually taught, seems to me utterly wearisome and unprofitable."

Mr. Routledge says he does not underrate its importance, but he disputes "its claim to be treated as the most suitable subject for children, with all its intricacies and subtle refinements." Several other inspectors also express similar views, and so far as I could find, but few of the inspectors expressed themselves distinctly in favour of grammar.

So far then from there being any strong and general testimony in favour of grammar, the evidence is rather the other way.

Passing on to history, Mr. Cornish gives as the result of his experience, that this subject has been taught "with very unsatisfactory results"; Mr. Pickard reports that it is taught in many of the schools under his inspection, "but not with good results"; Mr. Routledge, as the result of his experience tells us that: —

"As to the usefulness of teaching detached periods of history, where time is so short, I have my doubts. Scarcely any child remains at school long enough to get more than a very vague notion of history, and it is such a wide and varied subject that a 'century' without any notice of preceding and succeeding events is not very profitable."

Moreover it is remarkable, as showing how much different departments of Government differ even amongst themselves with reference to the choice of subjects, that there is one which is excluded in England, which has not even a place in the list of specific subjects, while it is in Ireland absolutely obligatory. On all hands it is I believe admitted that the Board of Commissioners in Ireland have exercised great wisdom and judgment in the scheme of education which they have introduced into the National Schools of the sister island. Now one of their obligatory subjects is agriculture, for which they have issued an excellent little manual. The children receive simple explanations of the different kinds of soil—clays, sands, etc.; of the advantages of drainage and manure; of the implements and machines used in agriculture; of the principal crops, and the rotation of crops; and the kinds of cattle and stock. Surely this is a very suitable and practical subject for country schools? And would, I cannot help thinking, be more interesting and important to children than some of our English subjects.

Moreover, I may be permitted to point out that her Majesty's Government is not always consistent with itself in this matter, for it is somewhat remarkable that out of fourteen specific subjects which are included in the Scotch code, no less than five, or more than one-third, are excluded from that of England. But even if the system adopted by Government were absolutely the best, who will maintain that the system which is best for most schools is necessarily best for all? Surely differences of locality, of district, of situation, are sufficient to negative this view. The Government admit this in principle, because in Northumberland they do not propose that the subjects should be the same as in Roxburghshire. But the differences between England and Scotland are not the only ones!

Very much must depend on the schoolmaster. One master may have special gifts in, or knowledge of some particular subject, which it would be most desirable to utilize.

Again, it is, if I may not say probable, at least possible, that in towns where there are special industries or manufactures, the children in the upper standards might with advantage receive some instruction which would lead up to the occupations of their after-life.

Of course we can never expect that the children in elementary schools can be made profound men of science, but on the other hand it is no less true that they do not become eminent grammarians or historians. No doubt, however, among the 2,500,000 children at present in our schools, there are a certain number, who though they may not be able, like Stephenson and Faraday, Newcomen and Watt, to triumph over all obstacles, yet if they had a first start, would make observations and discoveries of real importance to mankind.

But even if history, grammar, and geography be the best subjects, why should they absorb the whole of the time? The classes affected by the provision are five in number, that is to say, they cover five years of school life, and surely that is unreasonable. Even admitting that the favourable subjects should come first, ought not other subjects to come somewhere?

The second objection is that the pupils in the training colleges are already sufficiently, if not too heavily taxed. I refer to this because it was urged against me in the House of Commons; but it is merely necessary for me to point out that the alterations in the code which I suggest would really require no alteration whatever in the curriculum of the training colleges, nor put any additional strain on the teachers.

Why should not the local authorities, acting, as they have done, and would no doubt continue to do, in consultation with her Majesty's inspectors of schools, be permitted to select, in addition to reading, writing, and arithmetic, such other subjects as they may deem best? Why should a subject be compulsory in one part of the United Kingdom and excluded in another? Why should agriculture, for instance, be compulsory in Ireland and forbidden in England? And why should the subjects comprised under the head of domestic economy be restricted to girls?

Then as regards the system of teaching, surely more latitude might well be left to school committees. Take, for instance, the case of botany. The following are the rules laid down by the department:

1st year. Characters of the root, stem, leaves, and parts of the flower, illustrated by specimens of common flowering plants.
2nd year. Structure of wood, bark, and pith. Cells and vessels. Food of plants, and manner in which a plant grows. Functions of the root, leaves, and different parts of the flower.
3rd year. The comparison of a germ and a moss with a flowering plant. The formation of different kinds of fruits. The structure of a bean, and of a grain of wheat or barley. The phenomena of germination.

It will be observed that this system differs considerably from that recommended by Dr. Hooker. Still I would not so much criticize the actual proposals as deprecate the institution of fixed rules on such points.

There is, in conclusion, one other argument, which I am anxious to bring forward. Every one will certainly admit that centralization is in itself objectionable.

Perhaps, however, this is peculiarly the case in matters relating to education. It is most desirable that we should induce the very best

men and women to serve on school boards; but in order to secure
them we must not interfere with them more than can possibly be
avoided. We must leave them a real interest and responsibility; but
if all control over the system of education pursued in the school is
practically taken out of their hands, we certainly diminish very
considerably the interest they would otherwise feel, and thereby tend
greatly to impair the efficiency of our schools. A late Minister of
Education in France is said to have boasted that when he looked at
his watch he could tell what every child in an elementary school
was doing at that moment; but surely such centralization is quite
contrary to the traditions of our Government and the convictions of
Englishmen.

However this may be, every one knows that there are the greatest
differences of opinion as to the best system of Education. To many
it seems that our present methods rely too much on memory and too
little on thought; that they make too much use of books, too little
of things; that they sacrifice education to instruction; that they
confuse book-learning with real knowledge; that instead of training
the mind to act with freedom and judgment, they choke the
machinery of the brain with a dry dust of facts, which at best are
but committed to memory, instead of becoming a part and parcel of
the child.

This is peculiarly the case with the children in our national
schools. There, at any rate, our main object should be to train, rather
than to teach the child. Suppose a boy leaves one of our village
schools at twelve or thirteen. He may know the date of the birth,
accession, and death of every one of our Sovereigns from the time
of William the Conqueror, he may be able to parse any sentence, he
may be invincible at a spelling bee; but if you have given him no
intellectual tastes, your school has to him been useless.

There are, however, as I have attempted to show, very different
opinions as to how these tastes may best be cultivated and utilized,
and under these circumstances it is surely most undesirable to
impose one stereotyped system on the whole country. If, on the other
hand, with the improved system of payment introduced by Lord
Sandon, the power which they hitherto possessed were restored to
the school boards and committees, they would be able in certain
cases to adapt their schools, or some of them, to local specialties,
they would be in a position to avail themselves of any peculiar
power on the part of the schoolmaster, and we should gradually

ascertain what system does on the whole most tend to develop the moral character and intellectual powers of the children.

Once more let me repeat that I do not wish to make the instruction given in elementary schools more difficult or more abstruse; quite the contrary— my object is to make it more practical, more real, and more lifelike.

At present the education given in our elementary schools is practically limited to the rudiments of arithmetic, outlines of states and names of towns, to grammatical rules, and the series of crimes and accidents which is misnamed history.

We should surely endeavour to give the children some information with reference to the beautiful world in which we live, the commoner animals and plants of our woods and fields, some explanations as to the common phenomena of nature, the causes of summer and winter, of the phases of the moon, the nature of the sun and stars, the properties of air and water, the character of soils, some elementary knowledge of light and heat, of the rudiments of mechanics, etc. Such information—elementary, but not superficial—would be intensely interesting to children, would make them think, and be a valuable addition to the abstract rules of arithmetic, and to the book-learning which now reigns supreme.

I hope I shall not be thought pertinacious in urging these views, but I have done so in the conviction that, without under-valuing our present system of inspection and examination, the real mode of making our elementary schools most conducive to the good of the country is to make them most interesting to the children.

What children know when they leave school is comparatively unimportant. The real question is whether you have given them a wish for knowledge and the power of acquiring it. That which they have learned will soon be lost if it is not added to. The great thing is to interest them, and make them wish when they leave school to continue their education; not so much to teach them, as to make them wish to teach themselves. Unfortunately our system of education has too often the very opposite effect; and under it the acquirement of knowledge becomes an effort rather than a pleasure. I have been good naturedly criticized, both in the House of Commons and out of it, as an enthusiast on this subject, but every one who loves children must know how eager they are for information, how they long to understand the facts of nature, how every bird and beast and flower is a wonder and a pleasure to them.

Hitherto I have treated the subject mainly from a utilitarian point of view, and with reference to what studies would be most effective in developing the faculties and intellect of the children. I cannot conclude without a very brief reference to another side of the question. It is impossible to remove the vast difference in wealth and luxury that has existed in all civilized nations between different classes of the community. But the truest happiness and the most real pleasures are, or might be, within the reach of all.

Books cost little, and nature is free to all. Gibbon is said to have declared that he would not exchange the love of reading for all the treasures of India; Mr. Trevelyan in his charming *Life of Macaulay*, tells us, as is indeed evident enough, that it was 'a main element of happiness in one of the happiest lives which it has ever fallen to the lot of a biographer to record'. Others, again, prefer the book of Nature to those of Man. Under a wiser system of elementary education the dreary existence of mechanics in towns might be brightened; the agricultural labourer might have opened to him a new world of interest in his daily pursuits; and thus lives, monotonous with daily toil, and in the want of interest and variety too often brutalized by coarse indulgence or cruel amusements, might feel the refining influence of beauty and the still more elevating power of truth.

NOTES

1. On the teaching of history as a subject in the primary schools, James Welton in his *Principles and Methods of Teaching*, 2nd ed., 1909, says: 'In the primary schools, history was practically unknown before 1875, though here and there a school had, during the previous eight years, taken it as a specific subject, with a few chosen pupils. In 1875 history was made one of the optional 'class' subjects, on only two of which grants could be earned; but it was the least favoured among those subjects. In 1899 the official returns show that even of schools taking such subjects only about 25 per cent took history, whilst 95 per cent chose object lessons, 75 per cent geography, and 60 per cent grammar. In the following year history was included in the subjects commonly to be taught in primary schools.'
2. The Committee of Council and the system of inspection and report were introduced in 1839 with the introduction of a grants' system to schools.
3. It seems that even twenty-four years later little had changed. James Welton, ibid., states: 'In 1899 a Committee appointed by the American Historical Association to

investigate the study of history in schools reported that in England "the most noticeable features are a lack of historical instruction, a common failure to recognize the value of history and certain incoherence and general confusion". These strictures were only too well deserved.'

4. See too, for example, W. Kenneth Richmond, *Education in England*, Penguin Books, 1945, p. 67: 'The Rev. Richard Dawes, whose school at King's Somborne deserves honourable mention as having wrought a transformation in an agricultural community, protested that the National Society was a hindrance and a sham, an ecclesiastical device for perpetuating the rural status quo. Voluntarism had done its best, and failed. Dean Hook confessed as much in 1846 when he wrote, "we have lighted a lanthorn that only makes us more sensible of the surrounding darkness."'

Dean Hook—Dr. Walter Hook (1798–1875), Dean of Chichester—a tireless worker on behalf of the poor, wrote *The Means of Rendering more Effectual the Education of the People*. The Anglican clergy, with supervisory responsibility for the National schools—and who may well have established a school themselves—had the opportunity, before 1876, to direct the process of education beyond the customary three Rs, scripture and sewing. Some did take the opportunity—King's Sombourne was an effective 'activity–oriented' school for rural children.

'Mr Henslow' was the Reverend John Stevens Henslow (1796–1861), the Cambridge mentor and friend of Charles Darwin. Professor Henslow left Cambridge for the rectorship of Hitcham in Suffolk, where, amongst his multifarious activities, he established a village school, giving some of the lessons himself.

Dr Hooker—Sir Joseph Dalton Hooker (1817–1911)—was a prominent botanist and friend of Charles Darwin.

22

THE OLD BARK SCHOOL, 1876
— Some excerpts

Eurunderee, Mudgee District,
New South Wales, Australia
Henry Lawson

Henry Lawson (1867–1922), the Australian 'people's poet', was born on the goldfields near Grenfell, New South Wales. Lawson's schooling was brief and rudimentary. It began in a 'slab-and-bark' hut in 1876, and ended four years later at the Mudgee Catholic School. Lawson's first teacher, John Tierney, an Irishman, from whom Lawson learned more about Ireland than Australia, was part of Lawson's unhappy childhood.

The Australian system of education was secularized in 1880, following which the Catholics withdrew their children from the public schools and established an independent school system.

> It was built of bark and poles, and the floor was full of holes
> Where each leak in rainy weather made a pool;
> And the walls were mostly cracks lined with calico and sacks—
> There was little need for windows in the school.
>
> Then we rode to school and back by the rugged gully track
> On the old grey horse that carried three or four;
> And he looked so very wise that he lit the master's eyes
> Every time he put his head in at the door.

Henry Lawson, *A Book of Verse*, Angus and Robertson: North Ryde, Australia, 1990

And we learnt the world in scraps from some ancient dingy
maps
Long discarded by the public schools in town;
And as nearly every book dated back to Captain Cook
Our geography was somewhat upside-down.

It was "in the book" and so—well, at that we'd let it go,
For we never would believe that print could lie;
And we all learnt pretty soon that when we came out at noon
"The sun is in the south part of the sky."

And Ireland! *that* was known from the coast-line to Athlone:
We got little information *re* the land that gave us birth;
Save that Captain Cook was killed (and was very likely grilled)
And "the natives of New Holland are the lowest race on earth."

But the old bark-school is gone, and the spot it stood upon
Is a cattle-camp in winter where the curlew's cry is heard;
There's a brick-school on the flat, but a schoolmate teaches
that,
For, about the time they built it, our old master was
"transferred".

But the bark-school comes again with exchanges 'cross the
plain—
With the OUT-BACK ADVERTISER; and my fancy roams at
large
When I read of passing stock, of a western mob or flock,
With "James Bullock", "Grey", or "Henry Dale" in charge.

And I think how Jimmy went from the old bark school content,
With his "eddication" finished, with his packhorse after him;
And perhaps if I were back I would take the self-same track,
For I wish my learning ended when the Master "finished" Jim.

23

AN OXFORDSHIRE VILLAGE SCHOOL AND A VISIT BY HER MAJESTY'S INSPECTOR, 1880s

'Fordlow', Oxfordshire, England
Flora Thompson

Flora Thompson's trilogy (*Lark Rise, Over to Candleford* and *Candleford*) was considered, in the 1940s, to be the most evocative of all accounts of a transitional era in the English countryside. Grinding poverty (wages were not raised substantially until after the Great War), a community spirit and a structure that allowed those within it to support each other, and pride in rural skills, were some of the characteristics of this rural community. Flora Thompson's delightful portrait of the village school, its pupils, teachers and visitors, enables the reader to 'hear the people talking' and to observe the impact upon the hamlet and village children of the various pieces of Victorian educational legislation in England. 'Lark Rise' is actually Juniper Hill, a hamlet on the Oxfordshire-Northamptonshire border where Flora Thompson (1876–1947) was born.

The two most important voluntary school societies in the nineteenth century were the National Society (founded in 1811) and the dissenting British and Foreign School Society (founded in 1814)—see Introduction and 'Reminiscences of the Lancasterian School in Detroit, USA'. The 1870 Elementary Education Act left untouched denominational schools that were working well and met local needs. Elsewhere schools built by the new School Boards were subject to the Act's clause that stated, 'Religious instruction in the board schools should exclude any catechism or religious formulary distinctive of any particular denomination.' Hence Fordlow continued as a National school in the voluntary sector with daily

Reprinted by permission of Oxford University Press, Oxford, U.K. from Flora Thompson's, *Lark Rise to Candleford*, [1945].

visits by the Rector (portrayed vividly by Flora Thompson), who took
the older pupils for scripture.

The 1870 Act did not allow rate aid for denominational schools but
did increase their grants, hence the annual visit of the government
Inspector of Schools, of whom Flora (as Laura) again has vivid (and
unhappy) memories. The system of payment by results and inspection,
as discussed by E.M. Sneyd-Kynnersley and Sir John Lubbock,
determined (and limited) the curriculum; certainly it held back able
children (such as Laura) and forced the pace for the less able. The
system was finally abolished by 1898.

Flora Thompson vividly portrays her three consecutive teachers,
each of whom was known as 'Governess'. They were assisted by two
monitors (or possibly, pupil teachers) aged twelve years. The second
teacher, a fresh graduate from a teachers' training college, was given
barely supervised responsibility for all the pupils in the school. This,
unfortunately for one so well disposed to the teaching profession, led
to her embarrassment. Nevertheless, the authorities were tackling the
great problem, which had increased significantly after 1870 and again
after 1880, when attendance to eleven years of age became compulsory,
of providing trained teachers for the Board and Voluntary schools.

Flora Thompson's account illustrates the impact adherence to the
school-leaving age had on pupils who were anxious to leave school. At
this time, they must first pass the 'fourth standard' in the year in which
they were eleven years of age. This was a similar set of tests to those
of earlier standards, although of increased complexity, and entailed
reading, writing a passage dictated by the inspector and some
arithmetic.

School began at nine o'clock, but the hamlet children set out on
their mile-and-a-half walk there as soon as possible after their seven
o'clock breakfast, partly because they liked plenty of time to play
on the road and partly because their mothers wanted them out of the
way before house-cleaning began.

Up the long, straight road they straggled, in twos and threes and
in gangs, their flat, rush dinner-baskets over their shoulders and their
shabby little coats on their arms against rain. In cold weather some
of them carried two hot potatoes that had been in the oven, or in the
ashes, all night, to warm their hands on the way and to serve as a
light lunch on arrival.

Although they started to school so early, the hamlet children took
so much time on the way that the last quarter of a mile was always
a race, and they would rush, panting and dishevelled, into school

just as the bell stopped, and the other children, spick and span, fresh from their mothers' hands, would eye them sourly.

"That gipsy lot from Lark Rise!" they would murmur.

Fordlow National School was a small grey one-storied building, standing at the crossroads at the entrance to the village. The one large classroom which served all purposes was well lighted with several windows, including the large one which filled the end of the building which faced the road.

Beside, and joined on to the school, was a tiny two-roomed cottage for the schoolmistress, and beyond that a playground with birch trees and turf, bald in places, the whole being enclosed within pointed, white-painted palings.

The only other building in sight was a row of model cottages occupied by the shepherd, the blacksmith, and other superior farm-workers. The school had probably been built at the same time as the houses and by the same model landlord; for, though it would seem a hovel compared to a modern council school, it must at that time have been fairly up-to-date. It had a lobby with pegs for clothes, boys' and girls' earth-closets, and a backyard with fixed wash-basins, although there was no water laid on. The water supply was contained in a small bucket, filled every morning by the old woman who cleaned the schoolroom, and every morning she grumbled because the children had been so extravagant that she had to "fill' un again".

The average attendance was about forty-five. Ten or twelve of the children lived near the school, a few others came from cottages in the fields, and the rest were the Lark Rise children. Even then, to an outsider, it would have appeared a quaint, old-fashioned little gathering; the girls in their ankle-length frocks and long, straight pinafores, with their hair strained back from their brows and secured on their crowns by a ribbon or black tape or a bootlace; the bigger boys in corduroys and hobnailed boots, and the smaller ones in home-made sailor suits or, until they were six or seven, in petticoats.

Baptismal names were such as the children's parents and grandparents had borne. The fashion in Christian names was changing; babies were being christened Mabel and Gladys and Doreen and Percy and Stanley; but the change was too recent to have affected the names of the older children. Mary Ann, Sarah Ann,

Eliza, Martha, Annie, Jane, Amy, and Rose were favourite girls' names.

The schoolmistress in charge of the Fordlow school at the beginning of the 'eighties had held that position for fifteen years and seemed to her pupils as much a fixture as the school building; but for most of that time she had been engaged to the squire's head gardener and her long reign was drawing to a close.

She was, at that time, about forty, and was a small, neat little body with a pale, slightly pock-marked face, snaky black curls hanging down to her shoulders, and eyebrows arched into a perpetual inquiry. She wore in school stiffly starched holland aprons with bibs, one embroidered with red one week, and one with blue the next, and was seldom seen without a posy of flowers pinned on her breast and another tucked into her hair.

Every morning, when school had assembled, and Governess, with her starched apron and bobbing curls, appeared in the doorway, there was a great rustling and scraping of curtseying and pulling of forelocks. "Good morning, children," "Good morning, ma'am," were the formal, old-fashioned greetings. Then, under her determined fingers the harmonium wheezed out 'Once in Royal', or 'We are but little children weak', prayers followed, and the day's work began.

Reading, writing, and arithmetic were the principal subjects, with a Scripture lesson every morning, and needlework every afternoon for the girls. There was no assistant mistress; Governess taught all the classes simultaneously, assisted only by two monitors—ex-scholars, aged about twelve, who were paid a shilling a week each for their services.

Every morning at ten o'clock the Rector arrived to take the older children for Scripture. He was a parson of the old school; a commanding figure, tall and stout, with white hair, ruddy cheeks, and an aristocratically beaked nose, and he was as far as possible removed by birth, education, and worldly circumstances from the lambs of his flock.

He spoke to them from a great height, physical, mental, and spiritual. "To order myself lowly and reverently before my betters" was the clause he underlined in the Church Catechism, for had he not been divinely appointed pastor and master to those little rustics and was it not one of his chief duties to teach them to realize this? As a man, he was kindly disposed—a giver of blankets and coals at Christmas, and of soup and milk puddings to the sick.

His lesson consisted of Bible reading; turn and turn about round the class, of reciting from memory the names of the kings of Israel and repeating the Church Catechism. After that, he would deliver a little lecture on morals and behaviour.

The children must not lie or steal or be discontented or envious. God had placed them just where they were in the social order and given them their own especial work to do; to envy others or to try to change their own lot in life was a sin of which he hoped they would never be guilty. From his lips the children heard nothing of that God who is Truth and Beauty and Love; but they learned from him and repeated to him long passages from the Authorized Version, thus laying up treasure for themselves; so the lessons, in spite of much aridity, were valuable.

Scripture over and the Rector bowed and curtsied out of the door, ordinary lessons began. Arithmetic was considered the most important of the subjects taught, and those who were good at figures ranked high in their classes. It was very simple arithmetic, extending only to the first four rules, with the money sums, known as "bills of parcels", for the most advanced pupils.

The writing lesson consisted of the copying of copperplate maxims: "A fool and his money are soon parted"; "Waste not, want not"; "Count ten before you speak", and so on. Once a week composition would be set, usually in the form of writing a letter.

History was not taught formally; but history readers were in use containing such picturesque stories as those of King Alfred and the cakes, King Canute commanding the waves, the loss of the White Ship, and Raleigh spreading his cloak for Queen Elizabeth.

There were no geography readers, and, excepting what could be gleaned from the descriptions of different parts of the world in the ordinary readers, no geography was taught. But, for some reason or other, on the walls of the schoolroom were hung splendid maps: The World, Europe, North America, South America, England, Ireland, and Scotland.

During long waits in class for her turn to read, or to have her copy or sewing examined, Laura would gaze on these maps until the shapes of the countries with their islands and inlets became photographed on her brain. Baffin Bay and the land around the poles were especially fascinating to her.

Once a day, at whatever hour the poor, overworked mistress could find time, a class would be called out to toe the chalked semicircle on the floor for a reading lesson. This lesson, which should have been pleasant, for the reading matter was good, was tedious in the extreme. Many of the children read so slowly and haltingly that Laura, who was impatient by nature, longed to take hold of their words and drag them out of their mouths and it often seemed to her that her own turn to read would never come. As often as she could do so without being detected, she would turn over and peep between the pages of her own *Royal Reader*,[1] and studiously holding the book to her nose, pretend to be following the lesson while she was pages ahead.

Then there were fascinating descriptions of such far-apart places as Greenland and the Amazon; of the Pacific Ocean with its fairy islands and coral reefs; the snows of Hudson Bay Territory and the sterile heights of the Andes. Best of all she loved the description of the Himalayas, which began: "Northward of the great plain of India, and along its whole extent, towers the sublime mountain region of the Himalayas, ascending gradually until it terminates in a long range of summits wrapped in perpetual snow".

Interspersed between the prose readings were poems: 'The Slave's Dream'; 'Young Lochinvar'; 'The Parting of Douglas and Marmion'; Tennyson's 'Brook' and 'Ring Out, Wild Bells'; Byron's 'Shipwreck'; Hogg's 'Skylark', and many more. 'Lochiel's Warning' was a favourite with Edmund, who often, in bed at night, might be heard declaiming: "Lochiel! Lochiel! Beware of the day!" while Laura, at any time, with or without encouragement, was ready to "look back into other years" with Henry Glassford Bell,[2] and recite his scenes from the life of Mary Queen of Scots, reserving her most impressive tone for the concluding couplet:

Lapped by a dog. Go think of it in silence and alone,
Then weigh against a grain of sand the glories of a throne.[3]

But long before their school days were over they knew every piece in the books by heart and it was one of their greatest pleasures in life to recite them to each other. By that time Edmund had appropriated Scott and could repeat hundreds of lines, always showing a preference for scenes of single combat between warrior chiefs.

The selection in the *Royal Readers*, then, was an education in itself for those who took to it kindly; but the majority of the children would have none of it; saying that the prose was "dry old stuff" and that they hated "portray".

Those children who read fluently, and there were several of them in every class, read in a monotonous sing-song, without expression, and apparently without interest. Yet there were very few really stupid children in the school, as is proved by the success of many of them in after-life, and though few were interested in their lessons, they nearly all showed an intelligent interest in other things—the boys in field work and crops and cattle and agricultural machinery; the girls in dress, other people's love affairs and domestic details.

It is easy to imagine the education authorities of that day, when drawing up the scheme for that simple but sound education, saying, "Once teach them to read and they will hold the key to all knowledge."[4] But the scheme did not work out. If the children, by the time they left school, could read well enough to read the newspaper and perhaps an occasional book for amusement, and write well enough to write their own letters, they had no wish to go farther. Their interest was not in books, but in life, and especially the life that lay immediately about them. At school they worked unwillingly, upon compulsion, and the life of the schoolmistress was a hard one.

As Miss Holmes went from class to class, she carried the cane and laid it upon the desk before her; not necessarily for use, but as a reminder, for some of the bigger boys were very unruly. She punished by a smart stroke on each hand. "Put out your hand," she would say, and some boys would openly spit on each hand before proffering it. Others murmured and muttered before and after a caning and threatened to "tell me feyther"; but she remained calm and cool, and after the punishment had been inflicted there was a marked improvement—for a time.

It must be remembered that in those days a boy of eleven was nearing the end of his school life. Soon he would be at work; already he felt himself nearly a man and too old for petticoat Government. Moreover, those were country boys, wild and rough, and many of them as tall as she was. Those who had failed to pass Standard IV, and so could not leave school until they were eleven, looked upon that last year as a punishment inflicted upon them by the school authorities and behaved accordingly. In this they were encouraged by their parents, for a certain section of these resented their boys being kept at school when they might be earning. "What do our young Alf want wi' a lot o' book-larnin'?" they would say. "He can read and write and add up as much money as he's ever likely to get. What more do he want?" Then a neighbour of more advanced views would tell them: "A good education's everything in these days. You can't get on in the world if you ain't had one", for they read their newspapers and new ideas were percolating, though slowly. It was only the second generation to be forcibly fed with the fruit of the tree of knowledge: what wonder if it did not always agree with it.

Meanwhile, Miss Holmes carried her cane about with her. A poor method of enforcing discipline, according to modern educational ideas; but it served. It may be that she and her like all over the country at that time were breaking up the ground that other, later comers to the field, with knowledge of child psychology and with tradition and experiment behind them, might sow the good seed.

She seldom used the cane on the girls and still more seldom on the infants. Standing in a corner with their hands on their heads was their punishment. She gave little treats and encouragements, too, and, although the children called her "Susie" behind her back, they really liked and respected her. Many times there came a knock at the door and a smartly dressed girl on holidays, or a tall young soldier on leave, in his scarlet tunic and pillbox cap, looked in "to see Governess".

That Laura could already read when she went to school was never discovered.

"Do you know your A B C?" the mistress asked her on the first morning. "Come, let me hear you say it: A-B-C-" "A-B-C-" Laura began; but when she got to F she stumbled, for she had never memorized the letters in order. So she was placed in the class known as "the babies" and joined in chanting the alphabet from A to Z. Alternately they recited it backward, and Laura soon had that version by heart, for it rhymed:

> Z-Y-X and W-V
> U-T-S and R-Q-P
> O-N-M and L-K-J
> I-H-G and F-E-D
> And C-B-A!

Once started, they were like a watch wound up, and went on alone for hours. The mistress, with all the other classes on her hands, had no time to teach the babies, although she always had a smile for them when she passed and any disturbance or cessation of the chanting would bring her down to them at once. Even the monitors were usually engaged in giving out dictation to the older children, or in hearing tables or spelling repeated; but, in the afternoon, one of the bigger girls, usually the one who was the poorest needlewoman (it was always Laura in later years), would come down from her own form to point to and name each letter on a wall-sheet, the little ones repeating them after her. Then she would teach them to form pothooks and hangers, and afterwards, letters, on their slates, and this went on for years, as it seemed to Laura, but perhaps it was only one year.

At the end of that time the class was examined and those who knew and could form their letters were moved up into the official 'Infants'. Laura, who by this time was reading *Old St. Paul's* at home, simply romped through this Little-Go; but without credit, for it was said she "gabbled" her letters, and her writing was certainly poor.

It was not until she reached Standard I that her troubles really began. Arithmetic was the subject by which the pupils were placed, and as Laura could not grasp the simplest rule with such small help as the mistress had time to give, she did not even know how to begin working out the sums and was permanently at the bottom of the class. At needlework in the afternoon she was no better. The girls around her in class were making pinafores for themselves, putting in tiny stitches and biting off their cotton like grown women, while she was still struggling with her first hemming strip. And a dingy, crumpled strip it was before she had done with it, punctuated throughout its length with blood spots where she had pricked her fingers.

"Oh, Laura! What a dunce you are!" Miss Holmes used to say every time she examined it, and Laura really was the dunce of the school in those two subjects. However, as time went on, she improved a little, and managed to pass her standard every year with moderate success until she came to Standard V and could go no farther, for that was the highest in the school. By that time the other children she had worked with had left, excepting one girl named Isabel Mary, who was an only child and lived in a lonely cottage far out in the field. For two years Standard V consisted of Laura and Isabel Mary.

They did few lessons and those few mostly those they could learn from books by themselves, and much of their time was spent in teaching the babies and assisting the schoolmistress generally.

That mistress was not Miss Holmes. She had married her head gardener while Laura was still in the Infants and gone to live in a pretty old cottage which she had renamed 'Malvern Villa'. Immediately after her had come a young teacher, fresh from her training college, with all the latest educational ideas. She was a bright, breezy girl, keen on reform, and anxious to be a friend as well as a teacher to her charges.

She came too early. The human material she had to work on was not ready for such methods. On the first morning she began a little speech, meaning to take the children into her confidence:

"Good morning, children. My name is Matilda Annie Higgs, and I want us all to be friends—" A giggling murmur ran round the school. "Matilda Annie! Matilda Annie! Did she say Higgs or pigs?" The name made direct appeal to their crude sense of humour, and, as to the offer of friendship, they scented weakness in that, coming from one whose office it was to rule.

Thenceforth, Miss Higgs might drive her pigs in the rhyme they shouted in her hearing: but she could neither drive nor lead her pupils. They hid her cane, filled her inkpot with water, put young frogs in her desk, and asked her silly, unnecessary questions about their work. When she answered them, they all coughed in chorus.

The girls were bad as the boys. Twenty times in one afternoon a hand would shoot upward and it would be: "Please, miss, can I have this or that from the needlework box?" and poor Miss Higgs, trying to teach a class at the other end of the room, would come and unlock and search the box for something they had already and had hidden.

Several times she appealed to them to show more consideration. Once she burst into tears before the whole school. She told the woman who cleaned that she had never dreamed there were such children anywhere. They were little savages.

One afternoon, when a pitched battle was raging among the big boys in class and the mistress was calling imploringly for order, the Rector appeared in the doorway. "Silence!" he roared.

The silence was immediate and profound, for they knew he was not one to be trifled with. Like Gulliver among the Lilliputians, he strode into the midst of them, his face flushed with anger, his eyes flashing blue fire. "Now, what is the meaning of this disgraceful uproar?"

Some of the younger children began to cry; but one look in their direction froze them into silence and they sat, wide-eyed and horrified, while he had the whole class out and caned each boy soundly, including those who had taken no part in the fray.

Then, after a heated discourse in which he reminded the children of their lowly position in life and the twin duties of gratitude to and respect towards their superiors, school was dismissed. Trembling hands seized coats and dinner-baskets and frightened little figures made a dash for the gate.

But the big boys who had caused the trouble showed a different spirit. "Who cares for him?" they muttered. "Who cares? Who cares? He's only an old parson!" Then, when safely out of the playground, one voice shouted:

Old Charley-wag! Old Charley-wag!
Ate the pudden and gnawed the bag!

The other children expected the heavens to fall; for Mr. Ellison's Christian name was Charles. The shout was meant for him and was one of defiance. He did not recognize it as such. There were several Charleses in the school, and it must have been unconceivable to him that his own Christian name should be intended. Nothing happened, and, after a few moments of tense silence, the rebels trooped off to get their own account of the affair in first at home.

After that, it was not long before the station fly stood at the school gate and Miss Higgs's trunk and bundles and easy chair were hauled on top. Back came the married Miss Holmes, now Mrs. Tenby. Girls curtsied again and boys pulled their forelocks. It was "Yes, ma'am", and "No, Ma'am", and "What did you please to say, Ma'am?" But either she did not wish to teach again permanently or the education authorities already had a rule against employing married-women teachers, for she only remained a few weeks until a new mistress was engaged.

This turned out to be a sweet, frail-looking, grey-haired, elderly lady named Miss Shepherd, and a gentle Shepherd she proved to her flock. Unfortunately, she was but a poor disciplinarian, and the struggle to maintain some degree of order wore her almost to shreds. Again there was always a buzz of whispering in class; stupid and unnecessary questions were asked, and too long intervals elapsed between the word of command and the response. But, unlike Miss Higgs, she did not give up. Perhaps she could not afford to do so at her age and with an invalid sister living with and dependent upon her. She ruled, if she can be said to have ruled at all, by love and patience and ready forgiveness. In time, even the blackest of her sheep realized this and kept within certain limits; just sufficient order was maintained to avoid scandal, and the school settled down under her mild rule for five or six years.

Perhaps these upheavals were a necessary part of the transition which was going on. Under Miss Holmes, the children had been weaned from the old free life; they had become accustomed to regular attendance, to sitting at a desk and concentrating, however imperfectly. Although they had not learned much, they had been learning to learn. But Miss Holmes's ideas belonged to an age that was rapidly passing. She believed in the established order of society, with clear divisions, and had done her best to train the children to accept their lowly lot with gratitude to and humility before their betters. She belonged to the past; the children's lives lay in the future, and they needed a guide with at least some inkling of the changing spirit of the times. The new mistresses, who came from the outside world, brought something of this spirit with them. Even the transient and unappreciated Miss Higgs, having given as a subject for composition one day "Write a letter to Miss Ellison, telling her what you did at Christmas", when she read over one girl's shoulder the hitherto conventional beginning "Dear and Honoured Miss", exclaimed "Oh, no! That's a very old-fashioned beginning. Why not say, 'Dear Miss Ellison'?" An amendment that was almost revolutionary.

Miss Shepherd went further. She taught the children that it was not what a man or woman had, but what they were which mattered. That poor people's souls are as valuable and that their hearts may be as good and their minds as capable of cultivation as those of the rich. She even hinted that on the material plane people need not necessarily remain there, rising upon their own merits. She would read them the lives of some of these so-called self-made men (there were no women, Laura noticed!) and though their circumstances were too far removed from those of her hearers for them to inspire the ambition she hoped to awaken, they must have done something to widen their outlook on life.

Meanwhile the ordinary lessons went on. Reading, writing, arithmetic, all a little less rather than more well taught and mastered than formerly. In needlework there was a definite falling off. Miss Shepherd was not a great needlewoman herself and was inclined to cut down the sewing time to make way for other work. Infinitesimal stitches no longer provoked delighted exclamations, but more often a "Child! You will ruin your eyes!" As the bigger girls left who in their time had won county prizes, the standard of the output declined, until, from being known as one of the first needlework schools in the district, Fordlow became one of the last.

A Visit by Her Majesty's Inspector

The school inspector gave a test in reading, in writing a dictated passage and in arithmetic. As part of Lord Sandon's 1876 Act, designed to improve school attendance, it became the duty of every parent to see that his child received efficient instruction in reading, writing and arithmetic. A 'Scholar's Honour Certificate' was issued to successful pupils. It stated that: '_____, a scholar in the_____ School having, at the age of ___ years, made the required number of school attendances, and passed the required Standard, is qualified to claim payment from the Parliamentary Grant of School Fees for the three years commencing on the first of_____, 187__, in accordance with the terms of the orders of the Education Department issued under the 18th section of the Elementary Education Act 1876.' In the previous chapter, Flora Thompson pointed out that children who passed the Fourth Standard at the age of ten years were allowed to leave school— otherwise they must wait until they were eleven years old.

Her Majesty's Inspector of Schools came once a year on a date of which previous notice had been given. There was no singing or quarrelling on the way to school that morning. The children, in clean pinafores and well-blackened boots, walked deep in thought; or, with open spelling or table books in hand, tried to make up in an hour for all their wasted yesterdays.

Although the date of "Inspector's" visit had been notified, the time had not. Some years he would come to Fordlow in the morning; other years in the afternoon, having examined another school earlier. So, after prayers, copybooks were given out and the children settled down for a long wait. A few of the more stolid, leaning forward with tongues slightly protruding, would copy laboriously, "Lightly on the up-strokes, heavy on the down", but most of the children were too apprehensive even to attempt to work and the mistress did not urge them, for she felt even more apprehensive herself and did not want nervously executed copies to witness against her.

Ten-eleven- the hands of the clock dragged on, and forty-odd hearts might almost be heard thumping when at last came the sound

Reprinted by permission of Oxford University Press, Oxford, U.K. from *Lark Rise to Candleford*

of wheels crunching on gravel and two top hats and the top of a whip appeared outside the upper panes of the large end window.

Her Majesty's Inspector was an elderly clergyman, a little man with an immense paunch and tiny grey eyes like gimlets. He had the reputation of being "strict", but that was a mild way of describing his autocratic demeanour and scathing judgement. His voice was an exasperated roar and his criticism was a blend of outraged learning and sarcasm. Fortunately, nine out of ten of his examinees were proof against the latter. He looked at the rows of children as if he hated them and at the mistress as if he despised her. The Assistant Inspector was also a clergyman, but younger, and, in comparison, almost human. Black eyes and red lips shone through the bushiness of the whiskers that almost covered his face. The children in the lower classes, which he examined, were considered fortunate.

The mistress did not have to teach a class in front of the great man, as later; her part was to put out the books required and to see that the pupils had the pens and paper they needed.

Most of the time she hovered about the Inspector, replying in low tones to his scathing remarks, or, with twitching lips, smiling encouragement at any child who happened to catch her eye.

What kind of a man the Inspector really was it is impossible to say. He may have been a great scholar, a good parish priest, and a good friend and neighbour to people of his own class. One thing, however, is certain; he did not care for or understand children, at least not National school children. In homely language, he was the wrong man for the job. The very sound of his voice scattered the few wits of the less gifted, and even those who could have done better were too terrified in his presence to be able to collect their thoughts or keep their hands from trembling.

But, slowly as the hands of the clock seemed to move, the afternoon wore on. Classes came out and toed the chalk line to read; other classes bent over their sums, or wrote letters to grandmothers describing imaginary summer holidays. Some wrote to the great man's dictation pieces full of hard spelling words. One year he made the confusion of their minds doubly confused by adopting the, to them, new method of giving out the stops by name: "Water-fowl and other aquatic birds dwell on their banks semicolon while on the surface of the placid water float the widespreading leaves of the *Victoria regia* comma and other lilies and water dash plants full stop."

Of course, they all wrote the names of the stops, which, together with their spelling, would have made their papers rich reading had there been any one there capable of enjoying it.

The composition class made a sad hash of their letters. The children had been told beforehand that they must fill at least one page, so they wrote in a very large hand and spaced their lines well; but what to say was the difficulty! One year the Inspector, observing a small boy sitting bolt upright gazing before him, called savagely: "Why are you not writing—you at the end of the row? You have your pen and your paper, have you not?"

"Yes, thank you, sir."

"Then why are you idling?"

"Please, sir, I was only thinking what to say."

A grunt was the only answer. What other was possible from one who must have known well that pen, ink, and paper were no good without at least a little thinking?

Once he gave out to Laura's class two verses of *The Ancient Mariner*, reading them through first, then dictating them very slowly, with an air of aloof disdain, and yet rolling the lines on his tongue as if he relished them:

"All in a hot and copper sky," he bawled. Then his voice softened. So perhaps there was another side to his nature.

At last the ordeal was over. No one would know who had passed and who had not for a fortnight; but that did not trouble the children at all. They crept like mice from the presence, and then, what shouting and skipping and tumbling each other in the dust as soon as they were out of sight and hearing!

When the papers arrived and the examination results were read out it was surprising to find what a number had passed. The standard must have been very low, for the children had never been taught some of the work set, and in what they had learned nervous dread had prevented them from reaching their usual poor level.

Another Inspector, also a clergyman, came to examine the school in Scripture. But that was different matter. On those days the Rector was present, and the mistress, in her best frock, had nothing to do beyond presiding at the harmonium for hymn-singing. The examination consisted of Scripture questions, put to a class as a whole and answered by any one who was able to shoot up a hand to show they had the requisite knowledge; of portions of the Church Catechism, repeated from memory in order round the class; and of a written paper on some set Biblical subject. There was little nervous tension on that day, for "Scripture Inspector" beamed upon and encouraged the children, even to the extent of prompting those who were not word-perfect. While the writing was going on, he and the Rector talked in undertones, laughing aloud at the doings of "old So-and-So", and, at one point, the mistress slipped away into her cottage and brought them cups of tea on a tray.

The children did reasonably well, for Scripture was the one subject they were thoroughly taught; even the dullest knew most of the Church Catechism by heart. The written paper was the stumbling-block to many; but this was Laura and Edmund's best subject and both succeeded in different years in carrying off the large, calf-bound, gilt-edged "Book of Common Prayer" which was given as a prize—the only prize given at that school.

Laura won hers by means of a minor miracle. That day, for the first and last time in her life, the gift of words descended upon her. The subject set was "The Life of Moses", and although up to that moment she had felt no special affection for the great lawgiver, a sudden wave of hero-worship surged over her. While her classmates were still wrinkling their brows and biting their pens, she was well away with the baby in the bulrushes scene. Her pen flew over her paper as she filled sheet after sheet, and she had got the Children of Israel through the Red Sea, across the desert, and was well in sight of Pisgah when the little bell on the mistress's table tinkled that time was up.

The Inspector, who had been watching her, was much amused by her verbosity and began reading her paper at once, although, as a rule, he carried the essay away to read. After three or four pages, he laughingly declared that he must have more tea as "that desert" made him feel thirsty.

Such inspiration never visited her again. She returned to her usual pedestrian style of essay writing, in which there were so many alterations and erasures that, although she wrote a fair amount, she got no more marks than those who got stuck at "My dear Grandmother".

There was a good deal of jealousy and unkindness among the parents over the passes and still more over the one annual prize for Scripture.

Those whose children had not done well in examinations would never believe that the success of others was due to merit.

The successful ones were spoken of as "favourites" and disliked. "You ain't a-goin' to tell me that that young So-and-So did any better n'r our Jim," some disappointed mother would say. "Stands to reason that what he could do our Jimmy could do, and better, too. Examinations are all a lot of humbug, if you asks me." The parents of those who had passed were almost apologetic. "Tis all luck," they would say. "Our Tize happened to hit it this time; next year it'll be your Alice's turn;" no pleasure in any small success their own children might have. Indeed, it is doubtful if they felt any, except in the case of a boy who, having passed the fourth standard, could leave school and start work. Their ideal for themselves and their children was to keep to the level of the normal. To them outstanding ability was no better than outstanding stupidity.

NOTES

1. Thomas Nelson's *The Royal Readers* was a reading scheme that, with little change, retained its popularity in schools in the UK and the Empire until well into the second half of the twentieth century (See, also, the Introduction).
2. Henry Glassford Bell (1805–1874) was a Scottish lawyer, a Sheriff of Glasgow and an author and poet.
3. Mary, Queen of Scots, by H.G. Bell, was included in the Standard VI *Royal Reader* of the 1880s. The example below, is from Part II, verse 6.

   ...And on the scaffold now she stands   beside the block—
   The little dog that licks her hand, the last of all the crowd
   Who sunned themselves beneath her glance and round her footsteps bowed!—
   Her neck is bared—the blow is struck—the soul is passed away;
   The bright, the beautiful, is now—a piece of bleeding clay!
   The dog is moaning piteously, and, as it gurgles o'er,
   Laps the warm blood that trickling runs unheeded to the floor!
   The blood of beauty, wealth and power—the heart-blood of a Queen,—
   The noblest of the Stuart race—the fairest earth has seen,—
   Lapped by a dog! Go think of it, in silence and alone;
   Then weigh against a grain of sand the glories of a throne!

4. See 'A Discourse on Curriculum in Village Schools' in this volume.

24

MY VILLAGE SCHOOL, 1880–1886

Near Werneth Low, Cheshire, England
Sir Ernest Barker

On leaving his village school in 1886, Ernest Barker (1874–1960) was educated at Manchester Grammar School and Balliol College, Oxford. He was appointed Lecturer in Modern History at Oxford in 1899. From 1920 to 1927 he was Principal of King's College, London, and was thereafter Professor of Political Science at Cambridge until 1939.

The pupil teacher system, to which Sir Ernest refers, largely replaced the monitorial system. Dr James Kaye-Shuttleworth, secretary to the Committeee of Privy Council on Education, strongly supported the scheme. While formal teacher training began in 1832, from 1846 the pupil teacher scheme provided five-year apprenticeships for boys and girls over thirteen who had left school. In the 1870s and 1880s, there were more than twice as many pupil teachers as college trained certificated teachers employed in grant-aided elementary schools. Many teachers, however, especially in village schools, remained untrained. See also, in this volume, 'An Oxford Village School and A Visit by Her Majesty's Inspector', 1880s; 'Pupil and Pupil Teacher', 1885–1898; and 'Clogs and Cinders: A Typical Village School', 1927.

At the age of six or thereabouts, I began to go to the village school. My mother took me the first time I went: after that I found my way for myself—down the lane; then over a stile and across three fields; then over a railway bridge, down a winding road, until I came to the village church and the church school which stood under its shadow. There was of course no motor traffic: there were no bicycles; there were only a few slow-moving carts, and I went safely enough. It seems, in retrospect, a little curious that though we

Reprinted by permission of Oxford University Press, Oxford, U.K. from Sir Ernest Barker, *Age And Youth. Memories of Three Universities* and *Father of the Man*, Oxford University Press: London, 1953

belonged to a Congregational chapel, I had my schooling at a church school. I suppose that the compelling reason was one of geography. I might have gone to a school connected with the chapel; but it was much farther away, and the road which led to it wound over a hill at the back of 'the new stone-quarry', along a stony and twisting path where it would have been easy to get into trouble. (There was a dark and forbidding pool on the way, in a deep hollow, which I always disliked.) So I went to the church school; and I was happy enough there for six long years. I never went inside the church (at any rate until I was much older); but I not only frequented the church school on week days—I also attended the Sunday school which was held there every Sunday. I think I began to do so towards the age of ten, when I had already become a hungry reader. I remember an old miscellaneous collection of books belonging to the Sunday school; and that, I suppose, was my bait. Was it not from this collection that I borrowed a history (perhaps a translation from the Spanish) of the fighting of the Spaniards and the Araucanians in South America? And did I not also borrow stories of the navigations of the early English voyagers?

I still remember the infants' room in which I started my schooling. It was a separate room, at the back of the main school. In my memory it is a well-lit room, in which mixed infants were gently and kindly taught. The mistress won my simple but ardent allegiance at once: she put a soft hand on the back of my neck (I can still remember the physical happiness of that soft touch); and she gave me, unless I am romancing, sweets. Days ran pleasantly under her hand; and I daresay I learned apace. But there is a soft cloud over my memories of that infants' room, and indeed over all my memories of the school, at any rate till I come to the end of the time that I spent there. My memories of my teachers, and my recollections of what I learned, only begin to be clear when I think of my second school—the Grammar School in Manchester. Miss Gregory, my infancy's mistress, is hidden in that soft cloud. I cannot see her face; but I can still feel a sense of warmth and kindness.

I suppose I must have crossed the passage from the infants' room to the main school by the time that I was seven, or perhaps even earlier. But here also there is a cloud. I see a single big room, narrower at one end (the end nearest the infants' room), and broader at the other. Different 'standards' occupied the different parts, and I must have moved from standard to standard, year by year, during the five or six years I sat in the room. We were a mixed school, but the only girl of whom I have any memory is one called Lillian, the daughter of the rent-collector. I remember that once, when I had been ill, she came across the fields to see me; and I remember going shyly to thank her for coming. Many of the boys came to play with me, attracted by the farm and its opportunities of bird's-nesting and exploration. We played with marbles, and at hopscotch; but I have no memory of any organized games. There was not much, if anything, of that sort in my boyhood; and anyhow there was only a small asphalt yard, at the back of the school, for our play.

I do not know when I began to be a reader of books: perhaps it was about the age of ten. Until that time I think I learned mostly from talk. My great-grandfather used to come about the farm, and I liked to listen to him. He was my great-grandfather on my mother's side. I was the eldest child of the eldest child of his eldest child; and as marriages were early then (about the age of twenty) the generations were drawn together. I suppose my great-grandfather's talk went back to memories of the beginning of the nineteenth century: he could tell me of the quick canal boats, with their fast-trotting horses, which took you into the neighbouring town at five or six miles an hour.

He had married again in his old age, and I liked his second wife, my step-great-grandmother. She had a pew in the Congregational chapel to which all the family belonged; and until I was twenty, and perhaps even later, I used to go and sit with her in that pew, where the two of us were often alone together. But it was my grandfather (my mother's father) who bulked most in my life and meant most to me—not in any flow of kindness, but rather in a sort of dry severity, which always seemed, however, to thaw when there was real need. He was the ruler of the farm and the quarry; and he ruled over them with a firm hand. He had not many words; and he was a contrast to my father's ready flow of talk. His wife died when I was still young—I think by the time that I reached the age of ten. She had been closely knit to my mother, and she did us every kindness in her power. Things altered when she died; and a harder time began.

I had some little jobs to do about the farm when I was free from school. I might help, in a sort of way, with the feeding of the cattle; I might be sent to deliver some of the butter which my grandmother (and later my mother) made; and once, I remember, I was sent out to trundle through the village a can of buttermilk on a little wheeled vehicle and to see if I could sell any—which I failed to do. But the great thing I remember is the delivering of cans of milk to a little stone house at the top of the lane, just through the wood, where you reached the top of the hill and commanded a wide-spread view—a view of mill chimneys in one direction, and of the Derbyshire hills in another. Romance was waiting for me in that house, where an old gentleman and his wife lived quietly together. There were forty-eight volumes of Sir Walter Scott's novels in the house; and there came a day when they began to be lent to me, volume by volume. What a world they unveiled for me! I have been a reader of Scott ever since. Scott was not the first beginning of my reading, though he is the great and towering landmark. We used in school (I suppose in the upper standards) a copy of *Robinson Crusoe*. It may have been a little abbreviated; but it was not one of those over-reduced and over-simplified abbreviations which I sometimes see nowadays. It was a good substantial red volume in Defoe's own words; and it had a good preface, not written down to the level of the young, which gave an account of Defoe himself and the origins of his story.

My other reading in school was only of ordinary textbooks—a volume of English history, which I read through at once, being too curious to wait day by day for the portions set to us in our lessons; an illustrated volume of geography; and other books of that order. I do not remember any 'literature' which we read in school, other than *Robinson Crusoe*; but I remember our learning by heart some passages from the Bible. They are not, I must frankly confess, as vivid in my mind as *Robinson Crusoe*; but that is partly because they are overlaid by later memories of the passages I afterwards learnt by heart at my school in Manchester, while Defoe is a unique memory, connected purely with my village school.

The memory of one teacher, and one only, fills that school. It is the memory of the Headmaster, Silas Whipp. I owe an incalculable debt to him. I can hardly see him now, or recall his face to my mind. His physical colouring, in my memory, is red—a sort of red gold. But that is symbolic, or whether it was his actual colouring, I cannot tell. The other masters, or mistresses (save Miss Gregory), have entirely faded away: he survives by himself, the president and master of my early learning. I do not know when he began to notice me: perhaps in my last years at school, when I got into the standard that he taught. The sunshine of his presence began to warm me, my mind grew rapidly under his teaching; and I found a delight in knowledge. I still remember the books that he lent me from his own stores. One was Dr. Smith's *Smaller History of Rome*; and I think another was the companion *Smaller History of Greece*. Partly from these books (which now seem pemmican, but then seemed full of fresh juices, because they revealed a new world to me), partly from the books about the Araucanians and the English voyagers which I borrowed from the Sunday school library, but, above all, from the volumes of Scott which I was now being lent at the house in the wood, I began to get some feeling for general history. It was born of pure curiosity, and nothing more; but curiosity is the mother, or one of the mothers, of scholarship.

I now come to the days, at the end of my time in the village school, when an educational ladder appeared for me suddenly out of the blue. Our village lay ten miles to the east of Manchester. An old and honourable tradition of the Grammar School in Manchester was the provision of scholarships for promising boys from elementary schools in the neighbourhood. I fancy that, at the time of which I am writing, it was only the elementary schools in Manchester itself that knew, or took advantage, of this provision. None of the boys of my village school had ever, so far as I know, been candidates: I doubt if even the Headmaster knew of the opportunities open to his boys. But it so happened that at this time a Manchester business man, who kept a shop in Stevenson Square, came to live in a house on the hill above the farm—a house separated only by two fields from that other house at the top of the wood which contained the novels of Sir Walter Scott. He had a son of my age, whom he sent to the village school. He knew about the scholarships at the Grammar School open to boys from elementary schools; and he asked the Headmaster to prepare his boy for the examination on which they were given. The Headmaster—thinking, I suppose, that two would work better together and would serve to stimulate one another—put me to work with the boy. That was how my feet were directed to the first rung of the ladder. This happened in the course of 1886, when I was nearing the age of twelve. In that year, but before this idea of sitting for a scholarship had emerged, my Headmaster had thought of training me to become a pupil-teacher, and of preparing me for the career of an elementary schoolmaster. It seems, in retrospect, an early age to begin to prepare for teaching; and I am almost ready to doubt the accuracy of my own memory. But I can recollect still, very clearly, an early and hasty breakfast, soon after seven o'clock, and I can also remember stumbling across the fields in the dark, and coming into collision with manure heaps, on my way to some early instruction before regular school began.

This was all altered by the new idea of working with another boy for a scholarship at the Grammar School. I do not think that I ever worked with any hope of succeeding, or that I had any ambition to win a scholarship. I was something of a sleepwalker; and I walked blindly and securely, without any idea of where I was going. I was entirely content to be pacemaker to the other boy, who came of a better social class (at any rate in my estimation) and was certainly better dressed. So far as I understood, I was working with him to help him: he might get a scholarship, but I should only sit for a scholarship in order to keep him company. Anyhow I enjoyed the work which we did; and that was enough for me. My chief memory of our work is a memory of our study of Euclid. How far we carried the study I do not know; but there was clinchingness about Euclid's proofs that impressed me deeply. Here was something different from the airy world of Scott—something with a precision, and a sort of click as the pieces fell home, that stirred my mind and stimulated me to thought. I doubt whether my knowledge of Euclid was anything more than mnemonic; and yet I remember the Headmaster saying that I understood the propositions, and could argue them out for myself. I think he was optimistic.

The examination came, somewhere about the Christmas of 1886, when I was just over twelve years of age. I think the examination lasted only one day; and I believe that we had to go to Manchester, and to take the examination in one of the rooms of the Grammar School. The one thing I am sure of is that early in January 1887 I received a letter from the clerk of the Grammar School informing me that I had been elected to a scholarship, and directing me to 'join the school tomorrow (Thursday) morning at half-past nine o'clock.' The other boy had not succeeded. The pacemaker had run in first, and was sadly alarmed, and indeed dumbfounded, by what he had done. So too were his family. It was all very well to win a scholarship. But who was to pay for the railway ticket, for books, and for new clothes?

25

THE NATIONAL SCHOOL, STRATFORD-UPON-AVON, 1880s

Stratford-upon-Avon, Warwickshire, England
As told to Angela Hewins by George Hewins
(1879–1977)

Stratford-upon-Avon in the 1870s, when George's story begins, as Angela Hewins, the author and wife of George's grandson, points out 'was a close-knit community which Shakespeare would have no difficulty in recognizing'. George Hewins was a builder who included, in his colourful career, his participation in plays at the Royal Shakespeare Theatre.

The first school I went to was the National School, Alcester Road, cos Cal believed in keeping in with the Vicar. 'There's no pickins from Chapel,' she said.

It was in the days of the Reverend George Arbuthnot—Black George, we called him. Many a time he punched my ear-hole. 'Wipe that grin off your face, boy!' 'Now,' he said to the class, 'can anyone tell me why our Sunday school is so popular?'

My hand shot up. 'Please, sir, cos of the Clothing Club!'

You had a card marked twopence, every time you went—twopence a week for clothing. Some of us snook out the back, once we'd got our cards marked, and at the end of the year you got the money. Who would have gone, else?

I got another clout for that.

It was drill, drill, drill. We was paraded in four companies on the Vicar's cricket field, down Back Lane, even the tiny tots, with staves

Reprinted by permission of Oxford University Press, Oxford, U.K. from Angela Hewins, *A Stratford Story*, Oxford University Press: Oxford, U.K. 1994.

for guns. The best boy had sixpence. Timmy Large, the teacher, rushes over to me. 'You'll never get the sixpence, Hewins!'

I didn't care about his old sixpence and I reckon he knowed it.

That was what got his back up. Plenty of them did care—I was lucky, I was better off'n most. Cal gave me as much as I wanted. She'd say: 'Don't go to school wi'out some coppers in your pocket.'

They were always bribing us. There was the School Attendance Prize. The first Monday morning of the new year we was all stood up for the Vicar as usual in dead silence, you could hear a collar creaking or the softest fart. He stood in front o' the fire and he bellows: 'The reward which we offer for regular and punctual attendance 'as produced good results, and we are going this year to try an extend its usefulness by making CLEANLINESS a further condition for winnin it.

The untidiness and dirtiness of some boys, mentionin' no names, is a disgrace to the community. SOAP is cheap,' he says, 'and the new supply of WATER to Stratford will doubtless soon make this commodity plentiful, so i 'ope for good results from this NEW RULE.' He stared long and hard at one of two of us, and the Evesham Road boys started sniggering. I thought: 'I'll get you later, Fatty Taylor.' Our teacher looked upset. We knowed why. The lad who'd stood to win the prize lived on Meer Street: there was no hope of Danny Andrews getting cleaned up. I didn't like teachers' pets but I didn't like the Evesham Road lot neither. Danny was poor; that's all he done wrong.

Soon as the Vicar had gone, Timmy Large our teacher started shouting; he didn't talk to us, he shouted—well, he had to, to make himself heard. Some days if another teacher was took bad there was as many as a hundred of us, in one class. 'THE OLDER THE BOY THE GREATER THE ASS!' Then it was a different sort of education: threepence a week to go to school and once you'd paid they didn't care if you didn't go again till next Monday. If it was raining, or the steeplechases, or peapicking, a lot of us didn't. The School Attendance Officer, he never troubled once your money was paid in. And plenty o' kiddies spent a penny or a ha'penny of it on jibber-and-jumbles afore they got to school. They had a good swipe o' the cane: the teacher told them to bring another ha'penny—quick! 'The older the boy the greater the ass!' he shouted. Timmy Large was always in a lather about one thing or another: he reckoned the

School Attendance Officer weren't doing his job, or Lieutenant Hutchings of the Volunteers was drilling us that hard we couldn't learn when we got back to school, or the Vicar was coming, or we was laughing at him behind his back. It was true!

*****

We got off school as much as we dared. We ran wild in those days—those of us as weren't earning and didn't want no prize neither—down by the river, up the Tram...

26

A LOVE OF POETRY, 1882

Punjab, India
G.W. Leitner, LL.D.

Gottlieb Wilhelm Leitner, (1840–1899) was born in Budapest and educated at a maktab (or Qur'anic school) in Turkey, and at the Malta Protestant College. He was appointed, at fifteen years of age, Chief Interpreter to the British commissariat in the Crimean war, with the rank of Colonel. Leitner attended the Muslim Theological School at Constantinople. He entered King's College, London, in 1858, where, in 1861, he was appointed Professor of Arabic and Islamic Law. Between 1864 and 1885, he was the Principal of the Government College, Lahore. On retirement to Woking, England, he acquired the Royal Dramatic College for his Oriental Institute. He published many works on education, philology, trade, dialects, etc. He spoke, read, and wrote 25 languages.

Leitner's *History of Indigenous Education in the Punjab since Annexation and in 1882*, (1883), premises the destruction of the forms of traditional education prevalent in the Punjab prior to its annexation by the British in 1849. 'Through all schools there breathed a spirit of devotion to education for its own sake and for its influence on the character and on religious culture,' Leitner stated. However, through a policy of official discouragement and of resumption by Government of rent-free lands (i.e. endowments) where no title could be proven (the income from which was used for the support of a school), the British, Leitner said, destroyed the spirit and practice of indigenous education.

When I spoke about some of the moral and practical results of even the humblest indigenous instruction to one of the Secretaries of Government; who, along with Colonels, seem to constitute the

---

G.W. Leitner, LL.D., *History of Indigenous Education in the Punjab since Annexation and in 1882*, Lahore, 1883

normal population of Simla, he said, in a tone of surprise, "well, then, we had better leave the country, as it seems we do not give them a better education than they already have." Without sharing this feeling, in which there is much to admire, I certainly think that our advent has not been an unmixed blessing to the Punjab, at least in education; and that we do not deserve to derive our income from its taxation, if we continue to treat education from a purely departmental or scholastic standpoint, instead of in a national spirit.

    – G.W. Leitner, *History of Indigenous Education in the Punjab*,

p. 145

Perhaps unsurprisingly, it was Leitner who first left the country. He resigned from the university in 1885, after a series of stormy meetings with regard to its new constitution.[1]

Indigenous schools of this period are described by former pupil Syed Wajid Ali in 'Maktab and Pathsala'; see also, in this volume, Sir Alfred Lyall's poem, 'The Old Pindaree'.

The Punjab is classic ground. Not merely the celebrated country between the Sutlej and the Jumma, but also the whole province teems with noble recollections. The history of its culture will tell us of a simple worship which long withstood the superstitions of the priests and warriors whom it had itself sent to conquer the South; of an ardent republicanism allied to the most chivalrous devotion to chiefs; of a capacity for self-government not equalled elsewhere; and, above all, of the universal respect for learning and of the general spread of education. The priest was a professor and poet, and in several tribes, castes and classes, education was a religious, social or professional duty.

As the wanderer through villages or unfrequented suburbs of towns, remote from the visits of Europeans, passes unperceived along the deserted streets or lanes, after the oil lamp has been lit in the household, he will hear snatches of songs or fragments of poems telling of departed grandeur, of duty to the Deity, of the fear of God which overcomes the fear of man. Love, which has ever inspired poetry in all ages and countries, will be celebrated in chaste and tender strains, except where the influence of Urdu has coloured the description of that passion. Here a minstrel will praise Ranjit Singh or recount the glories of the 'Dharm Raj' when God's law alone was King. There a boy will chant a chapter from the Qur'an or a "sweet-voiced" reader recite portions of the Ramayana. Elsewhere, the sound of some saying of a Sikh sage or of the verses of a favorite Panjabi poet, unknown to print, but living in the mouths of the people, will strike the attentive ear. Indeed, the taste for poetry, chiefly Panjabi, Persian, and now Urdu, is still the native resource for a prosaic life. Few are the shops, houses or even huts in which there are not periodical gatherings, though their recurrence is rarer than before annexation, to hear readings or recitations from religious books; many there still are who have committed portions of the Mahabharata to memory in polyglot versions; in the humblest household will often be heard those charmingly compiled stories of prophets and saints which have been written for the use of girls; the driest grammatical or philosophical disquisition will collect and keep an audience in the Village Hall or shop whose owner wishes to become a public benefactor, and even the frivolities of the Holi are sobered at numerous places, as, for instance at Amritsar, by the concourse of pandits to discuss some subtle point in the Vedanta and of 'Mastersingers' in Panjabi. These "Battles of the Bards," whether of priests or poets, mubahisas or mushaa'ras, attract numerous listeners from all creeds, whilst every night at the Durbar Sahib of the sacred City of the Sikhs may still be heard, though in less enthusiastic tones, discussions on religion and science. Even at Simla, within the shadow of the stronghold of the Education Commission, and undeterred by the presence of several Lát and numerous *Bara Sahibs* and *Councilis*, there are, in the small row of shops near the Elysium Hotel, repeated nightly gatherings for prayer or praise, or to hear religious or philosophical recitations, which are generally hushed into temporary silence at the sound of approaching *jampanis* or of a cavalcade taking European riders to their belated rest.

NOTE

1. G.R. Elsmie, *Thirty five Years in the Punjab*, 1858–1893, [1908] Sang-e-Meel Publications: Lahore, 2001, pp. 320–321.

27

OBJECT LESSONS, 1880s

Cheshire, England
E.M. Sneyd-Kynnersley

Object lessons were short, conversational, lessons of no more than fifteen minutes each for the 'babies' or infant classes and thirty minutes for the seven to ten year-olds. They used visual aids and were intended to develop powers of observation and spoken language and as such they made sound educational sense. They were the means by which 'nature study' as a subject was introduced and developed as part of the school curriculum and, too, the means by which the teaching of such subjects as history and geography was moved away from the traditional questions-and-answers approach with which late nineteenth century teachers were familiar. Teachers were advised to use, as the subjects of object lessons, common natural objects—blackbirds and bluebells, rather than the giraffe and the sago-palm '...for neither diagrams nor models are effective as substitutes for the actual objects...' Lessons where india rubber may be preceded by one on a glacier and succeeded by one on coal with each lesson disconnected one from another, and with lists of miscellaneous information which the children were expected to remember, were 'tedious, formal and dull'.[1] The Education Department advised, in Circular 369 of 1895, that: 'A lesson on the elephant to children in village schools, who have no opportunity of visiting Museums or Zoological Gardens, may convey information and store the memory with interesting facts, but it does not cultivate the habit of obtaining knowledge directly and at first hand, or develop the faculty of observation.'[2]

The HMI, E.M. Sneyd-Kynnersley, here, good-naturedly criticizes these lessons. See also,'Change in the Village', 1912.

E.M Sneyd-Kynnersley, *H.M.I.: Some passages in the life of one of H.M. Inspectors of Schools,* Macmillan: London, 1908

To tell the truth, we did not profess to teach natural history as a part of the regular course. But we gave object-lessons; that is, lessons on an object placed before a class; and as the object was usually a picture, and as the picture usually represented either Scripture scenes, or animals, it followed that—after 10 a.m.—most of the lessons were on animals. Our menagerie was a small one. A new beast would require study. Moreover, the managers did not like buying too many pictures.

Will you accompany me through a large infant school? The head mistress greets me: "The first class was going to have a lesson on the elephant: will that do?" Oh yes; let us have the elephant.

The lesson is devoid of interest. How do I know, when admittedly my thoughts have been wandering? Because the children are better judges than I, and they have damned it by entire indifference. Would the Inspector like to ask any questions at the end? Only one:

"What does the elephant eat?"

"BUNS."

Will I take the second class? Certainly. I am offered the camel. The camel has been called the ship of the desert. He is very useful; he lives in very hot countries, where it is very hot. Tommy Jones, don't fidget; listen to teacher. And he lives in the desert, where there is nothing but sand all round. Mary Smith, if you don't give over talking, teacher will be very cross with you: yes, my word, etc., etc.

When the stream of drivel has run dry, I ask:

"Where does the camel live?"

"In very 'ot coountries."

"Yes: but whereabouts?"

"In the desert."

"And what does he live on there?"

"Sahnd."

"Sand? Yes; but I mean, what does he get to eat?"

"Sahnd."

"And what does he get to drink in the desert?"

"Water."

"And where does he get that from?"

"Out of the taps."

I had not thought of that. There comes up a recollection of a Norfolk country school, where, after hearing all the uses and the virtues of the camel, I asked whether there were any of these precious beasts in Norfolk? None. And if the camel was so useful, why not? The answer came from the gamekeeper's son:

"Cos that 'ud tread on th' young pheasants."

I looked at its sprawling feet as shown in the picture, and understood their unfitness for a game-preserving county.

We must move on again. The third class is hearing about the mole, and I pause for a minute on the way:

"The mole is useful because it eats the worms, which would eat the potatoes and get into our food. Is it ever idle? No, it is always working; digging fresh passages."

Good old mole! "Well said, old mole! Can'st work i' the ground so fast?" Let us try the next class. It is engaged on the lion, under an elderly dame. Etiquette requires that the lesson should conclude with some remarks on the use of the lion.

"What is the use of the lion? The use of the lion is to 'unt. What is the use of the lion, children?"

"CHORUS: 'To 'UNT, teacher."

I find she means "to be hunted": and, when the children are gone out to play, I put it to her whether she really thinks that beneficent Providence has created the lion on purpose that man should hunt him. She is a little staggered by this presentment of her own doctrine, but pleads that it is so stated in her book, and produces it. There it is in black and white! I have little doubt that a similar belief is held by fox-hunters and other sportsmen.

"Crewel?" said an old keeper, when reproached for badger-baiting, "Why, whatever do yo think as badgers was made for?"

In ten minutes the children return from the playground, and I am implored not to forget the babies: they are going to have an object-lesson, and the pupil-teacher is waiting for me. It is Mary Williams, whose pretty face and pretty ways make her the idol of the babies, and even draw a smile from my grimmest Sub. I yield to pressure. The babies are hot and dusty, and riotous, and have to be relieved with a song, just to blow off steam. What is next on the agenda paper? The cow? Let us have the cow. The whole class sees the picture of the cow brought down from the wall, but nevertheless we must approach the subject as tradition dictates:

Pupil-teacher: As I was coming to school this morning along the High Street I heard a great noise, and there was a man in a blue frock, driving a great big animal down the road. What do you think it was, babies?

CHORUS: A kyow, teacher.

Pupil-teacher: Yes, a cow, and here's a picture of a cow. (The class regard it with blank indifference born of familiarity.) Now the cow is a very useful animal: —

Billy Jones: I seen a kyow this mornin' as I was comin', an' it was a bull: and it run at a mon an' 'orned 'im nearly, only 'ee got away—(pauses for want of breath).

Pupil-teacher (coldly): That will do, Billy, you mustn't talk now till teacher has done. And it gives us milk. What little boy or girl had milk for their breakfast this morning, I wonder? (Alarums and excursions, many competing claims to have had two moogs full.) Yes, and that came from the cow. What has it got on its head? Horns, yes. And what can it do with its horns, Jenny?

Jenny: Hike yer. (i.e. toss you.)

Pupil-teacher (much shocked): Oh, Jenny! I told you never to say "hike." The cow would give you a great knock. And how many legs has it got?

My attention wanders, as if I were sitting under a dull preacher, and in the absence of mural tablets I study the pictures and general exhibits. With joy I hail a reading sheet for infants:

Bill is not well. He is ill at the mill. Bid Ann fill a can of jam, and get us a bit of ham, and we will go with them to him. Did Bill sip the jam? Oh yes, he sat up in his bed, and did sip jam till his lips were red. He did not have a bit of ham. We sat with Bill till six, and then we set off.

I infer that Bill succumbed to this novel treatment at 5.55, and that they fled in haste, when they were quite sure, you know. But I think if they had given him the ham, too, he would have gone off quicker, if that was all they wanted.

Over the fireplace is the time table for the babies' class. It is "approved by me as satisfying the Conscience Clause." (In those days our control over time tables went no further.) The babies have two lessons a week, each of fifteen minutes, on "threading a needle." I think the Conscience Clause might come in here. On Friday afternoon they have a lesson on riddles! And I never knew that! "Why does a miller wear a white hat?" "When is a door not a door?" For children who have gone through a year of this course of instruction, including the cow, the camel, and the cat, life has no further terrors, and death comes as a happy release.

The cow is nearly exhausted. "And it has a very, very long tongue, and when it wants to get some grass to eat it wraps its tongue round the grass, and tears it off. Isn't that clever? Yes, Sally, you shall go home directly, if you are a good girl."

The closure is applied: the lesson ends, and the cow "winds slowly" to its place on the wall.

NOTES

1. James Welton, *Principles and Methods of Teaching*, W.B. Clive: London, 1906, pp. 355–357.
2. Quoted by T. Cox, *The Suggestive Handbook of Practical School Method*, Blackie and Son: London, 1909, p. 63.

28

PUPIL AND PUPIL TEACHER, 1885–1898

West Kilbride, Ayrshire, Scotland
Lord Boyd Orr

John Boyd Orr (1880–1971) began training as a pupil teacher at the age of fourteen years. He became a medical doctor; a research worker; a distinguished officer in the army medical corps (and subsequently the Navy); the founder of a scientific institute in Aberdeen; a farmer; a banker; a Member of Parliament; a Director-General of the United Nations Food and Agricultural Organization; a Rector of Glasgow University and a Nobel Laureate for Peace. He was a lifelong social justice campaigner.

Lord Boyd Orr's village school exemplifies the Scottish practice and tradition, unlike that of England, by which schoolmasters in parochial schools were capable of preparing pupils for the university. In the highlands and islands of Scotland, in 1826, for example, over half the schools were said to teach Latin and book-keeping and one-third Greek and English grammar. Thus, while poor children would receive little more than religion and the three Rs, the opportunity for social advancement existed for the children of those who could afford to keep their children in school.

See also, 'The Village Philosopher', c. 1855, and 'Childhood Days', 1889–1894.

In the nineteenth century Scotland was probably the best educated country in the world. At the time of the Reformation in the sixteenth century, John Knox, who established a theocracy in Scotland, put a school in every parish, under the supervision of the local church which saw to it that religious instruction took a prominent place in

---

Lord Boyd Orr, *As I Recall*, MacGibbon and Kee: London, 1966

education. In 1874 the state took over the schools from the Church, but religious instruction was retained. Every pupil had a copy of the Shorter Catechism with theology explained by question and answer in simple language. On the back page was the multiplication table— an excellent primer for a religious life and a successful commercial career. Education in the parish schools was at such a high level that many pupils educated by the village schoolmaster were able to pass the university entrance examination, though this must have been lower standard than it is today. Scotland had a number of secondary schools which England lacked until an Education Act in 1902 promoted by A.J. Balfour made it possible for local authorities to establish secondary schools. The Scots were keen on education and many families sacrificed themselves to give at least one son a university education. Scotland had thus a far bigger proportion of university educated men than England.

When I was a boy religious instruction still formed a prominent part of education. We all had to learn the Shorter Catechism and parts of the Scriptures off by heart. We were examined once a year at the Christmas prize giving by three clergymen who were members of the Parish School Board. The school day opened with the singing of a hymn. One I remember was 'Rescue the perishing, care for the dying; Jesus is merciful, Jesus will save.' Another common one was 'Childhood years are passing o'er us, soon our schooldays will be done; cares and sorrows lie before us; hidden dangers, snares unknown'. The sentiments of the children, who were all anxious to leave school, were rather different. One of the older pupils amended the last two lines to 'A better future lies before us; no more lessons, much more fun.'

The schools were uncomfortable in winter. A coal fire at one end of the room had little effect on the pupils who sat shivering at the other end. The school hours were from nine till four o'clock with an hour off for lunch. Some of the children had to walk long distances to and from school. The discoverer of penicillin, Sir Alexander Fleming, was an Ayrshire boy, who had had to walk four miles to school. There was no provision for food. The children brought a 'piece', which they ate in the school shed. In the cold winter days the children were keen to get back into the shelter of the school and used to sing round the doors: "Teacher, teacher, let me in, my feet are cauld and my shoon are dune; ad if ye dinna let me in, I'll play truant in the afternune."

When I was thirteen I won a bursary and was sent to Kilmarnock Academy, about twenty miles from my home. Fortunately or unfortunately for my education, my father owned a quarry about two miles from Kilmarnock and I was sent to lodge with the tenant of a house near the quarry. I found life at the quarry among the navies and quarrymen much more interesting than walking two miles to the Academy in Kilmarnock. I was allowed to fire the engines and work the crane and mingled as I wished with the workmen who taught me to smoke, and from whom I gathered a wonderful vocabulary of swear words.

Part of my pocket money for lunch in Kilmarnock was spent on buying the penny and twopenny 'blood and thunder' stories of the Wild West. These were forbidden and had to be smuggled into the house when I went home. I still remember the stories and names of some of the books—*Panther Paul the Prairie Pirate*, *Icicle Isaac from Frozen Flats*, *Deadwood Dick in Denver City* and other alluring titles. Such was my first introduction to English literature! So far as I can remember they were good clean stories of adventure, suitable for a boy of thirteen or fourteen years and, on the whole, better than some of the Westerns on television today.

My report from the Academy must have shocked my parents for I was taken home and sent again to the village school where I was soon taken on as one of the four pupil teachers. It was customary then for one or two suitable pupils of about fourteen to be taken on to the teaching staff as pupil teachers serving a kind of apprenticeship to the teaching profession. The headmaster invited me to become one and I accepted. I was paid £10 the first year, rising to £20 in the fourth year.

At that time the family fortunes, following the disastrous quarry venture, were at the lowest level. My father was working very hard with only a few hired men so as to make as much money as possible. The spring was the busiest time with so much work that it was difficult to get it all done. Work began at six o'clock in the morning. In order to help my father I got up and worked from six till eight o'clock. At eight I went home for my breakfast and then on to the pupil teacher class at 8.30. We taught from nine to four, after which we had another half-hour of instruction and then home to study for examinations for an hour or two. It was a hard life, common at that time in many Scottish families who stinted themselves to get a son or daughter to the university.

The schools in those days were strong on the classics. Latin was the dividing line between boys wishing to go to the university and those with no such ambition. The schoolmasters were well up in the classics and though Peter McConkey, the headmaster, had never been to a university, he read Latin, Greek and French almost as easily as English. Indeed he published a book of translations of extracts which he thought the most beautiful. In my first session at the university I devoted nearly all my time to the study of Latin, neglecting mathematics, my other subject. I managed to get through the Latin degree examination and have never looked at a Latin book since. The only Latin author I was interested in was Tacitus who could give lucid expression to an idea or describe an event with fewer words than any other author I had ever read.

Having done little or no work on mathematics, I went up for the degree examination in fear and trembling; fortunately, from what I had learned myself before going to the university I was able to answer a sufficient number of the questions to enable me to scrape through. I still deplore the waste of time spent on Latin and Greek when I would much rather have studied mathematics. All our seven grandchildren study Latin, and the boys at Eton do Greek in addition. Our mediaeval education dies hard.

When I had got past the stage of the 'Penny Dreadful' literature, during any spare time left over after studying the examination subjects which, apart from mathematics and essay-writing I found a bore, I read a great deal about the stars and plant and animal life. Fortunately our house had lots of books including a Chambers Encyclopedia where one could always find information on anything one was wondering about. Some knowledge about the universe and the manifestations of life on our planet, can lay a better foundation for a full intellectual life than knowing by heart all the irregular verbs or other verbal niceties in Latin and Greek.

To get back to the old schooldays: for those who were not going to the university, life in the senior classes was pleasant. The old schoolmaster took the view that it was not worth while giving advanced education to a lot of farmers' and farm servants' sons who were going to spend their lives growing crops and tending cattle. He taught them a little book-keeping which he thought would be useful to them, and also a good deal of composition to enable them to write letters. He also tried to give them an interest in art by giving them drawings to copy. The older pupils had a good deal of spare time on their hands and were allowed to slip in and out of school pretty much as they pleased. With no hard studies, some of them got into mischief. On one occasion my elder brother slipped out of the classroom, managed to climb on to the roof of the school and placed a slate across the chimney of the headmaster's room. He then put a turf on top of the slate to prevent it being blown off. Soon the schoolroom was so filled with smoke that the pupils had to be allowed out. At night he went back and removed the slate and the turf so that when workmen came next day to see what was causing the obstruction, they informed the headmaster there was nothing wrong with the chimney. But next day, the same thing happened, and this went on for a day or two with an argument going on between the headmaster and the chimney sweep until some passer-by saw my brother edging along the rigging and watched him put the slate and turf on top of the chimney. The headmaster was informed and my brother was given a good caning.

Many other tricks were played on the headmaster. He wore a morning coat with two big pockets which were always full of newspapers and various other papers. At the threshing of the grain stacks at the farms some of the country boys caught mice, brought them to school in a box, and when the old man was passing up between the forms they slipped a few of the mice into his pockets. When he felt the movement in his pocket he would take out all the papers to see what it was and out jumped the mice to the great amusement of the class and the anger of the old man who could not find out which boy had presented him with the livestock!

The children weren't bothered with the many examinations they have today. Two school inspectors appeared once a year to examine the children and the pupil teachers. The headmaster gave them an excellent lunch, and the afternoon part of the examination was very pleasant. Unless there was something drastically wrong, the report was good enough to warrant the government grant which was estimated according to the number of pupils and attendances.

In my second year as a pupil teacher the old headmaster retired and was succeeded by John G. Lyon who, by studying at home, had won a London B.A. without attending a university. He was an excellent teacher devoted to his profession. Of the five pupil teachers under him, three of us went to the university and the other two to technical colleges, and all went on to more or less distinguished careers.

There has been a great improvement in primary school education since the 1880s when I went to school, or even later when I was a teacher. In those days the education authorities were interested only in book learning. There was little or no regard for the physical well being of the children. Though the children of the poor were probably as well educated as those of the wealthy in rudimentary subjects like reading, writing and arithmetic, they did not enjoy as good physical conditions. As late as the 1930s boys of fourteen years of age of the lower middle class were nearly three inches taller than those of the manual workers, and boys in wealthy families about five inches taller. In the industrial towns rickets and other evidence of malnutrition affected nearly half the children.

The introduction of school cheap or free milk and school meals, together with the big rise in the standard of living of the lower income group, enabled families to get a better diet, and there is now little difference between the health and physical well being and dress of children of different income groups.

After four years as a pupil teacher I won a Queen's scholarship which took me to a teachers' training college and, as I had passed the university entrance examinations, my fees were paid for university classes, and I had won a bursary sufficient to pay for my lodgings. I attended Glasgow University for some classes and the teachers' training college for others, but the university education was the most important.

29

CHILDHOOD DAYS, 1889–1894

Parkhead, Scotland
Thomas Bell

Thomas Bell (1882–1944) was born in Parkhead, then a semi-rural village in the east end of Glasgow. Handloom weaving was still an active industry. However, as Bell stated in his autobiography, 'The smell of oil and smoke, the thud of the Sampson hammer and the glare of furnace fires were fast banishing the scents and sounds and colours of the country.' Bell was a leading member of the Communist Party of Great Britain. He was imprisoned in Wandsworth with his colleagues in 1926 on the eve of the General Strike. See also, 'The Village Philosopher', c. 1855, and 'Pupil and Pupil Teacher', 1885–1898.

In my parents' childhood days there had been no Board schools. They were the more keen that we should attend regularly. When the Education Act for Scotland was passed in 1872 and the Board of Education for Glasgow took over all schools, the limited grant of the Government and the parsimony of the city ratepayers made it necessary for scholars not only to purchase their own books, pencils, slates and ink, but to pay seven pence a week for instruction. What this meant to a worker with three or more children at school can well be imagined.

Often when the date came round to pay the school fees (which were due fortnightly), my mother, having to decide with her limited means which were the most pressing debts, would not be able to afford them. I recollect the trouble she had to persuade my elder brother, Samuel, to tell the teacher the fees would be paid next week.

Thomas Bell, *Pioneering Days*, [1941] Oriental Publishing House: Benares, 1946

He was a proud, stubborn lad, and insisted on having the 1s. 2d when it was due or he wouldn't go to school. My mother would plead with him that she hadn't got it. Then she would take the family 'tawse'—a black strap with five fingers—to him and beat him, but to no purpose. Finally, in despair, she had to borrow the money from her brother or my grandfather.

With my keener sense of the difficulties at home I had, on the contrary, no hesitation in going to school and telling the teacher he couldn't get his fees till next week. This led to conversations with the teachers about our family circumstances, and I remember the sympathetic words of one teacher, in particular, who came of a miner's family himself.

I went to school in the spring of 1889 and left in the spring of 1894—at exactly eleven and a half years of age. But even this short period had taught me something in addition to the routine subjects. Resentment at the cruelty of certain of the teachers led to their being mobbed by the boys after school hours. More than once I took part in waylaying a teacher, booing and hissing and shouting names at him on his way home. The relief to our feelings was great, especially when we got rotten apples or other refuse to throw at him, though we knew well that this would lead to a 'court martial' next day. Finally feeling ran so high that we organized a strike. We had a daredevil of a boy, the son of a steel smelter—Jock Clyde—for our leader. We all stood outside the gate and when the bell rang we refused to go in.

Away we marched in formation through the cornfields, singing the popular songs of the times, and in a mood of defiant destruction. Gathering sticks on the way, we prepared to defend ourselves against the farmer, his dogs, or any other 'enemy' who might attempt to stop us. Nobody did. But this, my first crude experience of strike action, has vividly remained with me ever since. The immediate result was the removal of the teacher in question, and a better disposition on the part of the remainder of the teachers.

In later years I came to travel in many lands and have observed the living conditions of the workers there. But I verily believe there is nothing, with the possible exception of the conditions under the old Russian Czardom, to compare with the slums of Glasgow. There had been some improvement in the last thirty years, but when I was a boy they were appalling. We did not live exactly in a slum, but in something next door to it. Imagine a block of buildings less than fifty yards square, with a courtyard; twenty-five families, with an average of four to the family; one water-tap outside to each group of families; two open wet closets; a central open midden joining them, and one wash-house for the lot; the courtyard of earth full of mud puddles in the wet weather—and it seemed to rain about nine months in the year in Glasgow.

Each family had no more than two rooms. In our case there were eight of us in these two rooms. I knew families of ten who were our neighbours. The beds consisted of holes in the wall with wooden props to support the straw palliasses. To add to our discomfort, we lived above a hay and grain store, so that we were on familiar terms with rats, mice, bugs and fleas.

Scarlet fever, measles, influenza, chickenpox and smallpox were continuously present—if not the one, then the other.

It must have been a heartbreaking job for my parents, who were scrupulously clean, to keep us in decent health. Looking back I can understand now the reason for so much scrubbing, cleaning, airing of beds and whitewashing of walls that went on.

*****

The half-time system was prevalent in the days of which I am speaking. Boys and girls of ten and eleven were encouraged to go to the cotton mills or rope-spinning works or to take jobs as errand-boys. Many of my school chums were half-timers. My parents were very much opposed to this system, though, like other workers, they badly needed the extra shillings. But while we were not allowed to neglect our schooling we were encouraged to carry milk in the mornings for a local farmer.

Boys and girls would get up at six o'clock and go to the farm or dairy. There each was given as many as twenty pint or quart cans at a time, with long handles for carrying; and with this weight they made the round, climbing three and four flights of stairs to deliver the milk to the customers – for which they got the handsome wage of one shilling and sixpence a week. My older sister and brother had done this job, and when I reached the age of eight or nine I fell heir to the post. I can remember how on a winter morning our hands were cracked and bleeding with the cold and frost, and I cried. My mother made me soak them in a basin of hot water, after which she rubbed in Vaseline. The hot water caused excruciating pain, but it softened the skin and helped it to heal.

30

THE MAKTAB AND THE PATHSALA, 1890s

Bara Tajpur, Bengal, India
Syed Wajid Ali, B.A., (Cantab.), Barrister-at-Law

Syed Wajid Ali, (1890–1951), a lawyer, essayist and philosopher, was born in Bara Tajpur village in the Serampore subdivision in Hughli, Bengal. Following his studies in the village *maktab* and *pathsala*, Syed Wajid Ali attended the Shillong Mokar High School from 1906, Allahabad University from 1910, and Cambridge University from 1912. He was a lawyer at the Calcutta High Court from 1915 and Magistrate of Calcutta Presidency from 1923 until his retirement in 1945. As a liberal intellectual in the inter-war years prior to the subcontinent's independence in 1947, he made a significant contribution to the ongoing, mainly middle class, debate on Bengali Muslim cultural identity in Hindu-dominated India. He supported the ending of the purdah system; the education of girls and women; the development of the Bengali language and the intention and spirit of Islam within a moderate Qur'an-based society. Syed Wajid Ali first delivered 'Maktab' and 'Pathsala' as lectures. They were published with Syed Wajid Ali's account of his days as a student at Aligarh Muslim College (founded by Syed Ahmed Khan in 1875 and now the Aligarh Muslim University) on the occasion of the fiftieth anniversary of its establishment.

'Maktab' is a Persian word meaning 'place of learning'. G.W. Leitner defines 'pathsala' as 'a school in which Sanskrit, in however elementary a manner, is taught, and one of the aims of which, at any rate, is religious; Syed Wajid Ali does not inform us, however, whether the guru mahasay taught this classical language in addition to Bengali.

Syed Wajid Ali, *Aligarh Memories and A Persian Bouquet*, Gulistan Publishing House: Calcutta, c. 1926

MAKTAB

Those born and bred in the city have little idea as to how their country cousins acquire their first rudiments of knowledge. And yet the majority of the population of Bengal live and work in the village, and their education and mentality is a matter of no small importance to anyone who wants to acquire a real understanding of the political, social and religious outlook of the people of this province.

I was lucky enough (at least I think so) to begin my scholastic life in the village maktab, whence I migrated to the pathsala. I still retain many pleasant memories of both these ancient, but fast disappearing, institutions. I hope to speak of the pathsala on a future occasion. Today, I shall say a few words about the maktab as I knew it.

Muslim village boys in my time began their acquaintance with letters at the maktab, which generally had its local habitation in the village mosque. Ours was no exception to the rule. The mosque was situated in the centre of the village, and was a fairly imposing structure of brickwork surrounded by a little garden, whose tall and stately palm trees gave it a peculiarly oriental, or I should rather say, Saracenic appearance. It had an extensive ledge surrounded by brick work seats looking like benches, and was a rendezvous of the true believers of the village, who, in summer evenings, would sit there for hours together, discussing religion, politics, business and other topics in which they were interested.

The village *panchayet* also used to be held there whenever the occasion required. All the male members of the brotherhood would then assemble in the court of the mosque after the maghrib prayer. The *reis* or headman of the village would take his seat in the middle. The elders sat round him and round them again sat the less august personages of the village. We children used to sit on the outer edge of the assembly. The *reis* would then ask the complainant in a solemn voice what his grievance was. The complainant would state his case in a few brief words interspersed with many expressions of humility and of submission to the wise decision of the assembled elders. The accused would then be called upon to state his defence.

After both sides were heard a debate would take place in which all the important members of the assembly participated. The *reis* would then give his decision after consulting the elders of the assembly. It need hardly be said that the decision used to be as binding as a judicial decision in the regularly constituted courts of law.

The mosque was in fact the church, the club, the court of justice and the school of the village. It is necessary to make this clear as otherwise the influence of the maktab, which was really a branch of the mosque, on the life of the young Muslim children would remain unexplained. As a matter of fact we acquired very little book knowledge at the maktab, but we did imbibe a great deal of the spirit and the traditions of our fathers. That was the peculiarity of maktab training, as it existed in old-fashioned Muslim villages in my time. We had to attend not only the lessons in the morning but the prayers in the evening as well and we used to look forward to the *panchayets*, the *miladshareefs* (recitations in commemoration of the birth of the prophet) and the lectures of itinerant *maulvis* as great treats. Often did we sit on the ledge on summer evenings and listen wonder-eyed to the discussions of the elders on religion, politics and other subjects. These things really formed a part of our maktab education, just as residence in school forms a part of the education of an English public school boy. In both cases the education imbibed from the atmosphere of the place has a far more abiding influence on the life of the boy than the actual amount of learning acquired. We used to have our lessons in the mornings and afternoons and not at mid-day as is the case in modern schools. We never thought of going to the mosque without performing the customary *oazu* (ablution). We invariably had our caps on, and all of us used to go to the mosque in our best clothes, which in many cases were, however, humble enough.

We used to sit in a long row in the corridor of the mosque with our Arabic texts placed neatly before us on dainty *rehals* (a wooden stand shaped like the letter X used all over the Islamic world from Morocco to China). There sitting crossed-legged in front of the *rehal* we would go on for hours swaying backwards and forwards and repeating our lessons in a monotonous sing-song. The *maulvi*, who had a fine patriarchal presence, used to walk up and down the corridor correcting our mistakes in a loud stentorian voice. It is wonderful how in the hubbub he used to pick out his erring sheep and correct their mistakes.

In those days we only learnt Arabic at the maktab. It goes without saying that we did not understand a word of what we read. It was considered a sufficient accomplishment for a child to be able to read the Holy Qur'an in the original text, without bothering about its meaning. As a matter of fact the maktab existed to teach us to read the Holy Qur'an and to instruct us in the formal and ceremonial parts of our religion. We were made to say our prayers regularly at the mosque. We were required to observe the cleanliness enjoined so strictly in Islam. We were also taught etiquette and good manners in a practical sort of way. Above all we were made to dress, act, and live like good Muslims.

We learnt our Arabic alphabet from a book known as *Kaidaie Bagdadi*. It is a wonderful little book and has been doing service in all the Muslim countries of the world since the spacious days of the Caliphs of Baghdad. After mastering this book we were started on the Qur'an. That used to be a great event in our little lives. We felt so mighty proud of ourselves. Our parents celebrated the occasion by distributing sweetmeats among the neighbours and at the mosque. A *miladshareef* was held at the house on such occasions in which rich and poor were alike invited, and in which the praises of the prophet where chanted with a lustiness peculiar to these gatherings.

When promoted to the study of the Qur'an we felt we already belonged to the grand fraternity of Islam. Beautifully bound copies of the Qur'an used to be given to us on these occasions, which we preserved in velvet or satin covers. We would never dream of opening the Holy Book without first performing our ablutions, and except in our best clothes with our little caps (the symbol of Islam in Bengal) on our heads. After gently taking away the cover we would impress a reverential kiss on the sacred book and then spread it on the *rehal*. Whichever portion of the book we might be having our lessons from we always commenced with the grand words of the Qur'an "I ask for the protection of Allah from the accursed Satan. I begin in the name of Allah who is merciful and kind."

The old fashioned maktab did not teach us the use of our mother tongue nor did it teach us how to cast accounts. But be it said to its credit that it gave a tone of earnestness to our little lives, which has persisted in spite of so many vicissitudes. It created a reverence for holy things which will never be choked out by secular education. It gave us a firm anchorage in the religion of our fathers which will stand the buffetings of the storms of modern life. This is no small achievement for the modest seminary which introduced the Muslim child to the mystery of letters. On the debit side it has to be confessed that we learnt practically nothing of the three Rs. Our own mother tongue was woefully neglected. The first three or four years of a boy's life were spent in learning things of which he knew not the meaning, and in which we could not feel any real intellectual interest.

Considering the pros and cons of the subject it has to be admitted that the maktab as it existed ought to go, and yield place to somethings in which the intellectual and practical side of education is not neglected. While conceding this, however, I must say that the atmosphere of culture and tradition which hallowed the old maktab cannot now be sacrificed without real loss to the spiritual welfare of the Muslims. Under the old system the boy breathed religion, lived religion and felt religion. In the secular buildings in which the present day maktabs are generally located, this spiritual atmosphere is lost, and that, it has to be confessed, is a great loss. Perhaps the best of both systems may be obtained by locating the new maktabs in the mosque like the old maktabs and by making religious instruction compulsory in the former as it was in the latter. This principle is followed in the Roman Catholic seminaries and schools with excellent results. Why should it not be given a trial in the Muslim maktabs and schools?

PATHSALA

No Bengal village is complete without its maktab or its pathsala and until recently the Muslim villages used to boast of both these ancient institutions. Time, however, has brought changes in its train even in the remote villages of Bengal. And now, in the Hindu villages, the pathsala is fast yielding place to the matriculation and middle English schools and in the Muslim villages the older maktabs and pathsalas are being amalgamated in the 'new maktab' and in many of the bigger villages even the 'new maktabs' are being replaced by the junior madrassas. The pathsala also, where it still exists, is fast changing character and in the not very distant future we shall not be able to distinguish it from an ordinary English kindergarten school. The picturesque seminary which has done such yeoman's service in the cause of culture for countless centuries would then have passed away into the limbo of forgotten things. No lover of the antique and the picturesque can help regretting the passing of these institutions, but like reasonable men we must, I am afraid, bow to the inevitable. But we are only human and cannot help shedding a few drops of tears at the fall of things once so great and mighty.

I very well remember my first lesson (*Hate Khari* as it is called) at the pathsala where I migrated from the village maktab. The guru mahasay, or preceptor, an affable middle-aged Hindu gentleman, received me very kindly, and, after a few sage and paternal remarks about the value of learning and the utility of making oneself learned, wrote the first letters of the Bengali alphabet in chalk on the cement floor of the pathsala. The chalk was then handed over to me and after I fixed it between my thumb and my index finger the mahasay (as he was called for brevity's sake) caught hold of my hand and guided the chalk over the writing on the floor and as he did so made me repeat each letter as the chalk passed over it. Thus ended my first lesson.

My father who accompanied me promised a valuable present to the mahasay to celebrate the auspicious occasion. The mahasay on his part expressed great pleasure at having the scion of such a distinguished family of the village as his pupil and told my happy father that I had the appearance of a bright and intelligent young lad. Needless to say I went home highly elated with all that happened.

Next day, however, things did not develop so propitiously. I left for the pathsala in the morning with a cousin of mine who had joined the institution a few days earlier. As ill luck would have it, he started taunting me over my imperfect knowledge of the alphabets, he himself having mastered practically the whole lot of them. I bore with him for a little while and then suddenly caught hold of one of his chubby cheeks with my fingers and pinched it so hard that blood began to stream out of it in great profusion. There was consternation amongst the boys who were accompanying us and they assured me with great emphasis that the mahasay would lay the *bechuti* (a stinging plant used by the village gurus to punish particularly naughty boys) on my back with no sparing hand to punish me for my ferocity. The mention of the *bechuti* plant conjures up indescribable terrors in the mind of the village boy and I was no exception to the rule. So instead of accompanying my friends to the pathsala. I made straight for home as fast as my little legs would carry me. For over a month the pathsala did not see my face any more.

The mahasay came to my place several times to look for me but as soon as I got scent of him the vision of the *bechuti* plant rose in my mind with all its attendant horrors and I lost no time in making myself scarce. Gradually, however, the fear lost its pristine vigour and I was ultimately persuaded to face my guru again. He, however, turned out to be a much more kindly and forgiving person than I had anticipated and I was only too pleased to resume my interrupted lessons.

We did not have any forms or benches in our pathsala like they have in modern schools. We had to carry our seats with us. These consisted of little rush mats about three feet long and two feet wide and were known as *pattaries*. We used to spread them on the floor and sit on them with our books, slates and other belongings arranged round us. When the lesson was over we tied up our books and other articles in a neat little parcel called *daftar*, rolled up our pattaries with the palm leaves tucked inside, and carried the whole lot home under our arms, with the inkpot swinging by a little string from one of our fingers.

The palm leaves I have spoken of were used by us for writing the alphabets. We brought them to school and took them back home in our *pattaries* every day. After filling the leaves with our writing we used to wash them in the neighbouring tank, spread them on the ground, got them dried, and used them again. Children are children everywhere and we were often glad to get a brief respite from our work on the pretext of washing and drying these leaves. After we mastered the art of writing the alphabets on the palm leaves and later on banana leaves, we were promoted to the use of paper for more complicated forms of writing. This used to mark a definite stage in the career of the scholar at the pathsala.

As a matter of fact the boys were divided into two main classes on the basis of the material used for writing, viz., (1) those who wrote on palm and banana leaves and (2) those who wrote on paper.

We did not use any steel pens and very seldom even quill pens. We made pens for ourselves out of the branches of the bamboo plants and some of us were adepts in the art. For our ink also we were not dependent upon any foreign source of supply. We used to make quite a passable kind of ink from the soot of the chimneyless kerosene lamp and the washings of rice fried to cinders. Cheap modern inks were however creeping into vogue in our time and now and then an ultra-modern scholar sported a pen. Talking of pen and ink reminds me of a belief that universally prevailed among pathsala boys and their home folk. It was thought that if a boy got home with his face and hands smeared with ink he had done a good day's work. It need hardly be said that we made liberal use of this belief to our advantage and made it a special point to get back home with our hands and faces smeared with ink. Our mothers made such fuss of us on these occasions.

There was only one guru mahasay and the scholars were in diverse stages of development. The reader would be wondering how he managed to attend to the needs of such a motley assemblage. I can, however, assure him that the wisdom of the ancients solved this difficult problem fairly satisfactorily and, as usual, in a remarkably simple way. The method adopted was to give the charge of the instruction of a junior pupil to a senior one. By this simple device the guru mahasay always managed to have as many teachers as he wanted, if not more of course; he himself kept a general supervision over all these comical results. I remember when I first went to the pathsala a boy who was my senior by about a year was detailed off to teach me the alphabets.

I happened to be his first pupil and so he naturally felt very proud of the distinction and lost no opportunity in impressing on me his unapproachable eminence in learning. I, and like a neophyte, meekly submitted to his pretensions. Fates, however, were unkind to my worthy mentor, and, in a few months our roles were reversed. I now became the teacher and he the pupil. It was my turn to crow. Be it however said to the credit of my teacher-pupil that he accepted the new situation with the best possible grace and instead of harbouring any ill feeling towards me soon became one of my ardent admirers.

In the modern schools boys begin their lessons at 10.30 or 11 a.m. and finish at about 4 p.m. This gives them sufficient time for games in the afternoon. We however followed the traditions of an age when play was considered objectionable and barely tolerated by the guardians and preceptors of the Bengali youth. We used to attend the pathsala from 7 a.m. to 10 a.m. and from 3 p.m. to 6 p.m., of course, approximately. We had therefore to indulge in our sportive instincts in the middle of the day, no doubt, a most inconvenient time. Thanks, however, to the wisdom of the ancient sages of India, there were so many *pujas* during the year for which the pathsala had to be closed that we always had plenty of opportunities to indulge in our favourite sports and pastimes. Furthermore, the spirit of youth always created opportunities for itself, and on the whole, we had as much play and fun out of life as the modern boys, if not more. Of course, we did not play the favourite modern games of football, cricket and hockey. And yet, the games we played were quite as healthy and exciting as the new-fangled innovations from the West. What pathsala boys can think of *hadudu* without recalling moments of intense excitement and rapturous joy. What game could test the stamina of a player better than *ghol ghol*. I will describe an incident in a *ghol ghol* game we played which will show that it yielded to none in rousing the spirit of fortitude and resistance in the boy. The game is a simple one and does not require any mechanical aids and contrivances. A number of boys divide themselves into two parties, one being numerically larger than the other. A fairly large circle is drawn on an open space of ground. The larger party gets inside the circle and the smaller party remains outside. The outsiders then try to drag those inside out of the circle, and the insiders try to drag the outsiders inside the circle.

Members of each party have the right to help their comrades. Sometimes there is a regular tug of war over a particular player, at other times, the player is easily dragged out of the circle or into it as the case may be. If an outsider is dragged clear in, he is out so far as that game is concerned. But for an insider it is not sufficient only to be dragged out. His captors must make him say *ghol*. Hence the name *ghol ghol*. Of course, a boy would not say *ghol* and thus give away his comrades easily. Force has obviously to be used, and in this game, this is permitted to a limited extent. The captive might be given as many slaps and fist blows on the back as he would stand. The beating has to stop as soon as he says *ghol*. He is 'out' then. When all the members of any party are out, the game is over, and the surviving party is out, the game is over, and the surviving party is the winner. One evening a large number of us were playing this game. The inside party consisted of about a dozen boys and there were three or four boys in the outside party. I myself was in the inside party. The outsiders were all older and stronger boys than us. Several of us were dragged out and made to say *ghol* without much difficulty. Then a sturdy chap with a limp in his gait was dragged

A writing lesson at the Christian Foundation School in Raja Jang, Punjab, 1995

A parent–teacher meeting in Raja Jang, Punjab, 1996

The Principal (left), lady teachers and visiting Pastor are seated. Village Schools editor is centre, back row.

out. The outsiders tried to force him to say *ghol* but he would not yield. Slaps, fist blows, and even kicks, rained fast on the brave little lad but to no purpose. He lay on the ground with his broad and deep chest resting on his sinuous little arms, and received all the blows that came, without flinching. The outsiders lost their patience and started playing foul. They pulled up the stalks of some *rang chitra* plants (a hedge plant) and belaboured our comrade with them. We implored him to give in but he would not. His body was soon a mass of bruises and swellings and he was literally bathed in perspiration. We could not stand it any longer, and tried to stop the outsiders from assaulting our comrade further. A hubbub arose. Older people came and stopped the game. The issue remained undecided.

I have often thought of this boy and of his bulldog-like tenacity. Given a sufficient education what a powerful champion he would have made of any cause he espoused. His parents, however, were poor and could not keep him long even at the pathsala and now he earns a precarious living at his native village in a humble calling.

It often seems to me Gray had some such sturdy rural hero in his mind when he wrote in his Elegy:

Perhaps in this neglected spot is laid,
Some heart pregnant with celestial fire,
Hands that the rod of empire might have swayed,
Or waked to ecstasy the living lyre.
Some village Hampden, that with dauntless breast,
The little tyrant of his fields withstood,
Some mute inglorious Milton here may rest,
Some Cromwell guiltless of his Country's blood.

In any case I cannot think of a more apt illustration of the truth of these beautiful lines than the splendid heroism displayed by our comrade on this occasion.

A good deal of sentimentalism is indulged in by our fashionable city-bred reformers regarding the virtues of open-air teaching as advocated by modern European educationists. Our guru mahasayas do not talk about the matter, but as a matter of fact they have been acting on this principle from time immemorial.[1] In winter we used to sit mostly in the open space outside the pathsala. In the summer afternoons also, when the sun lost its fierceness and the trees cast their grateful shadow on the ground, we spread our *pattaries* in the open and did our work under the canopy of the blue sky! Outside the pathsala and bordering on the District Board Road there was a shady pepul tree. Our guru mahasay sat on a *pattari* under this tree, smoked his hookah and supervised our work in a leisurely sort of way. Along the great highway carts and carriages passed to and fro. Perspiring pedestrians trudged along the road to their far-off destinations. In the midst of our lessons we looked up every now and then to catch a glimpse of any vehicle that passed or of any interesting traveller who happened to attract our notice. Sometimes a sociable traveller walked up to our guru mahasay and asked for a smoke from his *chelam* (the bowl of the hookah in which tobacco is burnt), a hospitality that was never denied. The stranger would then seat himself comfortably under the shade of the tree and chat away about the outer world, which was so strange, so wonderful and so interesting to us. We dropped our pens and our books and listened to the guru mahasay with rapt attention.

All unconsciously, we drew closer and closer to the gossiping stranger, until suddenly the sharp voice of the guru mahasay rang out and sent us back to our lessons. Our rebellious ears however still strained to catch the syren call of the stranger. Sometimes, however, the traffic on the road led to startling developments. I can recall one such incident with vividness even now. It was in the year of the great plague which ravaged the length and breadth of India and created panic and consternation everywhere. There were very serious troubles in Calcutta over the handling of plague patients. People deserted the city in their thousands and flocked to the country where they spread highly coloured accounts of what was going on in the city. Doctors and their attendants were freely painted as a sinister band of kidnappers and murderers. Stories were abroad of how hale and hearty men had been seized on their way, and even from their shops and houses, hustled unceremoniously into dark covered carriages and spirited away into the unknown whence no man ever saw them return. Old pathsala boys who had recently gone to the great city to earn their living, or to prosecute their studies further and who now sought the safety of their village homes, came to the pathsala almost daily and made our flesh creep by recounting the horrors that were being enacted in Calcutta.

We huddled together and listened to them with an almost morbid interest and on these occasions even our worthy guru mahasay became so deeply absorbed that he forgot to send us back to our work with sharp words and expletives as was his wont on similar but less engrossing occasions.

One day while we were in this state of tense excitement a Bengali overseer in his exotic uniform appeared on the District Board Road with a batch of Sontal coolies. They were on their way to do some repairs somewhere. This obvious explanation however did not occur to us then. Some one suddenly cried out "the kidnappers" and in the twinkling of an eye the whole pathsala, guru mahasay and all, were making to the interior of the village as fast as legs would carry, leaving books, slates, *pattaries*, and everything else, behind. Ours was a Muslim village and in a few minutes some fifty stalwarts appeared on the scene armed with lathies and surrounded the startled Public Works Department Babu and his coolies. Matters would have gone hard with these worthy men but for the timely intervention of the soberer and better informed men of the village.

We were expected to take our seats and begin work before the guru mahasay put in his appearance. Any one who came late had to bring a supply of tobacco for the mahasay, and, in default he was given the stripe. Needless to say, we all managed to secure a supply of tobacco from somewhere whenever we happened to be late. A cynic might say that our worthy guru mahasay would, under such a system, naturally like his boys to be late. He, however, never openly expressed any such preference to my knowledge. Some of us presented him with supplies of tobacco even when punctual, just to please him, and thus managed to become his favourite pupils.

If a boy, however, willfully absented himself from school, drastic steps were taken to enforce his attendance. Four or five of the sturdiest boys were then detailed off to bring the culprit to school by main force. The arresting party would go up and down the village looking for him and more often than not find him plucking fruits in some one's garden, or perchance, catch him stealing birds' eggs in some sequestered bush. The pathsala 'bulldogs' would pounce on the truant before he had time to get away and lead him to school under arrest. Some of the bolder spirits sometimes resisted apprehension.

The bulldogs however were always more than a match for them, and, in pursuance of their warrant, they would tie the culprit's hand and feet with his own *dhoti* and *chaddar*, and carry him to school, swinging like a hammock, some holding him by his hands, and others by his feet. Needless to say his reception at the pathsala on these occasions used to be of a somewhat stormy nature.

The guru mahasay had a much ampler armoury of punishments than the modern schoolmaster. Birching, as in all countries and all schools was the common form of punishment, but there were others which were more indigenous, and I might also say, more ingenuous. Boys were sometimes made to stand on their toes; sometimes they had to sit with the weight of their bodies resting on their toes and brickbats inserted between their legs and thighs. They had often to box their own ears and pull their own noses and, in special cases of delinquency the offender had to rub his nose on the ground to the length of seven cubits. But the punishment that was par excellence, the pathsala punishment, and which, in the language of hotel managers might be called its 'specialty' was the application of the *bechuti* plant on the back of the offending boy. This plant, peculiar to the soil of Bengal, has a stinging quality that made its victim writhe and shriek with agony. He felt as if a thousand wasps were digging their angry stings into his poor unprotected skin. The boy naturally struggled and tried to push away the plant with his hands and in doing so got all his limbs brushed by it and the poor wretch was reduced in a few seconds to a writhing mass of agony. As an extra refinement of this punishment the plant was sometimes soaked in the foul water of the hookah. This gave its sting an atrociously painful character.

Be it however said to the credit of our kind guru mahasay that he seldom resorted to the *bechuti* plant, and in no case did he soak it in hookah water before application.

But this cannot be said of gurus of a more ruthless disposition. Of course, boys who were treated in this drastic fashion would be dealt with severely at any educational institution. Good and obedient scholars were never shown any particular severity.

Loud singsong style of reading was characteristic both of the pathsala and the maktab. It is also to be found in the modern Indian schools. But whereas, in the latter institutions, it is a failing for which apologies are often made, in the former, it was the approved system. We all read our lessons aloud and, while doing this, our instinct of emulation often made us drown the voices of others by the deafening din we made. And yet something can be said in favour of this age old-system of reading aloud; it fixes the words and ideas in the tender minds of children more effectively than silent reading;

and to a great extent it checks that lapse into absent minded reverie which is one of the pitfalls of early youth.

Anyway, multiplication tables were impressed in our minds by this system in a wonderfully effective way. In the evening, before dispersing, the guru mahasay used to muster us in a line on the ground outside the pathsala. He took his stand in front and with his face towards us repeated the multiples in a sonorous singsong. We took up his words and chanted them in a loud chorus. It was, I can assure the reader, a most effective method of teaching. Even at this distance of time, I can repeat my multiples without a moment's hesitation. Short Bengali poems also were taught in the same pleasant and effective way. Here the modern teacher can very profitably take a leaf out of the guru mahasay's book. As a matter of fact the guru mahasay taught us all that he set out to teach, effectively and well.

After a three years' course at his seminary we could read Bengali without difficulty, write letters, receipts and other minor documents tolerably, and could even keep *khatas* and other complicated books of account in an intelligible manner. A boy who spent an extra year at the pathsala could do all these things remarkably well, in fact, much better than a boy who spent an equal number of years at a modern school.

When a rival pathsala came into existence in our neighbourhood we tried to drown the voice of its scholars by chanting our multiples and poems with the utmost possible lustiness. It is hardly necessary to add that they on their part tried to pay us back the compliment. This introduced an element of tense excitement in our little lives, and our revelries often went far beyond mere shouting, and encounters between the scholars of the two institutions, somewhat in the style of the fights between the Capulets and the Montagues of Verona, often disturbed the peace of the countryside.

Our fees ranged from 2 annas to 8 annas and some of the poorer boys were taught by our kind guru mahasay without any pecuniary remuneration. There used to be about 50 scholars at the pathsala. At a most favourable computation the guru mahasay's income from fees could not have been more than Rupees 20 per month. This was hardly a sufficient income for a man in his station in life, and yet, he managed somehow to live in fair comfort. How then was this miracle achieved?

Well, to begin with the income from fees was to a considerable extent supplemented by *sidhas* or contributions in rice and vegetables made by boys once every fortnight. This used to ensure the food supply for the month. The sidha day being observed as a half-holiday the boys used to look forward to it but not so, I am afraid, many of the parents. But it was a time-honoured custom, and had to be respected.

Enterprising gurus sometimes attempt to increase the number of *sidha* days in the month. Boys welcome these innovations but the protests of parents, and the gradual falling off in the number of scholars soon bring the guru mahasay back to the path of orthodoxy and the innovation is regretfully abandoned. A little money the guru mahasay always makes by giving private lessons to some to the wealthier boys, but the chief source of his extra income is the writing of deeds and other documents for the village folk. Every guru mahasay is more or less of an unlicensed lawyer and as such he fills an important place in the rural economy.

The cultivators and other humble folk find in him a real friend, philosopher and guide. Our guru mahasay's income was derived from all these sources, and yet, it has to be admitted, it was not by any means a princely one. He was, however, like the majority of his calling a born philosopher, and often talked feelingly of the feud that has existed from eternity between Laksmi (the Goddess of wealth) and Saraswati (the Goddess of learning).

There is one thing which the old pathsala had and which is woefully lacking in the modern schools in this country and that is the intimacy between the teacher and the pupil. We used to look upon the guru mahasay as one of our own kith and kin and this, although we were of different religious persuasions, which meant a good deal more to us than it does to the city dwellers of today. If any one of us fell ill he was sure to come and enquire about the invalid's health. If he himself was indisposed we on our part made anxious enquiries about him at his *basha*. If there was a feast or a festival in the house of any of us he was sure to attend although his religion forbade him from taking any food at the house of a Muslim. On wet days we huddled round him in the centre of the pathsala house to avoid the draught and the drifting rain. One of the boys would then fill his *chelam* for him and puffing comfortably away at his hookah he would tell us wonderful stories of ghosts and spirits, of floods and famines, of snakes and tigers, and of saints and holy men. The aromatic fumes of the tobacco imparted genial warmth to the damp air and we listened to the stories with the zest which only childhood knows.

In spite, however, of friendship and familiarity we held our guru mahasay in the highest esteem; he on his part, although entertaining an almost filial affection for us, never relaxed his discipline and kept a vigilant supervision over our work. Under such conditions, it is hardly necessary to add, we put forth our best efforts and the few years we spent at the pathsala were by no means wasted.

Time passes, and, in our journey through the vale of life, we leave the old landmarks behind. It is now nearly a quarter of a century since I last attended my dear old pathsala, mighty changes have occurred in my life since then—I have left the happy days of childhood far behind and am now advancing steadily towards middle age.

Many old associations have I forgotten and many new associations have I made. But even time, the great dissolver has not dissolved the bond of affection between my old guru mahasay and myself. Even now he often honours me with his visits and makes anxious inquiries about my life and work. When success attends any of my endeavours no one is better pleased than he, and, when disappointment damps my spirit, he is one of the few genuine friends who come and administer the healing balm of consolation.

When a reminiscent mood comes over me the memories of many gorgeous institutions and surroundings fade away before the tender and vivid recollections of the thatched *atchala* (structure with eight separate *chals*) under the pepul tree at the junction of the village roads where I had my first lessons in Bengali at the feet of our dear old guru mahasay. A strange longing comes over me for the happy days of childhood, and the guru mahasay and his pathsala become a symbol and an inspiration.

NOTE

1. Increasing concern amongst the medical profession with regard to the health of children led to the open-air school movement in the UK. It was strongly supported by Margaret Macmillan (especially for children under seven years) and other leading educationists. A school, opened in 1904, in Germany, was an early inspiration. The movement influenced school architects in England from 1907. (See, for example, M. Seabourne and R. Lowe, *The English School: Its Architecture and Organization*, vol. II, 1870-1970, Routledge and Kegan Paul: London, 1977).

31

MY OLD SCHOOL, c. 1900

England
P.B. Ballard, M.A., D.Lit.

P.B. Ballard was a writer of school textbooks and a London County
Council school inspector when he included this poem in his English
textbook for thirteen to fourteen year-olds.

Long years have passed since last I saw
That little country school;
Strange things have happened since I left
Its melancholy rule;
And strange the things I still can see
In memory's magic pool.

I still can see the long low room,
With its battered oaken door,
And hear the drowsy drone of work
Oft rising to a roar,
And mark the clean and pungent smell
Of sawdust on the floor.

    The desks were old and stained with ink
    And scored with children's names;
    So thick they were that none would dare
    To portion out the claims;
    And who could say which separate J
    Meant Jacob, John, or James?

P.B. Ballard, *Fundamental English*, Senior Series, Pupil's Book Three, University of
London Press Ltd.: London, 1932

The leaden inkwells in the slots
Were narrow-mouthed and fusty;
The ink within was weak and thin,
Or else was thick and dusty;
And oft the pens with which we wrote
Were scandalously rusty.

But then we mostly wrote on slates,
And took them from a stack,
The new ones grey with ashen dust,
The old ones nearly black,
All smooth and shiny on the front
And greasy on the back.

And when a pupil had perchance
A pencil[1] with a squeak,
The boys around would glare at him
Or give his arm a tweak,
Although the poor offending one
Was penitent and meek.

The love of learning in his soul
Burned like a sacred flame;
And those who did not catch the glow
  Had but themselves to blame;
  And so to me he ne'er can be
An unremembered name.

No child saw pictures on the wall
To cheer him or to chide him,
But old, decrepit, varnished maps
Designed to teach and guide him,
And fearsome diagrams to show
The ghastly things inside him.

I see the master of the school,
Whose form was tall and slim;
His face was pale, his eye was cold,
His very smile was grim;
And those who worked and those who shirked
Were all the same to him.

They all were objects of his wrath
And targets of his fire;
For all would sometimes blunder,
And all would sometimes tire;
And the things we did and the things we didn't
Would stir the old man's ire.

And yet—and yet—I can't forget
The debt I owe to him;
'Twas only to the younger boys
His face was wholly grim;
To those who knew him well his ways
Were simply strict and prim.

He merely to the faults of youth
Was never weakly blind;
His features were a mask that hid
A nature deeply kind;
His very captiousness concealed
A cultivated mind.

And though the builders of the place
Had broken every rule,
And though the trappings scarce were fit
To educate a fool,
'Twas all redeemed to me because
the master was the school.

NOTE

1. The hard slate used in England for school slate boards came from the north Wales
slate quarries, while the softer slate required for slate pencils was imported from
Germany and Austria. Slate pencils were cut into long narrow strips, smoothed and
rounded and put into little boxes for sale. Generally, slates were used only for the
lower standards—too much slate practice, teachers under training were told, led to
careless and untidy work—hence they were advised to begin paper work as early
as possible.

32

A REMINISCENCE OF BHERA SCHOOL, 1902

Bhera, Shahpur Disrict, Punjab, India
Sir Firoz Khan Noon

Sir Firoz Khan Noon (1893–1970), Prime Minister of Pakistan, 1957 to 1958, was educated in the Punjab in Bhera, 1902 to 1905 and at Aitchison College, Lahore, 1905 to 1012, from where he went to Wadham College, Oxford. During his distinguished career he was Education Minister for the Punjab, 1931 to 1936, and the High Commissioner for India in London, 1936 to 1941.

Bhera was a small town with a population of five or six thousand people. It was on the banks of the river Jhelum because the only safe mode of travel was by river and towns on their banks were important, especially to the merchants. But after the British built the roads and railways, these towns dwindled and lost their importance. In the whole district of Shahpur between 1900 and 1912, Bhera was the biggest town.

Before the railway started in our district, circa 1890, everybody travelled to Lahore on horseback, which took about a week for the one hundred miles. We used the same horse throughout the journey. People used to say goodbye to their families fully realizing they might never return. Robbers and murderers existed all over the land. In 1902 my father decided that my brother Ali and I should go to school. Therefore, we were sent to Bhera town, ten miles away, where there was a public school like the grammar schools of England.

Reprinted by permission of Ferozsons Ltd., Lahore, from Sir Firoz Khan Noon, *From Memory*, Ferozsons Ltd., Lahore, 1966.

It was financed by the Government and went up to the tenth class. There was no boarding house, so we lived in a building belonging to Malik Hakam Khan Noon, head of our family. His son, Malik Sultan Ali Noon, also went with us and so did his grandsons, Malik Mohammad Sher and Gul Sher, from Kot Hakam Khan village. We used to come home on our ponies on Saturday and went back early in the morning to Bhera School on Mondays. One summer morning after I had picked up my half-uncle Sultan Ali Noon from Sardarpur Noon, a servant walking behind me shouted, "Snake, snake, snake." Somehow with a stick, the snake was pulled down and killed. In the summer many a bullock, cow and buffalo were killed by snakebites when feeding out in the fields. Today we do not seem to see so many snakes.

I remember one of the teachers who prided himself on wearing white clothes, a big turban and baggy trousers, had the habit of pulling up his legs and putting his knees against the table and swinging himself backwards and forwards on the hind legs of his chair. One day he over-did it and fell backwards on to the wall and could not right himself. We students were astounded for a few minutes and could not help feeling amused at his predicament. His turban had fallen off his head and we found that he was completely bald and his beard was sticking up towards the roof and his arms waved helplessly. The class left him in this position for a while but eventually two senior boys came to his rescue. Thereafter the rocking of his chair stopped. There was a story current about him that in the days gone by he had sent a student to fetch for him some milk. The boy drank half of the milk himself and filled up the glass with water from a bucket lying near the mouth of a well, without noticing that a little frog had gone into the glass. When the teacher had finished the milk and discovered the little frog, he said angrily to the boy, "Look, there is a frog in the milk!" The boy innocently replied, "Sir, you did not expect a camel for the two annas you gave me."

******

The most powerful persons in the city were the police sub-inspector and the tehsildar, but the most influential person was the doctor and after him came the headmaster. There was one schoolmaster who used to teach mathematics and had the reputation of being very hard on the students who did not do their sums. To punish them he would put pencils between their fingers and press them hard or pinch their ear lobes with his thumb and finger. The boys used to cry and weep. But no one dared to complain.

on the teacher's plathit but to their seats. In utter silence the round
pink pencils between their lips. It passes them out, or gives it two
children with his minute and The boys begin to try and write.
They are dazed in competition.

33

LANCASTERIAN SCHOOL, 1910s

Cork, Co. Cork, Ireland
Seán O'Faoláin

The author was a novelist, critic, biographer of Irish political figures, and
principally, a short story writer. Seán O'Faoláin (1900-1991) fought with
the Irish Republican side in the Irish Civil War and taught in the USA in
the 1930s. It would seem that his Lancasterian School was founded in
the early decades of the nineteenth century, possibly in the 1830s after
the British government made the first grant for education in Ireland. The
essay is abridged.

The school I speak of was the Lancasterian School in the town of
Cork, one of the first, and maybe the first, Bell and Lancaster
schools founded in Ireland. This I did not discover, until long
afterwards, for we all associated it with the enemies of the Tudors,
and the good monks who taught us, being mentally and emotionally
rather like children themselves, did not, I imagine, discover it at any
time. It was originally a barrack or a poorhouse, or maybe a
madhouse, but at any rate it was born weary like a Buddhist in his
fourth transmigration, and should never have been used in our time
for any purpose whatever. I do not know when it was founded, but
I am certain that it defied all the change and alteration that overtook
schooling since the days of Wordsworth, and I know that the hoary,
dusty, cobwebbed atmosphere of the place remained to the end the
atmosphere of Carleton rather than of Joyce—the atmosphere, that
is, of an enormous hedge-school in what, so bizarre was the life
there, must surely have been a discarded asylum.

Reprimted by permission of Rogers, Coleridge, and Wrights Limited, London from Seán
O'Faoláin, 'An Irish Schooling' in *The Hutchison Book of Essays*, ed. Frank Delaney.

At the centre of the school was the Big Room, what wealthier folk would have called the *Aula Maxima*. The roof was broken on either side of the roof-tree by a clerestory composed of hundreds upon hundreds of patches of glass; beneath this clerestory, 'dreadful and dizzy to cast one's eyes so low,' four or five classes would 'toe the line' in different parts of the hall, curved about a horseshoe, chalked on the floor, at whose centre stood the black-robed monk in charge. Every second boy was barelegged, with the mud drying between his toes and zoomorphic tracery on his shins from sitting in the ashes of his laneway home. At playtime, when other classes were howling in the yard, we would stand thus, each boy with a little penthouse balanced on his head, an open book, to protect him from the penalty of falling glass. For the great game in the yard outside was what I have since heard called the Roof Game. It began with the throwing of a ball, a thing of paper and twine, sideways on the slates, and it ended with a mad tangle fighting under the gutters to catch the ball, when, where, and if it fell.

East and west were the aisles to this nave, sheltering one or two more classes each, as well as the science-room, which was also office, drawing-room, monks' lunch-room, and place of more painful and less modest corporal punishment. The Infants were tucked away behind the apse; there was a black-hole where chronic offenders were sometimes flung to whimper among the coals and the rats; a gravelled yard ran on each side of the building; the foul jakes lined it behind; and there was, finally, the caretaker's cottage where he stored thrown-out copy-books for fuel and broke up old desks for firewood.

I always associate this school with Lowood School in *Jane Eyre*, not because we ever had any Reverend Mr Brocklehurst, but because in spite of much vermin, some disease, and no external beauty, in spite of the cold and the smells, we managed to create inside that crumbling hole a faery world of our own—and by we, I mean the monks and the children together, for these Brothers were truly brothers to us and I think we really loved them. They were country lads with buttermilk complexions, hats prevented from extinguishing their faces only by the divine prescience of ears, hands still rough from the spade and feet still heavy with the clay. I recall their complete lack of self-consciousness with us—which did not prevent them from being shy and blushing in the presence of other monks— the complete absence of the keep-the-boy-in-his-place rule which (perhaps largely in self-defence) is so common in High Schools. Some to be sure, were disliked—it is not in the nature of small boys to hate—and because they were mincing or had no sense of fun we called them names like Cinderella or Sloopy Dan.

****

The place is gone now; not a stone remains upon a stone, and a boot factory in red brick stands where it stood. A new, modern school replaces it, all white tiles and parquet, very anodyne and aseptic. That is all to the good, but it is not that which gives it an advantage over the old place. It is beside fields, and below it there are trees through which one sees the flowing river with cows in other fields beyond. In our old place there were a few ragged trees growing out of asphalt but not a blade of grass to be seen anywhere; and a school without a field is a prison.

If I were a child again and both schools stood, to which would I go? If not to some sterner, more ambitious school than either of them? Certainly, if it is a matter of getting on in the world, to neither. But if one places more value on other things, then this type of school is ideal, and according as you value these 'other things' the more, then the more reason to go to some old shack like mine where, although one learned little about the world, one imbibed a great deal about life—and perhaps a little about the next life, too.

34

CHANGE IN THE VILLAGE, 1912

The Bourne, near Farnham, Surrey, England
George Bourne

George Sturt (1863–1927), born in Farnham, Surrey, was a close observer of Surrey country life, on which he wrote numerous books and articles under the name of George Bourne. He was a grammar school teacher until 1894 when he took over the family wheelwright shop in Farnham.

This extract, from Sturt's best-known book, refers to the irrelevancy, as he saw it, of the content of education provided in the village school and the local night school during a transitional period in the rural areas of England. 'Unlike the industry of a peasantry, commercial wage earning cannot satisfy the cravings of a man's soul at the same time it occupies his body, cannot exercise his faculties or appeal to many of his tastes; therefore if he would have any profit, any enjoyment, of his own human nature, he must contrive to get it in his leisure time.' What is offered in school, according to Sturt, fails to meet villagers' needs. As an illustration, below, he describes the experiences of a young village coal-carter. In this passage, one can almost, but not quite—as Sturt wanted an improved curriculum—hear an echo of an earlier Farnham resident—William Cobbett—'All this increase of education has not been productive of any good...' Sturt was, at this time, a member of the management board of the school.

Although it was more than fourteen years since the end of the payments by results' system, the urban-oriented elementary school curriculum remained, according to its critics, inappropriate for large numbers of rural pupils. Compulsory education, particularly in England, was often subject to harsh criticism until the Great War proved the

George Bourne, *Change in the Village*, [1912] Augustus M. Kelly: New York, 1969 loyalty of men educated under the national system. Almost certainly, the coal-carter enlisted in Farnham or was conscripted into the army before 1918. Some critics were clearly motivated by a genuine concern for the pupils; others by a resentment of the passing of the traditional ways in the countryside. It is instructive to compare Sturt's strictures with Sir John Lubbock's discourse on rural elementary school curriculum in the 1870s, Flora Thompson's experiences in the 1880s and George W. Harding's experiences of rural elementary education in the 1930s.

But it goes almost without saying that the man's "education" did very little to enrich his mind. The ideas and accomplishments he picked up at the elementary school between his fourth and fourteenth years were of course in themselves insufficient for the needs of a grown man, and it would be unfair to criticize his schooling from that standpoint. Its defect was that it failed to initiate him into the inner significance of information in general, and failed wholly to start him on the path of learning. It was sterile of results. It opened to him no view, no vista; set up in his brain no stir of activity such as could continue after he left school; and this for the reason that those simple items of knowledge which it conveyed to him were too scrappy and too few to begin running together into any understanding of the larger aspects of life. A few rules of arithmetic, a little of the geography of the British Islands, English history, no fairy-tales or romance, no inkling of the infinities of time and space, or of the riches of human thought; but merely a few "pieces" of poetry, and a few haphazard and detached observations (called "Nature Study" nowadays) about familiar things—"the cat," "the cow," "the parsnip," "the rainbow"[1] and so forth—this was the jumble of stuff offered to the child's mind—a jumble to which it would puzzle a philosopher to give coherence. And what could a child get from it to kindle his enthusiasm for that civilized learning in which, none the less, it all may have its place? When the boy left school his "education" had but barely begun.

And hardly anything has happened since then to carry it farther, although once there seemed just a chance of something better. During two successive winters the lad, being then from sixteen to seventeen years old, went to a night-school, which was opened for twenty-six weeks in each "session," and for four hours in each week. But the hope proved fallacious. In those hundred and four hours a year—hours which came after a tiring day's work—his brain was fed upon "mensuration" and "the science of horticulture," the former on the chance that some day he might want to measure a wall for paper-hanging or do some other job of the sort, and the latter in case fate should have marked him out for a nursery gardener, when it would be handy to know that germinating seeds begin by pushing down a root and pushing up a leaf or two. This gives a notion of the sort of idea the luckless fellow derived from the night-school.[2] I do not think that the joinery classes at present being held in the night-school had begun in his time; but supposing that he also learnt joinery, he might, now that he is a man, add thoughts of mortices and tenons and mitre-joints to his other thoughts about wall areas and germinating seeds. Of course, all these things—like Jewish history or English geography—are worth knowing; but again it is true, of these things no less than of the childish learning acquired at the day-school, that whatever their worth may be to the people concerned to know them, they were very unlikely to set up in this young man's brain any constructive idea-activity, any refreshing form of thought that would enrich his leisure now, or give zest to his conversation. They were odds and ends of knowledge; more comparable to the numberless odds and ends in which peasants were so rich than to the flowing and luminous idea-life of modern civilization.

NOTES

1. Sturt is, of course, referring to what were earlier known as 'Object Lessons'—the forerunner of Nature Study. Much depended upon the teacher's interest in this subject—'The teacher of nature must find his subject matter and his inspiration in nature herself.' Unexpectedly, according to James Welton (*Principles and Methods of Teaching*, 1906): 'There are a few—a very few—books which will be of help to the teacher.'—And some did not even give elementary facts correctly. See 'Object Lessons', 1880s, in this volume.
2. Night-schools for pupils aged 12 to 17 years were first recognised officially in 1851 with the award of small grants. 'The Evening Continuation School Code' of 1893 raised evening schools to the dignity of a separate system. The maximum age limit was removed and the curriculum became similar to that of the secondary and technical schools.

35

THE PUNJAB VILLAGE SCHOOLMASTER, 1920s

Punjab, India
F.L. Brayne

The earliest memories of Frank Lugard Brayne (1882–1952) were of the primitive cottage in which he and his family lived in Norfolk. Brayne became Deputy Commissioner of Gurgeon District, in the Punjab of India, thirty miles south of Delhi, and Commissioner for Rural Reconstruction, Punjab. He was indefatigable in his zeal for development or 'uplift' and wrote numerous books on all aspects of village development. He saw the village schoolmaster as the agent of change and education as a major factor in the improvement of village life. He believed that village education must, as its main objective, lead to an improved quality of life in the villages and not, conversely, to the movement of educated people to the towns. The officials of the Punjab Education Department of the period were not, however, so sanguine with regard to rural one-teacher schools. For example, the *Report on The Progress of Education in the Punjab during the quinquennium ending 1941–42* (Lahore, 1943) stated that:

> Primary Education (Boys): Very gratifying advance has been made in the number and strength of primary schools; the number of schools has risen by 352 to 6,163; enrolment by 33,929 to 410,616 and the average attendance has outpaced enrolment. It is satisfactory also to note a drop of 492 to 480 in the number of branch schools that have definitely failed to achieve the object for which they were initially instituted. It is not so satisfactory to find that out of an aggregate of 6,163 primary schools the number of one-teacher schools is 2,117 or almost 34 per cent. Owing to paucity of pupils

Reprinted by permission of Oxford University Press, F.L. from Brayne, *The Remaking of Village India*. Oxford University Press: London, 1929.

in sparsely populated backward areas and primary education, such schools are undoubtedly a necessity in some areas for some time to come, and the alternative often is a one-teacher school or no school at all.

The report adds: 'Single-teacher schools, though often denounced as inefficient and undesirable, have increased in number in areas of scattered population where means of communication are unavailable or where uneconomical and unsuccessful branch schools have been converted with advantage into single-teacher schools.' The branch schools were established to provide educational facilities for the first two years to young children who could not travel far from home and were intended to feed the central schools. The report further states that:

Most of the primary schools continue to be housed in rented or rent-free buildings, which had not been built to serve as school-houses, and consequently primary schools continue to suffer for want of adequate, good and sanitary buildings...There are schools which have not even sufficient matting for pupils to sit on, and often boys have to provide themselves with mats or pieces of gunny bags to sit on. It is to the credit, however, of both the teachers and the pupils that life in schools has gradually become more interesting and cheerful.

F.L. Brayne wrote in the patronizing style beloved of the period, but clearly his sincerity was genuine and his advice sound.

The future of the village lies in the hands of the teacher, and he has an immense opportunity for good—and for evil too. What is he to do with his talent? Bury it in the ground? Too many do, and small blame to them either, with such colossal odds against them. No; the reward will be great—the affection and respect of everyone, parents as well as children, and a happy, contented village. Nothing is more encouraging than the way the villagers appreciate, and describe to me as I tour, a really good teacher. The boys come crowding to school, and so do the girls; he is spoken of with reverence by the villagers; and his little charges are happy and good-mannered and do him credit in after-life. What more could a teacher desire than a life of such usefulness? True, it does not tend to great distinction, but to be loved and honoured by one village is more than many a great man can boast.

The ideal of the village teacher is not to produce potential B.As and LL.Bs, and most of the good he does is outside the textbooks altogether. The temptation of the schoolmaster is to send his boys on to the high schools and colleges, and attract attention to himself as a producer of scholars.

But most of the boys that so leave the village are a dead loss to the village. The uplift and development of the village demand the best brains of its children, and if the betterment of the village is the final goal, the village schoolmaster should be always trying to keep his boys at home.

The object of a village school is to make better, more intelligent, healthier and happier villagers. If a ploughman's son comes to school, his schooling should so prepare him that when he comes to follow the tail of his father's plough he will pick up the work more quickly and display more intelligence in all his business than his fathers did. Above all, the children must learn at school how to lead healthy lives and protect themselves from epidemic diseases. Without health nothing is of any value at all, so health is the first and great lesson, and until its simple lessons are learnt it is no use going on to anything else. Health involves cleanliness, personal and general, and so this must figure largely in all the work of the village schoolmaster.

This desire of the village father to school his boy and send him away to earn his living is not, in Gurgaon at any rate, the effect of increasing pressure on the soil, as the population has decreased 20 per cent in the last two decades (1901–21). In Gurgaon it is a good sign, and means that the villager has begun to realize that all is not well in the village. The land does not seem to respond to his efforts as it should, and the village itself is unhealthy and uncomfortable. He desires to do well by his boy, and so sends him away. It is this beginning of a desire for better things which the schoolmaster must exploit. He must convince the boy and his parents that things can be put right, the land made to yield its increase, and the village made healthy, comfortable and pretty.

The village teacher has to teach the parents as well as the boys, and the first lesson the parents have to learn is that the goal of the village school is not an underpaid clerkship.

For a long time the villagers will refuse to believe that any improvement, either in their farming or in their conditions of life, is even possible, and will mock at the idea that the teacher has really got anything practical to teach them. By example as much as by precept, the teacher must convince the people that his aim is to turn out, and that he really can turn out, clean, healthy, happy, intelligent boys and girls, with a sufficient knowledge of reading, writing and arithmetic to enable them to carry on and improve their ancestral occupations.

The teacher must become a genuine village leader, a centre of light and culture, whom the people trust and to whom they refer their problems and consult when they are in doubt or difficulty. If he has absorbed the spirit and training of the rural school, his equipment for his new part will be complete. To take and hold his proper place in village life, however, he must practise what he preaches, and set the example of working with his own hands at all the uplift measures he recommends.

His gospel is the dignity of labour and the dignity of social service, and he must be as willing to set about cleaning the village or adjusting an iron plough as he is to teach reading and writing. Then, and then only, will the villagers respect him and his mission.

All healthy children want to play, and much time must be spent in teaching them good games. Vaccination, re-vaccination and, when plague is about, inoculation must come as a matter of course, and it must become impossible to find an unprotected child at school.

One of the biggest lessons I have left to the last. The little boy must be taught that his little sister at home is just as good as he is, if not better, and needs schooling just as much, if not more, than he does.

She must come too, and learn all the good things he is learning. Of course, she must come—and come she will if the master is respected in the village. And then the master will be able to begin the greatest of all lessons in the village school, the lesson of chivalry. The little boys will be taught to honour and respect their sisters, their mothers and all womenkind. And quickly will they learn when they see their sisters beating them at lessons, and when they see the master treating them exactly the same as, or even better than the boys.

It is a winning battle the teacher is fighting. When the time comes for the little girls now at school to send their own children to school, half the teacher's work will be done for him. Till then the teacher must do the work of both parent and teacher, with a touch of the country parson as well, and that is the ideal for him to aim at.

36

CLOGS AND CINDERS: A TYPICAL VILLAGE SCHOOL, 1927

Lancashire, England
W.H. Perkins, M.Sc.

This school, selected by W.H. Perkins, then Secretary of Elementary Education, Lancashire Education Committee, as a typical Lancashire village school, had three teachers and about 100 children on its roll. The average daily attendance was 88 pupils. The school served a population of some 600 persons who lived in the industrial village and its surrounding agricultural area.

Like most village schools it is a voluntary school, but in this case there is no complication in the form of a neighbouring school of another denomination. The buildings stand back from the main street of the village on a rectangular site of about one third of an acre, which is surrounded on three sides by a brick wall, the front boundary being an iron railing with a gateway to the street. The playground has a cindered surface with a few patches of gravel. Most of the children wear clogs, so that in dry weather the cinders are ground into fine dust, and in wet weather into a very unpleasant kind of mud. Mud and dust in turn find their way into the school buildings in large quantities.

The buildings themselves are of brick, about 70 years old, and they are beginning to be the worse for their age. Otherwise they have changed very little since they were erected, because even the smallest improvement involves a local effort to raise money, in

W.H. Perkins, M.Sc., 'The Problem of the Village Schools' in H. Bompas Smith (ed.), *Education at Work. Studies in Contemporary Education*, Manchester University Press: Manchester, 1927

which the teachers and pupils are called upon to take a prominent part. The school was originally planned for parochial as well as for educational purposes, and the buildings are consequently semi-ecclesiastical in type. The main room of about 40 feet by 25 feet accommodates the upper school in two classes, and there is a smaller room about 20 feet square for the infants. The recognized accommodation of these two rooms is 130.

Heating is provided by coke stoves, of which there are two in the main room and one in the small one. The windows in both rooms are of peculiar shape, rather small and awkwardly placed. Their lower panes are of obscured glass and a few of them have upper portions which open by swinging into a sloping position.

The larger room is open to the ridge of the roof, the exposed beams being inaccessible for dusting except by means of a ladder. To provide cloakrooms, the original porch has been enlarged and divided into two parts, one for boys and the other for girls. Clothes hooks are fixed to the boarded walls, and each cloakroom has one small lavatory basin. The infants must all pass through the main room whenever they enter or leave their classroom. New floors have recently been provided for the second time in the life of the school. Ninety per cent of the cost of this improvement was borne by the Local Education Authority on account of their responsibility for the wear and tear of the old floors. The walls of both rooms, which had previously been unplastered, were surfaced and renovated three years ago, the major portion of the cost being raised by means of a bazaar.

The sanitary conveniences are 50 yards away from the main buildings and are necessarily somewhat primitive, because the local sanitary authority has not yet established an up-to-date sewerage scheme.

Caretaking is in the hands of a widow who was appointed by the managers partly on compassionate grounds. Her duties include all scrubbing, sweeping and dusting both of the school and the out-offices, the lighting of fires and the carrying of fuel and ashes, and they are entirely performed outside school hours. The floors are scrubbed three times a year only, the outside of the windows being cleaned at the same time.

This school is definitely above the standard for inclusion in the Board of Education's 'black list'. Its accommodation is technically adequate, and its other defects are not so unusual as to merit condemnation. But we can readily conclude, from the above description, that its material conditions, as measured by modern standards, are distinctly imperfect. The caretaker's battle against dirt is waged on most unequal terms. She asserts that the whole of the playground is carried into the school once a year and that she has to sweep it out again. It is difficult to get the rooms warm before the pupils arrive at 9 a.m. If they are warm they rapidly become stuffy owing to the lack of proper means of ventilation. Hygiene, both in practice and as a subject of instruction, presents formidable problems, owing to the system of sanitation and the inadequacy of the cloakrooms and lavatories. Lighting is unsatisfactory, and the planning of the building makes it impossible for even three classes to have separate rooms or the accommodation suitable for effective teaching.

Beginning in the infants' room we find 28 children in charge of an uncertificated woman teacher. This teacher is a married woman, nearly 50 years of age, who has spent all her educational life in the school, first as a pupil, then as a pupil teacher, and finally in her present capacity. In spite of total lack of training she achieves a certain amount of success in her work, perhaps because she is so well acquainted with her pupils' parents and their homes. By attending summer schools as frequently as her domestic cares and limited means have permitted, she has just been able to keep herself conscious of the changes which have taken place in the last 25 years. Her methods would appear distinctly old fashioned to a girl coming today fresh from a Training College, but she would be found in conversation to be fully aware of her limitation and of the defective conditions under which she is compelled to work. She would frankly regret her lack of knowledge and training for certain branches of her work, but she would point out very reasonably that, even if she were more accomplished, her small room would not provide the space for the varied activities which she would then wish to prescribe for her pupils.

Although the room is recognized for 40 pupils it is obviously too small for 28, when their ages vary from three to seven. Free movement for the pupils and space for the storage of their material are restricted, owing to the presence of the stove and of certain large cupboards containing parochial and Sunday school stores. The only school piano has to be kept in the large room, but in any case its frequent use for younger children's games would be very disturbing to the upper classes. The formal work of the 'sevens' needs careful organization, which is not easy unless the movements and occupations of the 'babies' are unduly repressed. An impression always remains that elbowroom is lacking, and that the consequent immobility reacts on the spontaneity of the children's work and on their characters. The atmosphere is too solemn for proper freedom, and the spirit of play can take control only during the intervals in the grimy playground.

It appears, perhaps, to be a good thing rather than a bad one that the Infant Teacher's opportunities have not been unbounded, and that she has spent her whole life in making the best of her surroundings. Otherwise her impatience and discontent might display themselves to the inconvenience of the rest of the school. At present it is a little pathetic to hear her recall that she once had 40 children in the same room where she now teaches the 28, and that she cannot imagine how she ever managed them.

A special feature of this class is that the girls who leave it at the age of seven to eight are always capable of doing simple needlework suitable for their age with remarkable neatness and speed.

Boys of the same age can sew on buttons quite securely, and have been taught that this is a duty they should always perform for themselves.

In the next class there are 34 children varying in age from seven to eleven. The teacher is a young girl of 22 who left the Training College less than a year ago. The headmaster believes she will become a very competent teacher, but both she and he agree that this type of class and its problems were not visualized when she was being trained. She is, therefore, gathering experience slowly and somewhat painfully, and all the time she is in danger of being tempted to exchange to a post in a still smaller school nearer her home. Three teachers have occupied her present place during the last five years, and the managers do not think they will obtain a permanent teacher until a local candidate presents herself.

The problems of this middle class are obvious. 'Elevens' and 'sevens' cannot easily be fitted into the same educational community. But in this case they must be kept in it while they receive their most important equipment for future intellectual pursuits. The routine processes of reading, writing, spelling, and arithmetic have to be mastered. In a smaller or more homogeneous class the tedium of mastering them could be reduced to a minimum by avoiding needless repetition, and by suitable recreative occupations. A simple straightforward scheme of work and timetable would enable the teacher to use all her vigour (which is at present her main asset) in actual teaching. In a mixed class of this size a great deal of energy is dissipated in making arrangements and dispositions to keep everyone occupied. Real individual work on the tutorial system or the Dalton plan is scarcely possible at this stage, or with such a class. Repetition is therefore unavoidable, and the grading of the instruction is so difficult that its efficiency is bound to suffer.

It may be added that the teacher of the middle class lives twelve miles away from the school and is therefore unable to take part in all its social activities. Because she cannot teach needlework or drawing, but is the best teacher of music in the school, the classes have to be completely rearranged during certain hours of the week. The two mistresses exchange classes, and the headmaster and the uncertificated mistress then re-group their pupils for needlework and drawing. The re-grouping involves a most complicated rearrangement of the seating accommodation in the whole of the main room.

We may now pass to the top class and to the head teacher, whose task in dealing with pupils from nine to thirteen years of age may appear to be almost a hopeless one.

But there are compensations. It will be noted that he has temporarily an unusual proportion of older boys. For the first time for many years he can get together a fairly good football team. He will have great difficulty in finding a field to play in, but fortunately he is at the height of his powers, and is not likely to be daunted by minor obstacles. For one year at least, he hopes to organize boys' games on satisfactory lines.

Some facilities for practical work are also available. For one afternoon a week fifteen boys are engaged in the school garden, while eight elder girls are taught cookery by the headmaster's wife, in her own kitchen. During this afternoon the remaining sixteen pupils of the top class are necessarily engaged on a programme of private study, organized by the headmaster, and supervised by the certificated assistant mistress. For the rest of the week the headmaster's class is taught in two sections, but its large size and extensive age-range interfere with any satisfactory attempt to provide the kind of systematic advanced instruction, which the pupils require. There is no space inside the school to carry out practical work in science or handicraft, or to store the equipment for such work. Organization is further complicated because some of the younger pupils have to be prepared for the local authority's Junior Scholarship Examination and because the elder ones will leave during the coming year in four groups—one at the end of each term.

Apart from his duty to his top class, the headmaster has of course the additional task of supervising the whole of the organization of the school, dealing with the complicated details of registration, school attendance, supplies, and the promotion of pupils from class to class. He must continue for some time to give very careful attention to the proper training of his young assistant, and he must be prepared to receive, often without notice, all kinds of official visitors to the school (including attendance officer, doctor, nurses, managers, inspectors and officials of the local authority). The visitors are always welcomed, but it is obvious that each of the two sections of his class must always be ready to work alone at short notice, which means that they must always have something to do and an inclination to do it.

One comparatively successful way of dealing with such a situation is for the head teacher to specialize with the older children in some branch of work for which he himself has great enthusiasm, to the possible neglect of others, which might be regarded as equally important. In this school the older pupils are specially trained in the observation and drawing of natural objects (plants, trees, birds, etc.). The school possesses a simple microscope, and in its garden and its rural surroundings there is much to be learnt of plant and animal life, as well as a certain amount of local history from buildings and other features. By prescribing limited fields of observation and insisting upon carefully written reports, illustrated with effective coloured drawings, the headmaster has gone some way to develop a special character in his school. He undoubtedly gives his better pupils a definite intellectual equipment which may fit them for dealing intelligently with some of the problems of their later life. They are not ignorant children but there are many things they do not know with which some critics might expect them to be acquainted. The most evident weakness of the school is the absence of any advanced work in mathematics, geography, or science. As most of the pupils take up industrial careers such weakness does not pass unnoticed.

The equipment of both classrooms is affected adversely by the history and the original purpose of the school. The Education Authority is gradually replacing the older seating accommodation by more up-to-date furniture. But in the infants' room the installation of tables and chairs is delayed by the comparative lack of space, and in the main room there is a certain reluctance on the part of the managers to sacrifice the long desks without back rests which can so easily be converted into seats for adults at public meetings. Modern school furniture is not adaptable in this way, and as long as the room has to be used for other than school purposes, the exchange is not readily welcomed. Similar considerations affect the supply of suitable cupboards, blackboards, and pictures. The difficulty of accumulating a school library is less than the difficulty of storing it. The equipment for games is kept in the toolshed which the Education Authority has provided in the garden. The piano, which has already been referred to, was originally bought second-hand ten years ago, and, in spite of the fact that the headmaster guards the key very jealously, it is much the worse for wear and difficult to keep in tune. There is no sewing machine except one, which is occasionally carried into the school from the house of the infants' mistress.

A friendly critic, on reading the foregoing somewhat detailed catalogue of material and personal difficulties, has expressed the opinion that it presents a deterrent picture of the difficulties with which teachers in elementary schools are confronted. It certainly does not describe either comfort or efficiency. But it is not an unjust or prejudiced account of typical condition. There are many teachers and administrators who can tell far more forbidding tales.

37

FROM CASTLE CAMPS TO LINTON VILLAGE COLLEGE, 1930–1939

Cambridgeshire, England
William A. Harding

William A. Harding was born at Moat Farm, Castle Camps, Cambridgeshire, in 1925. Following his attendance at Castle Camps village school he became, in 1937, one of the first pupils to enter Linton Village College. Mr Harding was afterwards employed on the local airfield during its construction and operation and at Tilbury Docks prior to wartime service in the Royal Signals in England and India. He retired from the Meat and Livestock Commission in 1985 after thirty years' service.

The Cambridgeshire county education officer, Henry Morris (1889–1961), described in his 1925 report, *The Village College*, the all-age primary schools, inherited from the Board School era and in a then impoverished countryside, as 'ill-managed, ill-found, ill-taught'. He established through energy and determination (and with no increase in an already low budget), six village colleges, four more of which were established following his retirement in 1951.

Cambridgeshire village colleges were to be community centres for all village activities; they would provide meaningful education for all age groups—from three years to old age—and too, would assist in the regeneration of a declining countryside. Although economic developments partially overtook their aims, they have been a source of inspiration to educationists around the world.

William A. Harding, *From Castle Camps to Rawalpindi*, Haverhill and District Local History Group, c. 1995

The Castle Camps School was an impressive, substantially built, brick building of character and charm with playground space on two sides. It was central to the surrounding villages of Shudy Camps (a two mile walk), Camps End—about the same distance, and Nosterfield End—about a mile away. These were journeys that had to be walked by all attending children and at most times by disgruntled mothers. The school was built in 1866 to accommodate 150 pupils.

A schoolmaster's house, situated beside the school, was built in 1892. Each child was taken to the school at age five and introduced to Miss Ethel Greengrass, who taught the infants. She was a small frail person who commanded the respect of every child who was fortunate enough to go through her skilful hands. Under her guidance one learned the alphabet and the tables up to twelve times twelve, chanting them aloud every morning of every school day. Children learned to read and write and were taught mathematics, geography and history with the thoroughness of a university lecturer and with varying results of success and failure. The local church vicar, the Reverend Hoar, visited the school once a week to teach religious subjects to those who cared to absorb the freely given knowledge and teaching.

During early school years, cod liver oil and malt, by the dessertspoonful, was given to all infants once a week, the same spoon being used by the whole class! A daily treat was the half bottle of milk supplied free to each child by the local council since most families could not afford to pay the halfpenny per bottle charged from 1936.[1] Days dreaded by most children were the twice-yearly occasions when the travelling dental caravan parked in the playground. Those whose surnames began with A or B wished they began with Y or W as you were called to see the dentist in alphabetical order. School was not all maths and reading; learning about nature and the countryside were subjects also incorporated in the school curriculum. In nature studies children were encouraged to search for nuts, seeds and berries in the autumn and, in the spring, collect flowers to press in schoolbooks. Lizards, newts, frogs and toads were small animals everyone was familiar with. Glow-worms could be seen by any roadside on dark nights, but proved difficult to pick up! Glow-worms are really beetles; only the female "glows" and this she can switch on and off at will. Frogspawn was collected and placed in a jar in the classroom so that the development from spawn to tadpole and finally to tiny frogs could be watched daily.

On reaching age eleven children graduated to the senior classroom under the watchful eye of Miss Winifred A. Hodgekinson, who lived in the schoolhouse adjacent to the school playground with her mother. She was an excellent teacher in every sense and subject to the receptive student and more than a match for the biggest bully in her school. She and I had one thing in common she once told me: we shared the same initials – WAH. The only heating in the building came from two coke-burning, slow combustion, tortoise stoves which roasted you if you sat at the front of the class and allowed you to freeze if you sat at the back. Miss Hodgekinson always kept her handkerchief up her knickers leg and, although she was very discreet, it was possible to see the colour of her nether wear now and then, which caused quite innocent giggling.

Happy events at school were prize-giving days when those children who worked hard and showed promise were, with those who had not missed attendance, awarded certificates or books of learning as rewards for endeavour. This prize giving was different from Sunday school prize-giving day in so much as on the latter occasion, the behaviour—with the emphasis on behaviour—and the prizes—were usually well-known story books, sometimes of a Christian leaning. One year I was given *Robinson Crusoe* and my sister Phyllis was awarded *Little Women*. Up to 1937 the children of the locality spent all their school years at Castle Camps School, which, I am convinced, was an excellent seat of learning with exemplary staff of great dedication and character.

From 1937 all eleven-year-old children were taken by omnibus, which called at collection points in the surrounding villages, to the magnificently purpose-built Linton Village College in order to further their knowledge and talents until reaching the age of fourteen when most left school to take up employment wherever they could find a job. A few of the brightest children did go on to further education in public schools, the number being decided by who could afford to pay or by scholarships won.

Apart from the local Linton children, who walked to school, others from a large catchment area were disgorged from buses of all colours, shapes and sizes on arrival in the mornings, and were loaded back on to them in the afternoons. Inevitably there were accidents and sadly a fatality occurred when a young lad was killed in a bus accident just outside the school. He was from the Abington Land Settlement, established during the late twenties and early thirties to find homes and land for out-of-work northerners in a period of severe depression in their home area. It proved a very successful venture and was copied by many local councils throughout the country.

The college building was huge, the centre piece a grand assembly hall which doubled as a gymnasium. There was a large library, music room, science laboratory and many classrooms, with two all-glass sides, which made them light and airy and pleasant to work in. The staff at Linton College were generally good, knew their subjects well and often taught more than one subject. Discipline was strict; if you were sent to the Headmaster for some misdemeanor, you were caned.

I loved the Linton College with its added facilities for football, cross-country running, etc. I always enjoyed the outdoor activities, especially sport, but gardening was also part of the curriculum and, under the watchful eye of a Mr Jacobs, we had to dig and double dig a plot of land as our contribution to cheap school meals of which school-grown vegetables were an important addition. Double digging, which everyone hated, was necessary to get the farm manure well down below the surface, where it was most effective we were told. All too quickly the years at Linton slipped by and in September 1939 I reached school leaving age—fourteen, which meant that I left school at the start of the six week summer holidays.

On leaving school no one was given a certificate of achievement—there was no such document. For myself, I'm convinced that I was better able to face the world with the broader education received at Linton.

The next task for me was to get a cycle and try to find a job. I had already decided that I would not work on a farm, which was a disappointment to my father and the local farmer, to whom we owed our home and livelihood. So I started making enquiries and visiting workplaces.

NOTE

1. Unemployment and undernourishment were widespread in the 1920s and 1930s. Under the government 'Milk in Schools' scheme, schoolchildren could buy, each school day, one-third of a pint of milk for a halfpenny. The many who could not afford that were given the milk free while children suffering symptoms of malnutrition were given two-thirds of a pint. LEAs and voluntary bodies provided, additionally, free dinners for necessitous children. Professor H.C. Dent in his *1870–1970 Century of Growth in English Education*, (Longman, 1970), observed that the service 'certainly saved the lives of some at least of the half-starved wretches.' Universal free milk in UK schools ended, acrimoniously, in 1970; there is currently a scheme in place that considerably reduces the cost of milk in schools. (See also, on free school milk and children's health, Lord Boyd Orr's 'Pupil and Pupil Teacher, 1885–1898', in this volume.)

38

TO SCHOOL THROUGH THE FIELDS, 1940s

Near Newmarket, Co. Cork, Ireland
Alice Taylor

This school description comes from Alice Taylor's account of growing up on a farm in the 1940s. In her introduction she says: '...this is the story of a childhood. In its day it was an ordinary childhood but, with the changing winds of time, now it could never be... It was an interlaced community and its structure helped those within it to support each other.'

Going to school and coming back was so enjoyable that it made school itself bearable. My main objection to school was that I had to stay there: it was the first experience to interfere with my freedom and it took me a long time to accept that there was no way out of its trap. I could look out through a window in the back wall of the school house and see my home away in the distance, with the fields stretching out invitingly and with the Darigle river glinting in the valley. I made many an imaginary journey home through that window: it was not that I wished to be at home so much, but that I wanted to be free to ramble out through the fields. I envied the freedom of the crows on the trees outside the window, coming and going as they pleased. But school became an accepted pattern and even though it had its black days it had its good ones as well. The black days were mainly in winter when we arrived through the fields with sodden boots and had to sit in the freezing cold with a harsh wind whipping in under the door and up through the floorboards. The school was an old stone building with tall rattling windows and black cobweb-draped rafters, and when the wind howled the whole school groaned and creaked. The floor had large gaping holes through which an occasional rat peeped up to join the educational circle.

The educational process of the day was based on repetition: we repeated everything so often that it had to penetrate into our uninterested minds. A booster, by way of a sharp slap across the fingers with a hazel rod, sharpened our powers of perception. Learning was not optional and the sooner you learnt that fact, the freer from conflict life became. All the same, most of the teachers were as kind as the system allowed them to be, but inspectors breathed down their necks and after them came the priests to check our religious knowledge. One stern-faced priest peered down at me from his six-foot height when I was in third class and demanded to know: "What is transubstantiation?"

Education was certainly not child oriented but our way of life compensated for its shortcomings. Sometimes, though unaware of it, we tried to educate our teachers, especially the ones that came from nearby towns to do part-time duty. One of these asked us to write a composition on "Life on the Farm." I loved writing compositions and my problem was not how to start but how to finish. I included in my account a description of the sex life of a cow and when I got my copy back from the teacher this section was ringed with a red pencil. A red mark meant an error so I checked every word for spelling in my dictionary but found nothing wrong. I returned to school the following day to ask the teacher what was wrong.

"That sentence should be left out," she said.

"But why?" I asked.

"It's not suitable," she answered, giving me a strange look.

On returning home in a very confused state I explained my problem to my mother. She read my composition, smiled and said: "People from a different background do not always understand." It took me another couple of years to understand why the teacher did not understand.

Ours was a mixed school and this suited everybody because families and neighbours were not split up but could all go to school together. The boys played football at one side of the yard and the girls played hunt and cat and mouse at the other side. At the back of the school the boys' and girls' toilets, which consisted of a timber bench with a circle cut in it to facilitate bottoms of all sizes, were separated by a stone wall. The little toilet building was partly roofed with galvanized iron but this had grown to a complete roof by years of free-growing ivy.

The school had just two rooms. The master had a room to himself and the second room was shared by the two other teachers: one taught infants and first class at one side of the room, while second and third classes were taught by the second teacher at the other side. It was open plan education and if you got bored at your end you could tune in to the other side, at the risk of a slap across the ear if you were caught out.

We ate our lunch, which consisted of a bottle of milk and two slices of homemade brown bread, sitting on a grassy ditch around the school, and we fed the crumbs to the birds. In winter the milk bottles were heated around the fire during classes, often resulting in corks popping from the heat and, if the cork could not pop because it was screwed on we had a mini-explosion and a milk lake.

There was a cottage near the school from which we collected a pot of tea each day for the teachers, and this provided a welcome diversion, especially in summer. We went down a narrow lane, which led into a long garden abounding with rows of vegetables, fruit trees and flowers. These flowers overflowed onto the paths and climbed up over the windows and onto the thatched roof of the cottage: it was almost buried in flowers, and when you went down the steps and through the doorway you stepped into another world. Inside the cottage was shadowed and had an air of mystery because every available space seemed to be filled with the treasures of the old couple that lived there. All around was the smell of flowers and on the table were bowls of fresh fruit from the garden. When you arrived into the kitchen you were seated on a soft súgán chair and given a cup of scalding tea coloured with goat's milk and a cut of bread with a thick layer of homemade jam, and afterwards you got a fistful of strawberries or raspberries that were soft and luscious. The little window on the back wall of the cottage was frilled with a lace curtain tied back with a ribbon and through the sparkling glass you could see the back garden as profuse and colourful as the front. It was a dream cottage and John O' and Mrs. O' were ideal occupants. They were gentle people; she wore a long skirt with her hair coiled in a soft roll on top of her head, he was a neat little man

with a black moustache, and always wore a navy suit. The trip to
John O's cottage brightened up many a school day tinged with
monotony.

The day in school was just an unwelcome interlude then between
the morning trek and the return home, and if the journey to school
took about thirty minutes, the coming home could take anything up
to two hours.

****

Finally we arrived home sun-soaked and relaxed, with school almost
forgotten because it was, after all, only one part of a much larger
cycle of education.

39

FIRST DAY OF SCHOOL, c. 1940

Dakar, Senegal,
Nafissato Diallo

An author from Senegal, Nafissatou Niang Diallo (1941–1982) was born in Dakar. Following her mother's death, her paternal grandmother brought her up. She worked as a mid-wife and as a paediatric nurse. The original French version of *A Dakar Childhood*, one of the first literary works by a Senegalese woman, was published in 1975.

Time came for me to enter the Qur'anic school. It was the exception in those days for Muslim children to attend lay schools before they had been exposed for a long time to the advantages of a religious education. There were no kindergartens and the minimum age for entry to a lay school was seven. So, until we were seven we used to go to the Islamic school, and even afterwards we continued attending during the school holidays. The older children in our family had done so before me. But I only went for three years because I was extremely naughty. The instruction at the Qur'anic school was not free but the fees were very low: thirty francs a month and two francs extra on Wednesdays. However, as my religious teacher was my maternal uncle, Father was not obliged to pay, but he did so voluntarily. But the teacher never asked for his fees so I collected a little nest egg for myself, as I didn't get any regular pocket money. But one day I was caught.

Nafissato describes her first day at primary school, aged seven years

Reprinted by permission of Pearson Education Limited, U.K. from *A Dakar Childhood* by Nafissato Diallo, [1975] Longman Group Ltd.: Harlow, Essex, 1982.

My girl-cousins, green with envy, would not let me pass. I could
understand their feelings. I was the first girl in the family that
Grandpa in his old age had finally allowed to go to school. They
whispered loud enough for me to hear, 'Look who's here! The
princess herself! Just see what she's been hiding from us all this
time! That's why she was always wearing a scarf on her head. Have
you seen her dress? The next time I'm born I'll choose a namesake
who's a dressmaker. Just look at her neck, she looks as if she's
swallowed a poker!'

That day I didn't take any notice of anything they said. Papa
couldn't help a smile when he saw me. The school that had been
chosen for me was in the Medina, opposite the Tilène market, but
you couldn't enrol in advance, so that day there was a such a long
queue of prospective pupils and their parents, all in their Sunday
best, that Mame thought there was a risk of all the places being filled
before it was our turn, so she decided to try another school. We
made our way to the school near the racecourse where the
Headmaster, who was a friend of Papa's, enrolled me straight away
in the first class and showed me to my classroom. I had to let go of
Mame. We were both in tears. She gave me some last words of
advice and returned home after slipping some pocket money into
my hand.

It was easy to distinguish the new pupils from the old hands. The
former were intimidated and looked completely lost. The others
were full of assurance and were ready to show off in front of us
greenhorns, calling to each other ostentatiously, pushing and jostling
us on purpose as they played, pretending nothing was happening.
My first teacher was Madame Ndèye who is still teaching. There
were fifty of us in her class. She was very pretty with deep black
skin and often wore her hair in four plaits that came down to her
shoulders. I can still see her in her white blouse and blue flared
European-style skirt that came down to mid-calf. I admired people
who dressed in European style. In Muslim families girls had to wear
a long dress or a camisole and a pagne. Only Catholics and a few
girls who were considered 'intellectuals' were allowed by their
families to wear European clothes.

Madame Ndèye soon put us at our ease. As I'm not exactly shy
by nature she soon picked me out. Eventually she put me in charge
of the blackboard: I had to see that the chalk, the duster and

everything else she needed were all put out. And when she was not there I had to keep the class in order.

That first day went off without a hitch except that a few girls were so lost they just put their heads down on their desks and went to sleep. Others, like the girls sitting behind me, went into ecstasies over our teacher's beauty and elegance.

A bit later on we went to the Headmaster's study and were given all our books and stationery. Parents didn't have to buy anything, everything was given to us. When I had filled my satchel I went home, where I was able to put Mame's mind at rest that everything had gone off well. She had been so anxious about my first day at school.

The year passed quickly. With my mind already sharpened by my attendance at the Qur'anic school and with my avid curiosity to know everything, I had no difficulty in taking in what we were taught.

40

A TEACHER BEGINS HER CAREER, 1957

Near Haworth, Yorkshire, England
Margaret Renton*

On an autumn day in 1957, I set out my desk, wrote the day and date on the blackboard, and waited for the pupils to arrive. And so I began my teaching career in a Yorkshire village school not far from Haworth, were the Brontë sisters had lived.

My class of second year juniors filed in, sat down and waited for me to begin. I surveyed them, and suddenly the pleasure of running my own class swept over me, dispelling my earlier apprehension.

The headmaster, a respected, rotund and jolly man, frowned on anything other than the three Rs being taught in the morning because he felt this was the best time of day for children to concentrate on difficult academic tasks. This was no doubt true in our case as several pupils worked on the outlying farms for an hour or two before setting out on their two-mile walks to school.

The head took small groups of remedial readers from each class every morning and positioned himself next to a strategically placed window in his office while hearing them read. From this window he could observe the number of children visiting the outside toilets during lessons. If he considered that a child was going too often, he would rap sharply on the window. This would be followed by frequent public reminders to the teacher on playground duty that

* Dr Margaret Renton worked in special needs education until her retirement in 1992.

this child must visit the toilet every break in order to alleviate his or her weak bladder.

One morning after Christmas we had a visitor, a rare occurrence. It was the Nit Lady. The children knew the drill and lined up in front of the blackboard, which was angled so that there was a measure of privacy for each child to be inspected behind it. The school nurse, a bluff no-nonsense woman, signalled for me to join the end of the line, stating that I was as likely to be infected as the children. She was followed by the dentist, who referred children to the clinic if they needed treatment.

Polio was a very real threat, and every morning the headmaster and caretaker could be seen striding across the playground to the outside toilets with mop, bucket and disinfectant. Poor hygiene was one of the recognized sources of infection.

The children had a bottle of milk at morning playtime, and some would blow down the straw, making bubbles. Most became expert at blowing with just the right amount of pressure to reach the top of the bottle without spilling, the penalty for which was mopping up and missing playtime.

Helping individuals and answering their questions without long queues forming was difficult, especially at first. So it was not until playtime one morning that I noticed a pupil with his head in his arms on his desk, fast asleep. I left him there during playtime, when playground noise woke him up. I asked him sternly what time he had gone to bed. "Two o'clock, Miss," he replied. "I was helping a cow to calve."

The children were enthusiastic about all our projects. We explored history and geography together, and by spring we had a well-established nature table for science. They already knew the names of all the specimens they had brought in, and could identify most of the plant and animal life in the stream at the far side of the playground.

With the summer term came the end of my probationary year. I suddenly received a message from the deputy head that my inspector had arrived, so I had only a few minutes to prepare. The inspector was a huge man whom the children watched with amazement as he sank his bulk into one of their small chairs. He observed my lessons, read my notes, spoke to the headmaster and then said that I had passed my probationary year.

My long-suffering pupils and helpful colleagues were as pleased as I was as I boarded my bus for home, feeling like a veteran.

41

AN ADULT EDUCATION PROJECT IN THE SOLOMON ISLANDS, 1960s

Makaruka and Balo villages, Guadalcanal, Solomon Islands
John Proctor

This Adult Education Project was part of a strategy designed by the government to deal with the growing Moro Movement of the northern or Weather Coast of Guadalcanal, an offshoot of the New Guinea Cargo Cult. Members believed, in part, that only a reversion to traditional ways and beliefs would bring again the great wealth accrued in the islands as a result of military operations during the Second World War. The development plan also envisaged a coastal road, the building of which would be supervised in part by Voluntary Service Overseas personnel (VSOs).

A violent two-year civil conflict, between the Guadalcanal and the Malaita islanders, ended in 2000. Literacy, countrywide, is estimated at 62 per cent.

The writer of these excerpts from letters home was an eighteen year-old school leaver.

10th November, 1966

Before leaving for the Weather Coast of Guadalcanal where we will be for three months, we made a number of preparations—including ordering stores and collecting educational material from the Education Department. Most of this was sent by ship about two weeks before we ourselves left Honiara. Luckily most of our stores were landed even though the sea was particularly rough. Although Makaruka is only forty miles by air from Honiara it is completely cut off by mountain and bush.

Until recently only boats could reach the Weather Coast, but now an airstrip has been cleared (it was finished last year by a VSO) at Avu Avu, about eight hours walk from Makaruka. Soon planes will be more frequent—about one a week—and so the Weather Coast will be opened up a little more to the outside world.

A schoolroom was built by the villagers shortly before we arrived, in which the men sit on the grey gravel sand. We lived here too until a simple house was built. It is a leaf house strongly built with poles and thirty yards from the beach. It has a pebble floor, the stones being changed occasionally.

Most houses in the village are some ten yards long by ten feet wide with low sidewalls and steep roofs, rather like a large tent. The door is raised from the ground to keep out unwanted animals. The cooking fires are maintained inside the houses. When we arrived there was great activity as the Moro were having a feast day.

About ten pigs were slaughtered using a crude method of strangulation. They were then butchered and baked in earth ovens known as *oomas*. While this was being done, there was dancing by the women of the local villages. This was followed by a play, put on by the men, showing the arrival of the first missionary. Many of the men coated themselves from head to foot in green mud and wore only leaves. The play was very amusing.

The feast day was completed by the sharing of the food, which was done with much ceremony—first by village and then for families. There was another feast two weeks later. It was very similar except that a play was put on showing the exorcism of devils.

The Moro Movement is named after its founder and was started ten years ago after Moro had a vision. It is on the same lines as the old Marching Rule,[1] which believed that cargo-laden ships would arrive for its adherents—this being a memory of the war. The Marching Rule was anti-government whereas the Moro is not. The movement is also known as the Moro Custom Company. The 'custom house'—right behind mine—is a museum of relics of the old days in the Solomons. Unfortunately we are not allowed inside due to the superstition that has grown up about it. Many of the ideas of the Company are good—like that of a village piggery—but have not succeeded, possibly as Moro is not of the 'great leader' type.

We have been treating a lot of people for cuts and boils. Some of the cuts have been quite bad as it was tree-felling time when we arrived in preparation for yam planting. One boy fell from a tree on to a stick. I had to dry bandage a baby with burns all around its head due to it having fallen in the fire (a not uncommon occurrence here). Another bad case is that of the man with the rotten finger. It was badly infected and so he opened it with a knife. Now the whole finger has swollen up and is completely rotten. I think he will have to have an amputation in Honiara (although it is unlikely he will go there).

Yesterday there was a gale, the first of its kind for five years. Many coconut palms were blown down and a number of older houses ruined. The Alualu river is so high it may be impossible to get this letter to Avu Avu for the next plane.

10th December, 1966

The hurricane did a great deal of damage on the Weather Coast. In Malaita a great many places were flooded and there was widespread damage. The government gave £10,000 for the people. It was difficult going to Avu Avu (usually eight hours by foot). The mouths of the rivers had to be crossed by canoe. Usually the rivers are only waist deep. Sometimes there is a great danger of being swept out to sea—this is not uncommon and many people have drowned in that way.

The school is going on well. Three days a week and in the evenings the men come and sit in the classroom. They enjoy arithmetic. At the moment they are trying to understand the decimal currency. They are very interested in world geography and world events. They enjoy talking about the war and about the part they played in it. Most of those old enough acted as carriers, and in other roles, for the Americans. On the whole they liked the Americans and disliked the British. The British it seems did not want to 'spoil' the people. After the war the discarded property of the Americans, collected by the people, was taken from them by the British. The Solomon Islanders had never seen so much 'cargo' as when the troops came—they never knew such things existed. This gave rise to the Marching Rule or 'cargo cult' of which I have told you. The people's opinion of the 'Europeans' is quite low. They see them in Honiara in office jobs and cannot understand how they are so rich. Once, I was told, two men of the Moro Movement went to Honiara in order to buy 'the white man's secret' with £2000.

To get back to the school—we often explain the news heard on the radio, even putting the pidgin English news into simpler pidgin. We also hold discussions in the evenings, using a wide variety of educational material from the Education Office.

We will spend Christmas in Makaruka. Everyone intends going spear fishing that day. Yesterday we fished in the Alualu river, starting about three miles up river and swimming down, spearing fish on the way. We are not able to fish in the sea very often as it is usually very rough. There, the best place is from a rock about thirty yards out. It is usually more interesting in the sea though—one just has to keep a look out for sharks—however, people say that on this part of the Weather Coast no one has been taken by a shark as, they say, sharks form part of their pre-Christian (and present) religious system—they worship the spirit of the shark in other words. Nevertheless, a boy last year lost his foot—apparently a shark mistook it for a fish. Some of the men can dive to a depth of sixty feet, though these are few.

A man from Naho village, two hours walk away, has said that he will take us crocodile shooting. They are shot at night from a canoe; a light is first shone in their eyes. They have to be skinned immediately and the skin put into salt water, otherwise they will rot. The skins are sold to the Chinese traders who come occasionally by ship to Avu Avu. Unfortunately, he does not at present have any cartridges.

26th December, 1966

On Christmas morning, the women wore their best calico and looked very smart. Many men and children dyed their hair white according to the custom of the village.[2] After swimming, we greeted the people who gave presents of tapioca and coconut pudding. In the afternoon every man in the village left to go and fight the men of the next district along the coast. Not one man was left, including the old men. The excuse for this was that a man from Talisa, the 'enemy' district married a girl from Mali within Makaruka district and there was a problem with the dowry.

There has always been inter-village fighting, at least until the missionaries came. The difference now is that several villages have united against several others. Also of course they don't use clubs or spears now. They do use, however, a kind of knuckle-duster, known as the 'scouse,' made of bone. The idea was to 'beat up' the Talisa men but not to kill them. Not killing enemies in a fight they say is not something they think is right—it is just obeying the wishes of the government. However, on Christmas Day the Talisa men were nowhere to be found, probably because they were outnumbered. If the fight had taken place there would have been about 200 men taking part. Now it has been fixed for Wednesday in a bush village called Pichihila. We are in fact going there tomorrow as a feast is taking place. So, one day the men will be singing together and the next fighting. To get back to Christmas—everyone was disappointed when the battle didn't take place and came back to Makaruka. At first it was arranged to take place today but Moro, the leader, heard that a government official was spending the Christmas holiday at Avu Avu and he didn't want the Central District office to hear about it. We had our Christmas dinner at 7 p.m., first chasing our chicken all over the village. We boiled it in coconut milk and soup and it tasted delicious. We were unable to spearfish, as the sea was so rough.

11th February, 1967

The Community Education Project is moved to Balo village

We sent our equipment to Balo on a government ship that came around the island picking up the Council members.

All the Makaruka and Bokesugu people came to see us off and consequently the boat was much delayed. We are now installed in Balo and have begun the project in the same way as in Makaruka—with the exception of not having school in the afternoons. Probably due to initial enthusiasm the men in Makaruka insisted on afternoon school but invariably went to sleep, which is the custom of the village. Nevertheless they would not give up this afternoon school routine. Here school is held under the shade of the palms, the men sitting on the stones on the ground. Everything discussed is related to events in their own lives and many visual aids are used.

The people in Balo are just as keen on having their ailments 'doctored' as were the people in Makaruka—the hypochondriacs are also becoming known. When we left Makaruka we assured the people we would be back to see them and would stop in their village again but we didn't realise how soon it would be before going back.

About a week ago we were just setting off for the village of Sukiki, about forty minutes away, when a letter was brought from Makaruka saying that a man was very sick and may have broken his back. We therefore set off at once to the village at a rather fast pace in order to get back to Balo before it got dark. We arrived there in about two hours but the man, far from having a broken back, seemed to have just an acute attack of 'flu (not even a strained back; it was just that whenever he coughed it felt as if his back was broken).

As very few people were there in Makaruka, and as we wanted to get back to Balo before it was dark, we set off at once, though stopping in a couple of villages on the way.

20th March, 1967

In Balo, teaching has been going well as usual. The people are always very keen to have classes. Yesterday I discussed how other people adapt to their environments (other than in the Solomon Islands that is). They are interested in the European history of the Solomons; the elections and the electoral process; decimal currency; the Europeans themselves and their history, particularly with regard to their various methods of fighting.

Many people come for additional lessons in arithmetic and in reading and writing. Much time is spent in talking to the people, which helps in achieving our aims, the best time being when chewing betal nut in the evenings.

Just recently a lot of bonito fish came offshore. When they are seen leaping out of the water while feeding, the men immediately leave the school and fly off in their canoes perhaps for a mile or two out to sea. Sometimes they are too late and come back with nothing; at other times they are luckier and come back with about twenty. Fish make up a far greater part of the diet of Balo than it does at Makaruka. Apart from just boiling the bonito it is also made into a kind of soup with pounded yam and coconut milk....

NOTES

1. The early post-World War II nationalist movement *Ma'asina Rura* was generally known as the Marching Rule.
2. Traditionally a paste made from coral lime was used. It served the double purpose of bleaching and destroying vermin.

42

THE SCHOOL IS OUR OWN, 1974

Sunchia, Liaoning Province, China
Kao Yu-pao

This is one of six articles that appeared in Chinese newspapers and magazines following the Cultural Revolution of 1966–1968. They were published together as *My Hometown* in 1974. Although the revolution was an economic and political failure, and the articles illustrate the development of the Mao Zedung personality cult, *My Hometown* represents aspects of autobiography and experience to which many people in modern developing countries will easily relate. The author's reflections on the inability of some parents to provide even a basic education for their children and the poor facilities provided should they be able to put together sufficient funds, remain a reality for many parents today.

The author, Kao Yu-pao, was a soldier-writer in the Chinese People's Liberation Army. In his childhood, in the 1930s, he was a swineherd for a despotic landlord. In 1970, he returned to his native village in north east China for a visit after an absence of twenty years.

I made a careful inspection of the new primary school in my hometown. In front of the buildings was a spacious playground. The children were all out for recess. Some were singing snatches from a model revolutionary opera, while others were having a merry chase, running, dancing, playing games...

I couldn't help comparing this picture of youthful activity with the school of my childhood. In those days it had only three run-down rooms and some twenty pupils. It had become a very beautiful place now! I was impelled towards these vivacious children, hoping yet to enjoy some of the happiness denied me in my boyhood. Now

Kao Yu-pao, *My Hometown—Six Reportage Articles*, Foreign Language Press: Beijing, 1974

I was in army uniform, and they swarmed around me at once and greeted me warmly. A girl with pigtails flying ran to the office and brought back a young man in peasant dress. It was Yu Chih-sheng, son of the former poor peasant Yu Tien-sheng who had slaved for the landlord for many years. He had graduated from this school and been chosen by the poor and lower-middle peasants to head the school's revolutionary committee.

We went to the office for a talk. A child climbed onto my knee and others shook me by the arm, insisting on my telling them a story.

"All right," I said, "I'll tell you my own story in the old society—how I ached to attend this school but was not allowed, because we couldn't pay the fee."

The mention of the bitter past refreshed my inveterate hatred of the wicked old society!

"Boys and girls," I began, "you're very young, but you've already started school. You should realize that in old China it was more difficult for poor children to attend school than to climb up to heaven. When I was nine I cried and cried because I wanted to go to school like rich people's kids, but my mother could only say sadly, 'Son with your father sick abed, we haven't anything to eat or cover ourselves with. Where can I get the money to send you to school?' But she couldn't stand seeing me weep my heart out and borrowed from some neighbours to get me into the school. We couldn't keep up, however, and before long I was forced to leave the school and herd swine for Skinflint Chou. One day, in my spare time, I went to the teacher with the book I had managed to get with much effort, hoping to learn a few characters.

But unfortunately I ran into Skinflint Chou, who knocked me down and gave me a bad beating. Tearing my book to shreds, he swore, 'Learning is not for poor devils like you! Get back to my pigs and hurry up about it!' "

My story set the bright eyes of the children around me flashing with anger. A girl of about thirteen shot up her arm and led her schoolmates in shouting indignantly, "Down with Skinflint Chou! Down with Liu Shao-chi!"

Later, when I told how I had joined the People's Army after liberation, and how the Party and Chairman Mao had enabled me to study, even through university, this girl again led the other children in a full-throated shout, "Long live our great leader Chairman Mao! A long, long life to him!"

When I had finished my story, she grasped my hand and said seriously, "Uncle, believe us when we say we will follow Chairman Mao's teachings, study hard and make progress every day. We will be good successors of the revolution."

"What's your name?" I asked.

"Lu Hsi-yung."

The bell rang for class; the girl said goodbye to me and ran to her classroom with the others.

"A good girl!" I remarked, looking at her retreating figure.

"Yes, she's one of the many who wouldn't be here if not for Chairman Mao's proletarian educational line."

The change in this primary school was due entirely to the leadership of the Communist Party and Chairman Mao, Yu Chih-sheng told me. It could happen only after the liberation, especially since the Cultural Revolution, when the poor and lower-middle peasants here joined in running the school under the Party's guidance. They threw the school gate wide open to the children of poor and lower-middle peasants.

One day Yu Chih-sheng and some other teachers visited Lu Hsi-yung in her village to see why she could not attend school. They found the girl's father sick, her mother at work in the fields, and she herself burdened with the care of a younger brother and sister plus other household chores. So they decided to let the girl bring her two year-old brother to school with her. The young woman teacher Chou Yu-yuan said, "Admitting Lu Hsi-yung or not is a fundamental question of 'for whom the school gate opens,' " and took the girl into her own class. Teachers who were not holding class would take care of Hsi-yung's little brother. The school now had over three hundred students with thirty-some rooms, giving a free education to all children of school age. It had a small farm, tree nursery, and poultry sheds.

Looking at the happy faces of the pupils at class, with their story filled in by Yu Chih-sheng's vivid account, I could not help thinking of the miserable past and feeling great excitement at the changes. In the old days poor children were not allowed so much as a peep at the school gate. Today my childhood dream had come true—the school had become our own!

43

FRITTENDEN CE PRIMARY SCHOOL, 1997

Frittenden, Kent, England
Sue Thomas*

Children are leaving our school today...
It is the last day of the school year and the children, their teachers
and their parents are gathered for The Leaver's Service to say
goodbye and wish good luck to the pupils who are moving on to
secondary school after the summer holiday. By tradition the leavers
organize and present the service, choosing favourite poems and
songs to share with their audience of well-wishers. The six children
aged eleven years who are the leavers, have, as all leavers over the
years before them have done, prepared a short talk about their
memories of being a part of this very small village school. As we
sit to listen in the hall with its high ceilings and pretty arched
windows, Jamie reminds us that the school is now 148 years old and
he remembers the 'Victorian Day' three years ago when all the
children and the teachers came dressed as Victorians. Parents helped
the children to dress in the costumes of the times; the head teacher
looked frightening wearing a flowing gown and carrying a cane—
which, Jamie assures the audience, she didn't have to use on him!
He remembers that one teacher came dressed as that famous explorer
David Livingstone, with tales of elephants and hippos, the raging
Zambezi River and the huge waterfall he named after his Queen.
The history stories made him decide he will travel and explore far
continents one day when he is older.

---

* Sue Thomas lives in Sussex and is a textbooks' writer and retired teacher. Frittenden
CE Primary School had, in 1997, sixty-eight pupils and three teachers.

Rachel is motherly and loves the little ones. She fondly recalls the day the whole school went for a walk. Each of the older children had to look after a child from the infant class. Rachel helped five year-old John through gates, over stiles and across roads, carrying his coat when he got hot, talking to him about the things they noticed on the way. She smiles as she recalls leading him through a field of oilseed rape where little John couldn't see above the high crop. He held Rachel's hand tight as he thought he was in a jungle full of tigers. The children in the audience nod and smile too as they remember the experience of being part of a long crocodile of children, winding its way around the village lanes and fields. Another leaver, Clare, remembers that day too. It was the first time she had been on a country walk through the village orchards and meadows. She wrote a poem about one of the many stiles on that footpath route.

I'm an old rickety stile
My pole is lopsided,
So I'm told.
The bones on my back
Are aching and sore.
Heavy feet climb me
Ten, a hundred, more.
My favourites are the children
They're happy that's for sure.

Next we hear from Roy who admits that he doesn't like lessons much but his favourite times were helping to run the tuckshop, where he sold apples and snacks, counted the money, kept the accounts, made orders and payments. He also enjoyed raising money for charity by growing and selling plants, and again he counted the money and kept the accounts. Much better fun than lessons!

Craig has brought his trumpet to the service. He talks about the day all the local schools joined together in a music festival to sing and play music together. He said it was a great chance to meet children from other schools and learn new tunes and songs. He explains how to get tunes from a trumpet and Roy tries to blow a note, only to find that it is much more difficult than it looks. The audience gazes in wonder at this little trumpeter as he stands alone and plays his new tune for them.

Despite all the fun of the outdoor and extra-curricular activities, there's still plenty of formal work done at Frittenden School. Jane has vivid memories of the government's standardized tests. She remembers sitting in this large hall at a desk on her own, waiting silently for the test papers along with the other five children in her year group. Would she be able to do it? Would she get the answers right? Would there be enough time? All those worries and then the surprise as she discovered she understood the questions, knew the answers and finished the paper in good time. She's worried about going on to her new school, but her friend is going too so she hopes it will turn out all right. The other leavers nod, they understand, as they too are nervous about leaving this small village school for the large secondary in the town five miles away.

It's also my last day as a teacher at Frittenden Primary School. Teachers don't take part in the Leaver's Service but the children's memories have sparked off some thoughts of my own. The future of our school has often been in doubt as the authorities think that small schools are not educationally viable. The six children leaving today take with them not only the skills of reading, writing and arithmetic, but the benefit of a range of experience outside the classroom that will help equip them with the skills to live in the wider world beyond the village.

And what do I remember most about my village teaching day? A group of travelling gypsies visited our village, located in the heart of 'The Garden of England', for the fruit-picking season. Grace, aged eight, came to school, unable to read. Learning to read was considered the most important skill we could offer her. Every lesson focused on reading and with in a couple of weeks she started to read. Soon she was devouring every book put in front of her... Grace could read. One day she came to school and said.' "My mother has joined an evening class—she wants to learn to read like me." Our village school had reached beyond the classroom to influence the families in their desire for an education. The service is ending. The six children stand together and start the singing of a school song written by the 1991 leavers and now reserved for the last day of every school year. The audience sings loud and clear, albeit with a lump in some of their throats.

"Children are leaving our school today,
Saying goodbye to their teachers.

Saying goodbye to those left behind,
Ready for work and for play.
At their new school they will try to succeed,
Hope they'll be happy and welcome.
Children are leaving our school today,
We wish them well in the future."

44

TAKHTIES, TO START WITH... 1998

Punjab, Pakistan
Hamid Raza Wattoo

A typical village school conjures up many images in one's mind—an assembly of pupils chanting the table of two; classes taking their lessons on mats under the shady trees in summer and out in the sun in winter; quenching their thirst and washing *takhties* at the solitary school water pump; a few minor students running after a ball and a lot more...

A village school is, indeed, a place of wonderful things. Trains of students hurrying towards the school with the first tintinnabulation of morning bell, the assembly of school children and their singing a hymn or prayer in chorus, their sedate walk to the mats and wooden benches which form their classes, the loud voice of a school master echoing through the whole periphery and coy, diffident pupils, listening to their overbearing teachers with utmost awe and respect, are things which could open up a world of dreams and fantasies for city people. Many individuals who have stamped their impressions on the national and international scenario have taken their first lessons sitting on the jute mats of a village school.

Still adhering to the age-old methods of teaching that puts emphasis on *qalam*, *davat*, and *takhti*,[1] the village teachers have till late produced the future of the country with a religious zeal. Starting with the drilling of the letters of the alphabet and numerals in the callow minds, they nurtured and educated the village urchins up to secondary level with all possible faithfulness.

The headmaster of a village school has always been a centre of respect and authority within his jurisdiction. It is incredible both in concept and practice. His opinion and judgement on any village

Reprinted by permission of *The News*, 'Takhties' by Hamid Raza Wattoo, Lahore, 22 February 1998.

issue is considered the last word. Until recently even a Member of the Provincial Assembly or a bigwig of the area had to think twice before influencing a headmaster in favour of his ward. The way the village pupils love and respect their teachers is also amazing. This respect might be generated from fear but, whatever the reason may be, the pupils treat their teachers with an unusual respect and deference. They love to do anything for their teachers during the school hours or after. Often they cut fodder, look after the farm animals, work in the teachers' fields. And as the evening sets in, they go to the teachers' homes to pick up a few crumbs of knowledge.

The promotion of a pupil to the next class is a special occasion for the village parents. The teachers are garlanded and showered with presents. A village teacher enjoys the privilege of borrowing fodder, grains and any other commodity any time from the parents of his pupils. In fact, In most of the cases, such things are sent to the teacher's home as a token of respect and deference.

At school, this bond is even stronger with the teachers taking pains to ensure their pupils acquaint themselves well with both studies and behaviour. As the pupils in villages are of all kinds and ilks, the teachers love the bright students but have equal preference for bringing up the refractory ones by 'hand.'

The village schoolteachers still believe in the age-old maxim 'spare the rod and spoil the child.' In corporal punishment, boxing the ears is the most popular but sometimes the punishment can be far more severe. Often it is ceaseless caning and spanking. But despite all this, the sense of community and belonging that exists between the pupils and teachers at village schools can only be imagined.

In most village schools there is no concept of uniform. As most of the parents can't afford to buy it, the teachers do not insist on observation of hard rules and pupils are allowed to come to school in any casual dress. Either taking advantage of the concession or due to the usual quirks of childhood, a fair number of minor pupils do not even bother to wear shoes and traverse vast distances to their schools in any weather with full ease and comfort.

The medium of instruction in village schools is the regional language as it helps the teachers to easily explain lessons to the pupils in their mother tongue. Interestingly, if a teacher opts for Urdu, he or she is mocked at by his fellows and pupils, who term him in their private talks a braggart who shows off his knowledge of the national language by 'casting pearls before the swine.'

As regards studies, the village pupils are a little below average. They manage to put up a good show in all subjects, especially in Mathematics which is the forte of village students; but when it comes to English they end up nowhere. Most of the village school pupils fail in their board exams due to English which is taught to them by teachers who have neither proficiency nor interest in the subject.

The shortage of qualified teachers has been the bane of education at these schools. While teaching the pupils, they place a *khulasa* (guide book) on the table, and as they speak a sentence from the book they see its Urdu translation in the book in front. Worse still, there is no communication whatsoever between the teacher and the pupils, and soon the lesson ends up as a stolid demagoguery that ultimately alienates the pupils from their studies.

Although lack of education in the village is due to the shortage of good teachers, the onus equally lies on the 'disinterested' parents who, until recently, were reluctant to send their children to school, arguing that they could not afford to send their children to colleges in far-off towns or that education up to Matric level would hardly help their sons get a government job. Due to this chicanery, the education of pupils comes to an end after middle or matriculation and they are engaged in farming and shepherding by their parents to add to the granary of the house.

The situation, however, has started changing now the village people have realized the importance of education in this high-tech age. They are now more willing to send their children to schools even by sparing them from other domestic requirements.

Extra-curricular activities and facilities in village schools are almost non-existent. The schools which were pride of the district in games like *kabbadi*[2] and football have gone into oblivion. With the non-provision of funds for the promotion of sports, most of the village schools have opted out of the annual tehsil or district level tournaments. Football has ceased to exist while the interest of village youth in *kabaddi* is also dying down—thanks to inexplicable media coverage of cricket and hockey.

Partly, this poor condition of schools can be attributed to the village people themselves, as all those influentials and village landlords, who by dint of their social and political leverage and by taking personal interest in the welfare of schools, could well have raised the standard of education, have sent their children to convent schools in cities, leaving the village schools to suffer their own fate. And, not only the village lords, even the education department officials have turned their backs on them.

They are not willing to release funds for the repairs or development work of schools and are equally negligent in conducting official visits to analyze the state of affairs prevailing in these schools.

With all this happening, it should, indeed, be a matter of satisfaction and pleasure for the powers-that-be that the village schools are managing to send out scores of matriculates to the city colleges for higher education. And who knows—if given proper funds and care, these village schools could uplift the provincial educational scenario that, at present, looks very bleak.

NOTES

1. *qalam*: bamboo pen; *davat*: inkpot; *takhti*: wooden writing board.
2. A wrestling game (see also, 'The Maktab and the Pathsala', 1890s).

POSTSCRIPT

Child labour statistics, worldwide, are truly shocking. According to the International Labour Office in Geneva, there are 73 million working children less than ten years of age; 246 million children are involved in labour that is damaging to their mental, physical and emotional development; some 22,000 children die in work-related incidents every year and many are engaged in the worst forms of child labour, including trafficking, armed conflict and slavery. In Pakistan, the government is making efforts to curb and control child labour. However, the employment of children, including those in hazardous occupations and environments, as bonded labourers and as domestic servants, continues.

> I am small because I am a little child. I shall be big when I am as old as my father is.
> My teacher will come and say, "It is late, bring your slate and your books."
> I shall tell him, "Do you not know I am as big as father? And I must not have lessons any more."
> My master will wonder and say, "He can leave his books if he likes, for he is grown up."

Rabindranath Tagore, *The Crescent Moon*, Macmillan: London, 1913

KEY EVENTS IN EDUCATION, 1696–2004

1696   In Scotland, an Act ordains a school and a schoolmaster in every parish.

1698   In England, the charitable Society for Promoting Christian Knowledge (SPCK) is founded and establishes schools.

1701   A branch of the SPCK is founded in America.

1711   Queen Anne further encourages charity schools.

1764   Frederick the Great establishes village schools in Prussia.

1780   Robert Raikes founds the popular Sunday school movement in Gloucestershire, England.

1782   Pestalozzi publishes his theories of education in Berne, Switzerland.

1785   In the USA, the first Land Ordinance is passed; every township is to contain 36 sections of 640 acres; the sixteenth section is to be sold in support of a school.

1789   In the USA, by the tenth amendment of the constitution, education becomes the responsibility of the states.

1794   The French Assembly decides on free and compulsory elementary education from 6 to 8 years but this could not implemented. The first normal school (for the training of teachers) is founded in Paris.

1797   Dr Bell, an army chaplain, after teaching in Madras, returns to England and publishes a report on his method and use of pupil-monitors. He establishes schools using these methods.

1798   Joseph Lancaster, a Quaker, opens a school in Southwark using the monitor system.

1808   The Royal Lancastrian Institution for Promoting the Education of the Poor, afterwards the British and Foreign School Society (the 'British') is formed to further promote Lancaster's system.

1811   The National Society for Educating the Poor in the Principles of the Established Church (the 'National') is formed to further promote Dr Bell's system.

1816   William Cobbett's *Political Register*, the first cheap periodical, is published.

1818   Lancaster migrates to the USA.

1825   The University of London is founded.

1831   A school system in Ireland is founded and a grant of £30,000 is made.–Physical science and modern languages are adopted in the curriculum of the Jesuits' schools.

1833   The first government grant of £20,000 is made to English schools.–Children under nine are excluded from cotton mills and inspectors are appointed. Older children employed in the textile industry are to receive two hours of schooling, six days a week.

1835   Macaulay's 'Minute': the use and study of the English language in India and the introduction of western culture is determined. –University College, London, is permitted to grant degrees.

1836   London University becomes solely an examining body; teaching is carried out by University College.

1837   Froebel establishes his first kindergarten. –Education is reformed in Massachusetts, USA.

1839   The Committee of Council–and a schools' inspection system–is introduced in England and Wales.

1840   The first UK government funded training college for teachers opens at Battersea, London.

1841   Degrees are granted to women in the USA.

1842   The Royal Commission on Mines describes the evils of women's and of children's employment–The Factory Act says children working in factories must go to school for six half-days a week.

1843   The Committee of Council provides grants to the 'National' and 'British' Societies for the building of normal schools and training colleges.

1846   The pupil teacher system is started by Dr (later, Sir John) Kay Shuttleworth.

1847   State aid is extended to Wesleyan and Roman Catholic schools. Jewish schools received recognition in 1851.

1848   The Ten Hours' Bill for women and children of 13 to 18 years is passed.

1853   Capitation grants are instituted for rural elementary schools, at a scale varying from three shillings to six shillings per head. The school must be under a certified teacher and three-quarters of the children must pass a prescribed examination. In 1856 the grant was extended to urban areas.

1857   The Universities of Calcutta, Bombay and Madras are founded.

1858   Oxford and Cambridge Local Examinations are instituted.

1861   Report on the State of Popular Education in England: the Duke of Newcastle's Commission describes the inadequate state of elementary education in England.

1862   A college, in each state of the USA, is founded for scientific and technical studies.–In England and Wales, Robert Lowe's 'payment by results' system is initiated.

1863   University College, Lahore, is founded.

1867   In England and Wales, extra payments are made to schools teaching history and geography.

1868   Disraeli introduces the Reform Bill.

1870   W.E. Forster's Elementary Education Act creates Board schools where no voluntary school provision exists.

1872   The Education Act for Scotland creates Board schools; it provides for compulsory attendance for all children, 5 to 13 years.

1875   Syed Ahmed Khan founds the Mohammedan Anglo-Oriental School (MAO) at Aligarh, India, to impart modern and Islamic education.

1876   Lord Sandon's Act, designed to improve school attendance, made it the duty of every parent to see that his child received efficient instruction in reading, writing and arithmetic.

1877   The MAO School is upgraded to the status of a college.

1878   The University of the Punjab, Lahore, is founded as an examining body with affiliated colleges throughout the province.

1880   An Education Act makes school compulsory for all children to the age of ten in England and Wales.

1882   In India, Lord Ripon's Education Commission recommends that primary education should be funded by local educational funds, and from provincial revenues. School Boards are established to control and administer these new resources. With regard to higher education, greater encouragement is to be given to private institutions. In addition, in all schools and colleges, arrangements should be made for games, sports and drill, and that in government institutions, where religious neutrality prevents religious instruction being given, moral education should be part of the curriculum.

1883   Status of 'University of the Punjab' is awarded to colleges in Lahore.

1891   In England and Wales a capitation grant enables schools to cease charging fees.

1897   In the UK, the payment by results' system is finally abolished and is replaced by block grants.–The proposal to grant degrees to women at Cambridge is rejected.

1898   The London University Bill creates a teaching university.–
The school leaving age is raised to twelve in the UK.–A government Board of Education is created, uniting the Education with the Science and Art Department.

1902   Balfour's Education Act is passed. The Board School system is abolished in the UK; local education authorities (LEAs) are established to run all elementary schools. A national system of free education for all children is implemented. LEAs are given power to provide secondary education.

1907   All secondary schools receiving grants from LEAs will reserve 25 to 40 per cent of free places for children from elementary schools.

1917   Mississippi makes education compulsory, the last state in the USA to do so.
1918   In the UK, Fisher's Education Act raises the school leaving age to 14; the fees remaining in some schools for elementary education are abolished.
1919   The Punjab Primary Education Act attempts to make education compulsory in selected areas of the Punjab but, for many reasons, fails.
1926   In the UK, the Hadow Report is published: elementary schools are to become primary schools with transfer at age of 11 to secondary schools.
1944   In the UK, Butler's Education Act raises the school leaving age to 15; free secondary education is to be provided in grammar, technical and secondary modern schools; primary education is to be reorganized into infant and junior schools.
1951   In the UK, the General Certificate of Education (GCE) replaces the School Certificate.
1965   In the USA, the Elementary and Secondary Education Act extends the role of the national government.
1973   In the UK, the school-leaving age is raised to 16 years.
1976   In the UK, an Education Act requires LEAs to submit secondary school reorganization (comprehensive school) proposals.
1988   In the UK, the Education Reform Act establishes a national curriculum for pupils aged 5 to 16 years.–The General Certificate of Secondary Education (GCSE), with a coursework assessment component, replaces the GCE O-level.
1993   In the UK, an Education Act makes changes to the ways in which schools are organized in England and Wales—it becomes easier for schools to become grant-maintained; a new School Curriculum and Assessment Authority (SCAA) and the Office for Standards in Education (OFSTED) are established.
2001   Fees to Matric level are abolished in the Punjab, Pakistan.
2004   Textbooks are provided free of cost in the Punjab, Pakistan.

BIBLIOGRAPHY

The source for each chapter is given on the chapter's title page. The editor has referred to, or has otherwise found helpful, the idiosyncratic list of titles, below.

Ali, Parveen Shaukat, *Pillars of British Imperialism. A Case Study of the Political Ideas of Sir Alfred Lyall*, Aziz Publishers: Lahore, 1976.

Aldrich, Richard, *An Introduction to the History of Education*, Hodder and Stoughton: London, 1982.

Anderson, G., *British Administration in India*, Macmillan: London, 1930.

Barker, Sir Ernest, *Political Thought in England, 1848 to 1914*, Oxford University Press: London, 1915.

Best, Geoffrey, *Mid-Victorian Britain, 1851–1875*, Weidenfeld and Nicolson Ltd · London, 1971.

Bhatnagar, Gulshan Rai, *A Course in Indian Civics*, Macmillan and Co., Ltd.: London, 1938.

Bhatti, M.A., *et al*, *Female Teachers in Rural Pakistan (Problems and Remedies)*, National Education Council: Islamabad, 1988.

Bohn, Henry G., *Cyclopedia of Political, Constitutional, Statistical and Forensic Knowledge*, The Standard Library: London, 1849.

Boswell, James, *The Life of Samuel Johnson, LL.D.*, [1791] Macmillan: London, 1914.

Brayne, F.L., *Better Villages*, Oxford University Press: London, 1937.

Briggs, Asa, *Victorian People, A Reassessment of Persons and Themes, 1851–61*, [1954] Penguin Books: London, 1990.

Brooks, G. and A.K. Pugh, (eds.), *Studies in the History of Reading*, University of Reading School of Education with the United Kingdom Reading Association: Reading, 1984.

Brooks, Ron, *Contemporary Debates in Education: An Historical Perspective*, Longman: Harlow, 1991.

Buckland, C.E., *Dictionary of Indian Biography*, [1906] Al-biruni: Lahore, 1975.

Cobban, Alfred, *A History of Modern France*, vol. II: *1799–1871*, [1961] Penguin Books Ltd.: Harmondsworth, 1972.

Cox, T.A. and R.F., MacDonald, *The Suggestive Handbook of Practical School Method. A Guide to the School-Room and Examination Room*, Blackie and Son, Ltd.: London, 1909.

Cunningham, W., *The Growth of English Industry and Commerce in Modern Times*, Cambridge University Press: London, 1917.

Daiches, David, *A Critical History of English Literature*, 2nd. ed., Indian reprint, n.d.

Derry Stephen (ed.), *Everyman's Poetry. George Crabbe*, J.M. Dent: London, 1999.

Disraeli, Isaac, *Curiosities of Literature*, [1784] George Routledge and Sons: London, 1867.

Duggan, Stephen, *A Student's Textbook in the History of Education*, [1916] D. Appleton-Century Company: New York, 1936.

Dunville, Benjamin, *Teaching, Its Nature and Varieties*, University Tutorial Press Ltd: London, 1933.

Elsmie, G.R., *Thirty-five Years in the Punjab, 1858-1893*, [1908] Sang-e-Meel Publications: Lahore, 2001.

Ensor, R.C.K., *England. 1870–1914*. Oxford University Press: London, 1936.

Evans, George Ewart, *The Cracked Scythe. An anthology of oral history*, Faber and Faber: London, 1993.

Fay, C.R., *Life and Labour in the Nineteenth Century*, Cambridge University Press: London, 1920.

Fay, C.R., *Great Britain from Adam Smith to the Present Day. An Economic and Social Survey*, Longmans: London, 1929.

Forster, John, *The Life of Dickens*, Cecil Palmer: London, 1874.

George, Dorothy, *England in Transition. Life and Work in the Eighteenth Century*, Penguin Books: Harmondsworth, 1931.

Gooch, G.P., *Annals of Politics and Culture (1492-1899)*, Cambridge University Press: London, 1905.

Hammond, J.L. and B., *Lord Shaftsbury*, [1923] Penguin Books: Harmondsworth, 1939.

Hammond, J.L. and B., *The Black Age*, [1934] Penguin Books: West Drayton, 1947.

Hans, Nicholas, *Comparative Education. A Study of Educational Factors and Traditions*, Routledge and Kegan Paul Ltd.: London, 1949.

Harrison, J.F.C., *The Early Victorians, 1832-51*, Weidenfeld and Nicolson Ltd.: London, 1971.

Hobsbawm, Eric, *The Age of Revolution, 1789-1848*, Weidenfeld and Nicolson Ltd.: London, 1962.

Hobsbawm, E.J., *The Age of Empire, 1875-1914*, Weidenfeld and Nicolson Ltd: London, 1987.

Hood, Thomas, *The Serious Poems of Thomas Hood*, Ward, Lock, & Co.: London, 1876.

Hunter, W.W., *The Indian Musalmans. Are they bound in conscience to rebel against the Queen?* [1871] Lahore, 1974.

Irving, Washington, *The Life of Oliver Goldsmith*: The University of Adelaide Library at http://etext.library.adelaide.edu.au/i/irving/washington/goldsmith/chapter1.htm/) (12-02-2005).

Jackson, Donald, *The Story of Writing*, Parker Pen International: London, 1981.

Jathar, G.B. and Beri, S.G., *Indian Economics. A Comprehensive and Critical Survey,* vol. I, [1928] Oxford University Press, 1949.

Jillani, Anees, *Child Labour: The Legal Aspects*, SPARC: Islamabad, 1997.

Jones, M.G., *The Charity School Movement; a study of eighteenth century Puritanism in action*, Cambridge University Press: Cambridge, 1938.

Khan, Syed Ahmed, *The Causes of the Indian Revolt*, [1873] Oxford University Press: Karachi, 2000.

Keith, A.B. (ed.), *Speeches and Documents on Indian Policy, 1750–1921*, vol. ii, Oxford University Press: London, 1922.

Kumarappa, J.C., *Why the Village Movement?* The Hindustan Publishing Co. Ltd.: Rajahmundry, 1939.

Lamb, Charles, *Essays of Elia*, [1823] Macmillan and Co, Ltd: London, 1927.

Lee, Laurie, *Cider with Rosie*, The Hogarth Press: London, 1959.

Legouis and Cazamian, *A History of English Literature*, Indian reprint: 1971.

Leitner, G.W., *History of Indigenous Education in the Punjab since Annexation and in 1882,* [1882] Republican Books: Lahore, 1991.

Lucas, John (ed.), *A Selection from George Crabbe*, Longmans, Green and Co. Ltd.: London, 1967.

Macaulay, Thomas, 'War of the Succession in Spain', [1833] in *Critical and Historical Essays,* vol. II, J.M. Dent: London, 1907.

Macaulay, Thomas, *Lord Macaulay's Miscellaneous Writings*, vol. II, Longman, Green, Longman and Roberts: London, 1860.

Mantoux, Paul, *The Industrial Revolution in the Eighteenth Century,* Jonathan Cape: London, 1928.

Mason, Phil, *Nothing Good Will Ever Come Of It: A History of Parliamentary Misgivings, Misjudgments and Misguided Predictions,* Warner Books: London, 1993.

Mingay, G.E., *Rural Life in Victorian England*, William Heinemann Ltd: London, 1977.

Mitra, K.P., *Indian History for Matriculation*, Macmillan and Co., Ltd.: Calcutta, 1933.

Moses, Brian, *A Victorian Schoolroom*, Wayland Publishers Ltd.: Brighton, 1997.

New Popular Encyclopedia, The, vol. 12, The Gresham Publishing Co.: London, 1902.

Primary Education, HMSO: London, 1959.

Raymont, T., *The Principles of Education*, Longman, Green and Co. Ltd.: London, 1924.

Report on the Progress of Education in the Punjab during the quinquennium ending 1941–42, Lahore, 1943.

Richmond, W. Kenneth, *Education in England*, Penguin Books: Harmondsworth, 1945.

Russell, George W.E., *Collections and Recollections*, Thomas Nelson and Sons: London, 1909.

Savailal, Harilal, *Samaldas Parmananddas, Scholar and Statesman. A Biographical Sketch*, B.H. Shindi: Bombay, 1912.

Seaborne, M. and Lowe, R., *The English School. Its Architecture and Organization*, vol. II, Routledge and Kegan Paul: London, 1977.

Spring, Joel, *The American School, 1642-1993*, 3rd ed., McGraw-Hill, Inc.: New York, 1994.

Stacpole, W.H., *Victorian England*, Dean and Son Ltd.: London, n.d., c. 1901.

Temple, Richard, *Oriental Experience*, John Murray: London, 1883.

Thabault, Ragor, *Education and Change in a Village Community. Mazieres-en-Gatine, 1848–1914*, Schocken Books: New York, 1971.

Trevelyan, G.M., *English Social History*, Longmans, Green and Co. Ltd.: London, 1942.

Usher, A.P., *An Introduction to the Industrial History of England*, George G. Harrap: London, 1921.

Weiner, M. and Noman, Omer, *The Child and the State in India and Pakistan. Child Labour and Educational Policies in Comparative Perspective*, [1991] Oxford University Press: Karachi, 1995.

Walton, James, *Principles and Methods of Teaching*, W.B. Clive: London, 1906.

Walton, James, *Principles and Methods of Teaching*, 2nd. ed., W.B. Clive: London, 1909.

Woodward, E.L., *The Age of Reform, 1815–1870*, Oxford University Press: London, 1938.

Selected school textbooks and other books for children

Reading and recitation

Blackie's English-Study Readers, Fourth Reader, Blackie & Son, Ltd.: London, c. 1920.

Chambers's Stepping Stones to Literature, Book VI, In Pastures Green, W. & R. Chambers, Ltd.: London, c. 1927.

Longmans' British Empire Readers, Book V, Longmans, Green and Co.: London, 1910.

Macmillan's King Readers, The King Readers, I, Macmillan and Co., Ltd.: London, 1911.

Robertson, Eric, *The Orient Readers, No VI*, Macmillan and Co.: London, 1894.

The Beacon Study Readers, Book Three, Ginn and Company Ltd.: London, 1928.

The Royal School Series, *The New Royal Readers, No VI,* Thomas Nelson and Sons, Ltd.: London, 1948.

The Royal School Series, *Highroads of Literature, Book VI – 'Thoughts and Voices',* Thomas Nelson and Sons Ltd.: London, 1927.

The Royal School Series, *Nelson's Indian Readers, Third Book,* Thomas Nelson and Sons, Ltd.: London, 1947.

The Tales The Letters Tell, Book Three, The House of Grant, Ltd.: Glasgow, c. 1934.

West, Michael, *New Method Reader, Four,* Longmans, Green & Co: Bombay, 1930.

Geography

Brooks, Leonard and Finch, Robert, *Columbus Regional Geographies, First Series—Book 4, The British Isles,* University of London Press Ltd.: London, 1928.

Bartholomew, J.G., *The Royal Indian World Atlas,* T. Nelson and Sons: London, c. 1895.

Lay, E.J.S., *The Empire Geographies, Book II, Life in Canada and Australia,* Macmillan and Co., Ltd.: London, 1934.

Morrison, Cameron, *A Junior Geography of India, Burma and Ceylon,* Thomas Nelson and Sons, Ltd.: London, 1924.

The Royal School Series, *Highroads of Geography, Book V, Britain Overseas,* Thomas Nelson and Sons: London, 1913.

The Royal School Series, *Highroads of Geography, Book VI, The British Isles,* Thomas Nelson and Sons: London, 1914.

The World And Its People, A New Series of Geography Readers, The British Isles, Thomas Nelson and Sons: London, 1904.

The World And Its People, A New Geography Reader, The World With Special Reference to Greater Britain, Thomas Nelson and Sons: London, 1909.

History

Aston, John, *The Oxford History Readers, Stories from English History,* Oxford University Press: London, c. 1914.

Frew, David, *A Survey of The British Empire, Historical, Geographical and Commercial,* Blackie & Son, Ltd.: London, c. 1910.

Gardiner, S.R., *Longmans' 'Ship' Historical Readers, The Seventh Reader To The Accession of George V,* Longmans, Green, and Co.: London, 1913.

Gateways to History, Book IV, Warden of Empire, Edward Arnold: London, 1910.

The Royal School Series, *Highroads of History, Book VII, Highroads of British History,* Thomas Nelson and Sons, Ltd.: London, 1930.

Thompson, F.W., *A History of India for High Schools and Colleges*, Christian Literature Society: London and Madras, 1915.

Others

Connor, Ralph, *Glengarry Schooldays*, [1902] Project Gutenberg: www.gutenberg.org, 2003.

Fabre, J. Henri, *The Life of the Grasshopper*, Hodder and Stoughton: London, 1917.

Fabre, J. Henri, *The Sacred Beetle and Others*, Hodder and Stoughton: London, 1918.

Kingsley, Charles, *The Water Babies*, [1863] Oxford University Press, Ltd.: Oxford, 1995.

Moles, T.W. and Moon, A.R., *An Anthology of Longer Poems*, Longmans, Green and Co.: London, 1938.

Teter, George, *One Hundred Narrative Poems*, Scott, Foresman and Co.: Chicago, 1918.

INDEX